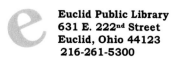

**Euclid Public Library
631 E. 222nd Street
Euclid, Ohio 44123
216-261-5300**

THE ROER RIVER BATTLES

THE
ROER RIVER
BATTLES

Germany's Stand at the Westwall, 1944–45

David R. Higgins

CASEMATE PUBLISHERS
Philadelphia & Newbury

Published in the United States of America in 2010 by
CASEMATE
908 Darby Road, Havertown, PA 19083

and in the United Kingdom by
CASEMATE
17 Cheap Street, Newbury, Berkshire, RG14 5DD

ISBN 978-1-935149-29-3

Cataloging-in-publication data is available from the Library of Congress
and from the British Library.

Printed and bound in the United States of America.

10 9 8 7 6 5 4 3 2 1

For a complete list of Casemate titles, please contact:

In the United States of America:
Casemate Publishers
Telephone (610) 853-9131, Fax (610) 853-9146
E-mail casemate@casematepublishing.com
Website www.casematepublishing.com

In the United Kingdom:
Casemate-UK
Telephone (01635) 231091, Fax (01635) 41619
E-mail casemate-uk@casematepublishing.co.uk
Website www.casematepublishing.co.uk

CONTENTS

For Walter and Agnes

Preface

The period between Allies' Operation Market Garden in September 1944 and the Germans' Ardennes Offensive in December–January 1945 remains an underreported period in military history. With history being written by the victors this may be understandable. Following the Allied breakout from Normandy, the heady race across France had given both soldiers and civilians hope that the war would be "over by Christmas." Once its hard crust had been penetrated at Normandy, the German Army in the West appeared to be on the verge of total collapse as it streamed back to the border of the Reich. When the situation suddenly changed in the autumn of 1944, American, British, and Commonwealth forces were presented with a reinvigorated *Westheer* that had been given time to reorganize, was closer to its sources of supply, and was now directly fighting to keep an invading enemy from its homeland.

In attempting to depict the events between the US and British forces coming to a strategic stop before the *Westwall*, and their eventual crossing of the Roer River five months later in February 1945, I have employed several elements to help illustrate and simplify an often complex situation.

- Army Groups, Armies, Corps, and Divisions are written as: i.e., 12th Army Group, Second Army (spelled out); XXX Corps (roman numerals); and 2nd Armored Division (ordinal).
- German formations are italicized to visually differentiate them from Allied formations.
- German designations are equivalent and partially anglicized to preserve flavor, while keeping it easily understood (i.e. *I.SS Panzer-Korps* being *I SS Panzer Corps*).
- The designation of German "infantry" was changed to "grenadier" in

1

1942 on Hitler's order to honor the infantry arm (i.e. *grenadier regiment*).

- Except in certain cases, formation names have been spelled out to lessen confusion.
- A formation's TO&E is described only once (coinciding with its first mention in the text), and structures above division are generally omitted to save space, as corps and army attachments would have been too numerous, complex, and likely not addressed in the text.
- Because most of the Roer battles involved the Allies in offensive operations I chose to structure sections based on actions rather than reactions.

Any errors or omissions in this work were certainly unintended, and for which I alone bear responsibility.

Acknowledgments

I would like to thank the following individuals for their kind support, without which this book, and my other military history endeavors, might not have been possible. Joseph Miranda, editor-in-chief (*Strategy & Tactics* magazine); Colonel (ret.) Jerry D. Morelock, PhD, editor-in-chief (*Armchair General* magazine); Captain (ret.) William F. Atwater, PhD, former director (US Army Ordnance Museum); David Fletcher, curator (Bovington Tank Museum); Charles Lemons, curator (Patton Museum of Cavalry and Armor); Colonel (ret.) David M. Glantz; Alan Wakefield, curator (Photograph Archive, Imperial War Museum); *Oberleutnant der Reserve* Otto Carius; Thomas Jentz, for taking the time to talk with me atop an Aberdeen *Jagdpanther*; the armor restoration crew at Richardson Motor Park in Ft. Knox, Ky.; 3rd Armored Division veterans and their spouses for welcoming me to their 2009 annual reunion; Troy and Lorie Dalrymple; Gilbert and Vi Lamb; F.W. and Lois Meine; Heinz and Klara Meine; Erin and Chris Bouten; my mom, and intrepid historian and geocacher, Carin; and my wife, Diana—especially for putting up with me while I wrote this.

Chapter 1

Strategic Overview
(Summer 1944)

For several weeks after their landings at Normandy on June 6, 1944, Allied forces struggled first to expand and then break out of their beachhead. To best organize this multinational command, Supreme Headquarters Allied Expeditionary Force (SHAEF) bisected the lodgment between Lieutenant General Courtney Hodges' US First Army and General Sir Bernard Montgomery's British Second Army to its east. The integration of differing national customs, doctrines, and aerial elements under SHAEF control was greater than previous Allied undertakings in North Africa and Italy, and under General Dwight D. Eisenhower, misunderstandings, diversions of effort, and internal friction were considerably reduced. Had this unifying command not been realized, it would have been necessary to coordinate the various national staffs along parallel, probably independent lines (as the Free French under General Charles de Gaulle had threatened before Paris), without overall guidance or arbitration.

With the British occupying eastern Normandy, supplies and reinforcements were shuttled in by ship from across the English Channel. The terrain in their sector was predominantly dry, open ground, but their commander, and that of the overall landing until the buildup became sufficiently stabilized, Montgomery, implemented his trademark cautious, casualty-minimizing strategy to the detriment of progress. Britain had been at war for the last four years and suffered from a chronic lack of replacements that could ill afford to be expended without results. With one eye on the political front, Montgomery would do what he could to avoid repeating the mistakes of criminally incompetent generalship of the previous war, when tens of thousands of British soldiers were sacrificed for negligible gains at places such as the Somme and Ypres.

In contrast, US forces had not experienced significant defeat at the hands of the Germans, save for Kasserine Pass in Tunisia in February 1943. After 16 months of marching across North Africa, Sicily, and Italy, the Americans were confident in their ability to quickly win the war. Historically over-supplied during wartime, the US ground elements in Normandy were no different, with most materiel arriving directly from the United States via the port of Cherbourg at the northern end of the Cotentin Peninsula. Progress remained slow due to the region's bocage farmland, with its numerous "hedgerows," hills, streams, and woods that compartmentalized the battlefield and restricted movement and firepower. This force multiplier that favored the German defenders, and an initial lack of combat experience for many of the American formations, added to Allied difficulties.

Although stifled on the ground, British and US control of the strategic airspace over France represented a considerable asset. Over the previous two years their coordinated bombing campaign had steadily grown in strength, and through a policy of attacking en masse, had disrupted German industry, stifled imports of oil and coal, and harried enemy air bases and forward repair facilities. For the next year this Anglo-American effort focused on a variety of targets, especially enemy fighter aircraft and ball bearing production, and class III supplies such as petroleum, oil, and lubrication facilities (POL).

This campaign reached a crescendo during an unrelenting, six-day bombing campaign against the enemy's dispersed aircraft production facilities in February 1944. "Big Week," as it was later called, resulted in irreplaceable losses in *Luftwaffe* pilots, and forced that service to abandon its strategic effort against enemy daylight raids. Instead, the Germans had to adopt a more modest system of localized hit-and-run attacks that remained the norm for the remainder of the war. Although still potent on the tactical level when it believed it had local superiority, or when high-priority ground targets were under attack, of its roughly 500 in-theater aircraft to contest the Western Allies' landing at Normandy, only about a third were available at any one time due to a lack of spare parts and fuel.[1]

As a prelude to D-Day, the Allied bombing campaign was supplemented by tactical elements that destroyed bridges and transportation routes along the Seine and Loire Rivers to "seal" the Normandy operational zone from enemy reinforcements and interference. With such an extensive rail and road network to target, however, the defending German *Seventh Army* remained able to steadily insert men and material into the fight. Under its commander, *Waffen SS Oberstgruppenführer* (Colonel General) Paul Hausser, damage done by bombs or French partisans was repaired in good time. Travel remained a predominantly nighttime activity to avoid patrolling Allied ground-attack aircraft such as the US P-47 Thunderbolt and British Typhoon. Providing replacement personnel for the front, however, had become an increasingly difficult endeavor for the Germans after five years of war.

In addition to a general manpower shortage, many *Ersatzheer* (Replacement Training Army) senior officers were reluctant to release units from their control. Their plans to assassinate the Supreme German Commander, Adolf Hitler (Operation Valkyrie), before the Allies gained such an overwhelming strength as to negate any possibility for generous surrender terms for Germany, called for these elements in Vienna, Cologne, Munich, and Berlin to secure a government takeover following the scheduled July 20 coup. These forces were to be redirected from their internal security duties, such as defending against any civil unrest from the millions of foreign workers within the Reich's borders. The Commander in Chief of the *Ersatzheer*, *Generaloberst* Friedrich Fromm, would not agree to such explicit resistance. Although having favored a negotiated peace with the Soviet Union since 1942, he remained non-committal towards his conspiratorial subordinates, namely General Friedrich Olbricht, Colonel Claus von Stauffenberg (*Ersatzheer* Chief of Staff), and Colonel Albrecht Mertz von Quirnheim, all of whom looked to take matters into their own hands if necessary.

Between June and August 1944 Fromm oversaw the creation of 62 divisions for frontline duty (48 infantry, 9 *schatten*—shadow formations around which to rebuild battle-worn divisions, or to simply confuse enemy intelligence—and 5 occupation). None of these, however, were immediately sent to front line duties. It was only after "Valkyrie's" failure, and the removal of the conspirators that the infantry and *schatten* divisions were released to front line duty.[2] Nevertheless, the Germans remained unable to keep pace with attrition against an enemy that was closer to its source of supply and could rely on considerable resources to make good losses in men and material.[3] These deficiencies also degraded German combat effectiveness at a time it was needed most—to contest both the Normandy invasion and the Soviet Union's Operation Bagration.[4] Across all fronts in July and August, 800,000 Germans became casualties, whereas the previous monthly average had amounted to a much lower figure of 100,000.[5] Beyond the battlefield this had a cascading effect as skilled labor was steadily transferred from civilian to military functions, and the economy correspondingly suffered as they were replaced by lower caliber, on less motivated foreign workers and slave laborers.

Normandy Breakout

To best economize their available forces, the Germans manning the 110+km Normandy perimeter weighted their forces, especially armor, against the British sector north of Caen. The German *Army Group B*, under *Generalfeldmarschall* Günther von Kluge (after July 19), reasoned that with this area's suitable tank country it was conceivably the most likely sector for a major Allied attack. Being so distributed, the armor would also be in a more advantageous position to protect Germany should an enemy breakout occur. To contest a second Allied invasion, anticipated to take place further east along the Channel coast, von Kluge arrayed his formations accordingly, with *Seventh Army* in the west of Normandy, *Panzergruppe West* blocking the British, and *Fifteenth Army* around Calais.

With the failure of Montgomery's air/ground attempt to break beyond the German lines at Caen (Operation Goodwood), Lieutenant General Omar N. Bradley, now commander of US forces as part of 12th Army Group, would try his luck in the west. This time heavy bombers were to be even more numerous. They would also use smaller bombs to limit the kind of cratering that had hampered the earlier British advance. At just 6.5km, the frontage to be struck was much narrower than with past American offensives. As the day of the offensive approached, Bradley stressed that "when we pull it, I want it to be the biggest thing in the world. We want to smash right through it."[6]

When the Germans' weaker western sector finally faltered along the St. Lô-Périers highway, US ground forces quickly pushed southward as part of Operation Cobra (July 24–31, 1944). VII Corps exploited the situation and maneuvered to outflank and trap the Germans from the south. VIII Corps would simultaneously initiate a pursuit of what remnants escaped or were peripheral to the battle. Although the Germans were forced to fight at a numerical disadvantage, and man a front line that was correspondingly shallow, and with few mobile reserves, they remained a cohesive, tenacious opponent. Across the Normandy front, what had been estimated by SHAEF to take a few weeks had evolved into a 49-day ordeal.

Once the front was ruptured, Hitler responded with one of his characteristically unrealistic orders to sever the US spearheads as they rushed south. This was to be accomplished by attacking due west through Mortain to the coast at Avranches, but the overextended and dispersed German strategic strength proved unable to accomplish the task. At a time when it would have been better to withdraw behind the Seine River to organize and to reestablish a cohesive defense, the *Westheer* was thrust in the opposite direction. *Oberbefehlshaber* (Army Command) *West* under von Kluge (also commanding *Army Group B*) favored pulling back, but his fear of being discovered as an accomplice in the failed July 20 plot to assassinate the German supreme commander made him unwilling to deviate from *der Führer's* orders.

With the Germans in an exposed position, Allied commanders saw the possibility of trapping and destroying *Seventh Army* and von Kluge's armored reserve, *Panzergruppe West*. By attempting to remain equally strong across their lines, the seven German infantry and six *panzer* divisions, all considerably depleted, were unable to effectively contest the seventeen nearly full-strength Allied divisions. The US First Army's VIII Corps soon fanned out into Brittany to capture several ports as possible supply embarkation points, while the remaining Corps—V, XIX, VII, and XV—initiated an encircling counterclockwise movement intent on linking up with a British/Polish/Canadian thrust southeast from Caen.

Von Kluge, with no strategic recourse save withdrawal, finally superseded Hitler's calls for another counterattack on August 16 and ordered a general retreat. The following day, Hitler, believing rumors that the field marshal had attempted to surrender his command to the newly arrived US Third Army commander, Major General George S. Patton, replaced him with *Generalfeldmarschall* Walther Model. Two days later this proven defensive specialist, dubbed the "Führer's Fireman," arrived from his Eastern Front duties as commander of Army Group Center, which was soon to be destroyed in Operation Bagration to the tune of 350,000 casualties.[7]

When Model began his new command at Normandy, his experience on the Eastern Front led him to believe that he could correct the situation in Germany's favor, if only by his mere presence. Allied air and artillery superiority soon changed his perspective and he dejectedly agreed that his predecessor's actions had been sound, and the eastward exodus was allowed to continue in an effort to extract as many formations as possible. When the Argentan-Falaise pocket was finally sealed on August 21, some 80,000 Germans were removed from Army records. The lost formations, however, would remain active in nucleus for rebuilding and possible reuse at a later time.[8] Partly the fault of an overly cautious Montgomery, but also resulting from Bradley's tardiness in swinging sufficient forces into position, the Allies failed to accommodate for such an eventuality and were unable to organize the complete elimination of the *Westheer*. With some 40,000 German soldiers having escaped destruction during the final battle, and many more before the Allied pincers had begun to close, Model merged what remained of his *Seventh Army* with that of *Panzergruppe West/Eberbach* (re-designated back to *Fifth Panzer Army*) and attempted to organize a strategic fighting withdrawal.[9]

By August 26 Allied forces had taken Paris and were quickly progressing beyond the Seine River. Every advance, however, placed an increasing strain on their logistical system, especially for fuel. Advanced Section (ADSEC) and Forward Echelon (FECOMZ) "communications zones" (rear areas) had been created to support a steady pace across France as well as evacuation facilities and repair shops. When the pace of operations increased following Normandy, this "base" to FECOMZ to front line ADSEC provided a successful logistical framework as it became increasingly difficult to establish fuel and heavy ammunition stocks close to the fighting. What standard operating procedures that hindered the process were ignored, such as the temporary doing away with the use of ammunition supply points, as valuable time would be lost for unloading. Equipment and supplies were often left aboard trucks as they leapfrogged depots forward in an attempt to keep up with the armored and mechanized formations.[10]

In an effort to make the most of available resources, the respective armies took on many transportation duties themselves. Bradley even ordered that heavy artillery be left west of the Seine to free up transports to haul more supplies. This translated into higher vehicle attrition and parts cannibalization that severely strained existing maintenance facilities. It also meant that of the 10,500 tons and 16,300 tons of supplies coming into Cherbourg and the Normandy facilities, respectively, upwards of ninety percent remained in local depots at any one time. First Army, for example, required roughly 5,500 tons of supplies per day, but received just 2,225 tons through the end of August, even with its priority designation.[11]

With the Brittany ports remaining German-occupied or in some stage of destruction, nearly eighty percent of all supplies had to be trucked from Normandy. While Antwerp offered potentially the greatest capacity, it remained firmly under control of the Germans. Of the Allied-captured ports, Cherbourg (and soon Marseille) were the most important, followed by La Havre and Brest. The remainder along the English Channel and Brittany were of little strategic value. A lack of local French labor hampered the reconstruction of bomb-damaged French railways. A line from Cherbourg to Chartres was at least completed by September, which kept some traffic from having to return the extra distance to St. Lô. With POL and ammunition resupply only amounting to half of Allied daily requirements, a limited capacity gasoline pipeline was also constructed up to Alençon to provide gas for consumption estimated at up to 10,500 daily tons by D+90 (days after the landings).[12] These figures, however, were greatly underestimated considering the rapid pace of the advance, and units consumed what fuel they received almost immediately. Commanders increasingly resorted to draconian rationing to retain their strategic momentum.

To make the process more efficient, Allied logisticians established a system based on the amount of supplies that could be hauled by truck and rail instead of according to which army had priority. This resulted in a required supply rate (what commanders expected) and a combat supply rate (what could actually be supplied). Improvisation became the primary means of continuing the Allied ground offensive, especially when one considers that just their forces in northwest Europe needed, according to Eisenhower, monthly replacements averaging 36,000 small arms, 700 mortars, 500 tanks, 2,400 vehicles, 100 field pieces, and 8,000,000 rounds for artillery and mortars.[13] While fuel was now a priority, ammunition was a close second; and its considerable variety made it the most difficult item to transport. With food a lesser concern, captured enemy stores were often used as a supplementary source. Air supply helped, but it was limited by having to divert transport and supplies from frontline formations to the roughly 6,000,000 urban Parisians, and other civilians behind the Allied front, as per political considerations.

As a temporary logistic solution, a specially designated inbound and outbound truck route was established between St. Lô and the front. Under ADSEC supervision, the "Red Ball Express" used an average of 900 trucks to deliver 89,939 tons between August 25 and September 6. By the end of its 82-day existence it had transported 412,193 tons of essential fuel, ammunition, and supplies. With the average Allied division requiring 600 tons of supplies per day and corps consuming 2,500 gallons of fuel per kilometer, the "Red Ball Express" used up 3,750 just to move the supplies that distance.[14] Along the "Red Ball Highway" various maintenance organizations and ordnance teams initiated quick vehicle repairs, often in the field, where they salvaged and cannibalized what parts they could. Additional supplies could eventually be brought in through the Mediterranean Sea following Operation Dragoon, Lieutenant General Alexander Patch's seaborne invasion of southern France on August 15. However, Patch would still need time to organize his own Seventh Army once it was in France, and overcome enemy resistance before sending it north to join the Allied effort striking out of Normandy.

Footnotes

[1] Generalleutnant Dr. Hans Speidel. MS #0017.

[2] Walter S. Dunn speculates in *Heroes or Traitors: The German Replacement Army, the July Plot, and Adolf Hitler* that this was intentional to retain a strong post-coup military force in Germany.

[3] Bernhard R. Kroener, Rolf-Dieter Müller, and Hans Umbreit. *Germany and the Second World War*, Vol. 5, Part 2. Oxford Press, p. 1030.

[4] Roland G. Ruppenthal, *Logistical Support of the Armies*, Vol. I and II, United States Army in World War II (Washington, 1953).

[5] Ibid.

[6] Lieutenant Colonel Chester B. Hansen. "Operations to Secure a Lodgment Area," Nevins Papers, 5, U.S. Army, Diaries, 8–9 June 1944.

[7] Christer Bergstrom, *Bagration to Berlin: The Final Air Battles in the East: 1944–1945* (Surrey: Ian Allen, 2007), p. 82.

[8] Carlo D'Este, *Decision in Normandy: The Real Story of Montgomery and the Allied Campaign* (London: Penguin Books Ltd, 2004), pp. 430–431.

[9] Sources vary between 20,000 and 50,000, although Blumenson, Elting and MacDonald agree on 40,000 in *World War II: Liberation* (Alexandria, VA: Time-Life Books, 1978), p. 334

[10] *Flaming Bomb: The Story of Ordnance in the ETO.*

[11] Roland G. Ruppenthal, *Logistical Support of the Armies*, Vol. I and II, United States Army in World War II (Washington, 1953).

[12] Ibid.

[13] Historical Section of the G-4 (COMZ, ETOUSA) [8-3.4 AA Volume 7] "Outline of Operation Overlord."

[14] Roland G. Ruppenthal, *Logistical Support of the Armies*, Vol. I and II, United States Army in World War II (Washington, 1953).

Chapter 2

Approaching the Reich
(Late August–September 12)

Although the United States and Britain were coalition partners throughout much of the war, and their respective armed forces were well-coordinated and controlled under SHAEF, differing political considerations continued to play a role in the decision-making process. For the US, an isolationist, indirect policy had largely changed to one of overt involvement following the Japanese attack on Pearl Harbor on December 7, 1941. Hitler's declaration of war against the US four days later, although issued in accord with Germany's military alliance with Japan, was also in reaction to unpublicized armed provocations by the US Navy. As the self-proclaimed Axis about which the world would revolve, the pact between Germany and Japan resulted in many governments viewing them not as separate nations, but as a single political and military threat.[1] Along with Italy (and other minor Axis states), all would be contested equally. With Germany considered the most dangerous menace to the Allies' global interests, it would remain their primary target.

US president Franklin D. Roosevelt considered German Prussianism a major causative factor in the three previous European wars and focused on its elimination as a prerequisite to lasting peace. He further felt that as there had been no Allied occupation of Germany proper following the First World War, many Germans retained a belief that they had not lost, but had been politically sold out. This time Germany would be made to internalize and accept defeat, and the lingering militarism and nationalism that had led to the present situation would not be repeated. At the Casablanca Conference in January 1943, and with the rather reluctant agreement of Britain's Prime Minister Winston S. Churchill, Roosevelt determined to adhere to a mutual policy of Unconditional Surrender. Although this might provide incentive for the Germans to fight harder, and distance many within the United States who remained opposed to involvement in the European War, the perception of a moral crusade against a perceived global danger became widely accepted.

Britain's political perspective was predicated on its overseas empire when it officially stood alone against the Axis until the middle of 1941. Faced with German domination and a total loss of these colonial possessions, it advocated for, and received, American support and participation. British attempts to control and manipulate strategic objectives to coincide with those of its political, economic, and military achieved mixed results as it was steadily forced to acquiesce in face of its almost total dependence on American war production. While ultimately Britain's policy favored the military defeat of Germany, it did not want a post-war dismantling of the nation. Instead, they called for a balanced policy that would not repeat the mistakes of the 1919 Versailles Treaty, in which Germany was de-militarized and bankrupted by the victors of the First World War. Soviet Premier Joseph Stalin's expansionist policies into Europe were considered too great a threat to allow anything other than an intact German nation to act as a buffer.

Allied Operational Planning

During the planning stage for Operation Overlord, the seaborne invasion of Normandy, Allied commanders believed that once they had broken into the open terrain and compromised the enemy's position, the German Army would initiate a series of organized, successive withdrawals eastward behind the numerous river barriers in France and Belgium. They estimated that by September 4 (D+90) enemy defensive positions along the Seine River would be manned in strength, and that the Allies would possess 12 divisions with which to contest them.[2] In reality, when the Germans withdrew over the river they were in full retreat ahead of an Allied force comprising 16 divisions. The combination of a rapid advance, and having to support a larger-than-anticipated force, meant American and British commanders had to continually improvise and prioritize men and material to take advantage of their extraordinary, and unexpected, success. By the time they had reached the Seine at the end of August the Allies had largely expended their operational reserves, and SHAEF struggled to best use their material and mechanized advantage with available logistic capabilities.

SHAEF believed that the goal of crippling German warmaking capability hinged on capturing the Ruhr industrial complex, with its

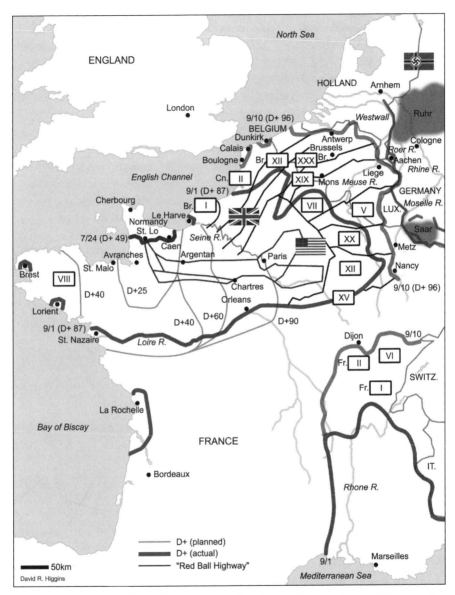

Strategic view of the Allied advance (planned and actual) across France following the Normandy breakout in mid-1944.

considerable coal and crude steel production, as well as the Saar basin to the south. To accomplish this, four options were initially considered, but two were soon found to be undesirable. A thrust across Flanders, while offering open terrain and a secured left flank along the English Channel, seemed too risky due to the area's low altitude and numerous waterways that were prone to flooding. The second, an offensive through the Ardennes-Eifel region, was equally unattractive due to the locale's rough, heavily wooded environment that would hamper large-scale maneuvering, and command and control.

As Eisenhower considered the remaining pair of options, he advocated that Allied forces should "avoid a line of advance which leads us to a head-on collision with the main German forces without opportunity for maneuver," and that they "must advance on a front sufficiently broad to threaten an advance by more than one of the 'gaps' into Germany...to keep the Germans guessing as to the direction of our main thrust, cause them to extend their forces, and lay the German forces open to defeat in detail."[3] Sending Montgomery along a Maubeuge-Liége-Aachen axis would secure additional ports, and eliminate the threats to English civilians posed by the region's numerous Fieseler Fi 103 jet (V-1) and A-4 rocket (V-2) launch sites. The second offensive option would be conducted through Metz-Kaiserslautern by Patton's Third Army in the south as a subsidiary action intent on the capturing the Saar Basin's substantial iron and coal mines, lead and zinc deposits, and industry.

German Operational Planning

While the Allies organized a unified, multinational authority under Eisenhower (SHAEF), the Germans suffered from a partitioned command structure in which Hitler held ultimate authority over a mix of "fiefs" such as the, Army, Police, *Ersatzheer* (Replacement Training Army), and the National Socialist combat arm, the *Waffen-SS*. As commander of both the *Oberkommando der Wehrmacht* (OKW, or Armed Forces High Command) and *Oberkommando des Heeres* (OKH, or Army High Command) his pathological desire for secrecy meant that strategic information became centralized, only parceled out to senior commanders to provide them with little more than what was deemed appropriate to carry out their localized duties.

The German Supreme Command routinely micromanaged and interfered with operational and tactical details below Corps level. Hitler's increasing distrust of senior leadership, especially after the failed July assassination attempt, prompted him to progressively control situations in the combat zone where his orders were to be unadulterat-

A view from the loophole of a concrete gun emplacement near Steinfeld on March 3, 1940. (NARA)

ed and carried out to the letter. This was in part because it became increasingly necessary to coordinate the different theaters and allocate resources. The tighter he retained control, however, the more front-line command changes occurred. Command and control was subsequently degraded for the units involved, as new officers needed time to acclimate to their new situations and responsibilities.

While this type of centralized command structure may have produced a quicker transmission of orders, the degree to which Hitler accentuated the process, and disregarded or was ignorant of local circumstances hundreds of kilometers from his headquarters in East Prussia, created innumerable problems for commanders on the spot. Many officers were forced to act against their better judgment and either acquiesce to *der Führer's* wishes or conceal their actions that were contrary to his commands. While the latter might save lives, and the battlefield situation, it was also done at great personal risk. Although it was planned to correct this problem by establishing a command center for Hitler at Soissons, France, the massive Soviet Bagration offensive, aimed at Army Group Center in the East, forced the idea's cancellation. Whether uninformed of the benefits of an active defense, or unwilling to suffer what might be seen as embarrassing battlefield "reverses," Hitler's "hold fast" orders negated what tactical flexibility the Germans retained. The accumulation of such operational imperatives relegated the German military to the same kind of static defense and exposure to disastrous envelopments that it had unleashed on Soviet forces in 1941 and 1942.

The Race Across Northwest Europe

Elated by the recent cessation of hostilities around Argentan-Falaise, Montgomery called for a meeting with Eisenhower on August 23 to pitch his idea for a single strategic thrust into northern Germany. Contrary to the accepted "broad front" approach, Montgomery believed that with the Germans in full retreat and that if he was to be given 30 divisions, "one really powerful and full-blooded thrust toward Berlin is likely to get there and thus end the German war."[4] The Supreme Commander, however, wished to avoid disproportionately favoring one command over another. Besides, existing supplies were insufficient in the short term until the extensive port facilities at Antwerp were opened to naval traffic, and the risk of poor weather and reduced shipping across the English Channel was deemed to be too great. The decision was later proven wise as German forces in Lorraine were preparing their largest armored counterattack to date in the West to stop what they believed would be the main Allied offensive by Patton's Third Army.

While Eisenhower would not alter his "broad front" approach, he did at least compromise by shifting focus further north across the previously disregarded plain of Flanders. On August 26 he granted supply priority to Montgomery's 21st Army Group, which naturally interpreted it as "absolute priority," while the US First Army was given similar status as it anchored the British right. "Monty" was also given the Allies' theater reserve, First Airborne Army. Bradley and Patton were incensed by the potentially detrimental side effects this would impart to their efforts. Bradley wanted a "modified double thrust," where one US corps would be sent to help Montgomery, while the remainder of the First Army joined the Third south of the Ardennes.[5]

Montgomery's influence as both an army group commander and top British military representative in the theater won out, at least

Reinforced concrete "dragon's teeth" under construction along the Westwall near Tettingen on March 31, 1940. (NARA)

temporarily. Even though the Allied effort had shifted to the northeast, Eisenhower had no intention of abandoning Bradley's and Patton's subsidiary thrusts, especially since SHAEF planners estimated that an isolated thrust by Montgomery was only feasible as far as the Rhine and was thus unlikely to force a decisive result. First Army was subsequently moved north to take responsibility for seizing the key "Aachen Gap," penetrating the *Westwall* ("Siegfried Line" to the Allies) and the Roer River, and gaining access to the open Cologne Plain. From such a springboard the Rhine could be crossed and the Ruhr exposed to envelopment, and with it the presumably large German strategic reserve positioned for its defense.

During the late summer of 1944, Allied forces had steadily raced across northern France against remnants of the German *Fifteenth* and *Fifth Panzer Armies* that seemed beyond salvation and without recourse save to remain ahead of their pursuers. *OB West, Generalfeldmarschall* Gerd von Rundstedt, unsuccessfully advocated limited withdrawals to more defensible positions in order to shorten lines and provide for mobile reserves. Although he was theoretically the supreme commander in the west, he did not have full control over attached *Waffen SS* formations, which provided operations and supply, but remained under *Reichsführer SS* Heinrich Himmler for disciplinary and administrative matters.

Following the debacle at Argentan-Falaise, German commanders struggled to impart stability into "the void" that had become their front lines, and organize effective running defenses and rearguard actions with ad hoc battlegroups. An inability to retain communications in such a frenzied combat environment, however, caused many formations to fight, and make command decisions, in uncoordinated isolation. A subsequent breakdown in transportation forced the abandonment of large quantities of material as movement was increasingly reduced to foot traffic.

At the end of August, Hitler continued to look for ways to concentrate the *Westheer's* available *panzer* forces into a strategic strike force to arrest the Allied advance. With such an offensive having proved to be beyond von Rundstedt's means at Mortain, *OB West* was ordered yet again to assemble a new grouping of four armored divisions and two armored brigades. From their assembly positions southeast of Paris around Chaument-Chatillon-Sur-Seine-Langree, German commanders moved quickly to organize an attack deep into the US right flank. Patton's rapid advance, however, preempted the operation and forced its cancellation.

About 100km to the south, *Army Group G* had been holding the area around Dijon to provide an escape corridor for German forces withdrawing from the French interior. Allied forces moved too quickly, though, and it was decided to recommit the German mobile strike group further north around Chalons-sue-Marne-Reims-Soissons for a counterattack between Aisne and the Marne. Again, Allied speed negated this as a strategic option, and the Germans wondered if the canals offered a better springboard, or whether they needed to pull back further to the *Westwall*. Concerned about the rapid Allied advance in the West, Hitler became adamant that ground was now to be relinquished grudgingly, and that encirclement by the Allies was to be avoided. Plans to stop the Allies now relied on making a stand along the canals in the north, the *Westwall* in the center, and Lorraine in the south. Although still largely disorganized, the Germans were falling back on ever-shorter supply lines, and at a time when their armaments factories were just approaching their wartime peak under the *Reichsminister* of Armaments and War Production, Albert Speer.

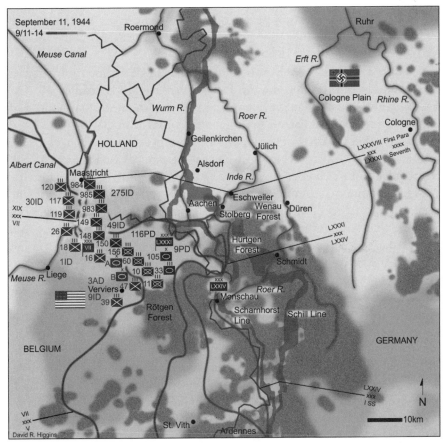

Campaign map showing the September 11, 1944 positions of the US XIX and VII Corps, and the German *LXXXI Corps* before the *Westwall*.

To the German Border (September 1–11)

By the first of September, Allied forces were approaching the absolute limit of their ability to sustain the offensive. Intelligence estimated that the main German forces west of the *Westwall* were grouped in a strength equivalent to two armored and ten infantry divisions.[6] Eisenhower wished to engage and destroy this concentration before they reached the German border, but Montgomery (now a Field Marshal) felt that the divisions he could assign to the task were insufficient. Eisenhower subsequently repositioned two corps from the US First Army north toward Antwerp in preparation for encircling and destroying as much of the retreating enemy as possible near Mons. The execution of the maneuver shifted 12th Army Group's center of gravity away from Patton's Third Army, which had to halt along the Marne and the Meuse Rivers until sufficient supplies could be made available.

SHAEF looked for ways to regain the strategic momentum as soon as the supply situation permitted. Eisenhower met with Bradley, Patton, Hodges, and Major General Hoyt Vandenberg, the new commander of Ninth Air Force, to discuss his immediate goals "to permit the Third Army and the V Corps of the First Army to move to the Siegfried Line and seize and hold that line with at least a part of each Corps."[7] On September 5, Eisenhower decided to "advance rapidly on the Rhine by pushing through the Aachen gap in the north and the Metz gap in the south. The virtue of this movement is that it takes advantage of all existing lines of communication in the advance towards Germany and brings the southern forces on the Rhine at Koblenz, practically on the flank of the forces that would advance straight through Aachen. I see no reason to change this conception."[8]

Eisenhower was certain that the overwhelming Allied airpower would continue to smooth the progress of the ground forces. Close cooperation between the two services, however, had become tenuous as airmen complained about unnecessary demands on pilots and aircraft, and their benefactors voiced displeasure with the seemingly frequent, unintended bombing of friendly forces. Eisenhower, and his senior subordinates, would make every effort to eliminate friendly fire casualties as had occurred at the St. Lô-Périers Road (Cobra), Caen (Goodwood), and Falaise (Totalize).

In early September 1944, total German forces numbered 327 divisions and brigades, and of these, 252 divisions, and up to 20 brigades, were actually serving in the front lines. The majority of the 3,421,000 soldiers in the Field Army—some 2,046,000—were fighting in the East. With the German High Command fixated on the Eastern Front since June 1941, only a fraction had been allocated to contest the Western Allies. Following the near collapse of German forces in France in August, Hitler ordered that an "operational reserve" of 25 new divisions be created between October 1 and December 1 to help address this issue.[9]

After being temporarily replaced by Model, von Rundstedt was reinstated as *OB West* on September 3 with command over some 48 infantry and 15 *panzer* divisions, plus several *panzer* brigades; all of which were considerably below their authorized strengths.[10] The next day the newly-assigned commander of the Maastricht-Aachen-Bitburg sector of the *Westwall*, the tenacious *General der Panzertruppe* Erich Brandenberger, began to reconstitute his *Seventh Army*. As *LXXXI Corps* covered the Aachen sector it prepared to take on the US VII and XIX Corps by aggressively gathering retreating German soldiers at various collection points and returning them to the fight. The *353rd Grenadier Division*, for example, little more than a headquarters, was thrust into defending the *Westwall* with help from several *Luftwaffe* and *Landesschützen* (local militia) battalions.

In addition to a strategic disparity in infantry, German artillery and armor in the Aachen sector operated at a disadvantage approaching 2.5:1 and 20:1, respectively. As the Allies pushed into the *Dreilaenderecke*, the area where German, Belgian, and Dutch territory intersected, von Rundstedt knew that the Aachen and Rhine-Westphalia sector would be the enemy's goal and called for up to an additional 10 divisions, with accompanying artillery, armor, and anti-tank elements, to establish an effective countering force. At present, only the skeleton *9th Panzer Division*, a weak armored assault detachment and two *Sturmgeschütz* (assault gun) brigades were available, with the *12th Volksgrenadier Division* en route.

The threat of an enemy airborne landing behind the German *Westwall* was also a concern, but von Rundstedt felt this would be a possibility only after the enemy successfully penetrated east of the Roer River. With an estimated 135,000 men under his command, plans to bring the *Westwall* up to combat readiness were estimated to take six weeks—time that could only be gained by fighting and containing the enemy for as long as possible.[11] Hitler, and many staff members of *OKW*, wishfully professed a great reliance on the fortifications as an effective barrier against invasion from the west.

What mix of German forces that were thrust into combat were in general poorly trained, organized, and equipped, and could make little more than a defensive showing. As the German soldiers took up positions, many bunkers were found to house homeless civilians that had been using them as shelters, especially during air raids. Most of the fortifications' weapons had long since been relocated to the Atlantic Wall defenses, and interior fixtures, and anything else of value, had largely been removed by recently evacuating administrative personnel. Four years of neglect had resulted in considerable undergrowth that covered the defenses and reduced the defender's visibility (though this also helped to conceal them from aircraft). When originally built, the pillboxes were designed to house small, now antiquated, 37mm guns, and no fixed weapons larger than machine guns were in place. Police and party agencies that oversaw the civilian labor that had been directed on August 20 to dig trenches and other fortifications were expressly prohibited from being subordinated to the army. As a consequence, the two efforts were seldom integrated, and many of the defenses created under party supervision served little purpose save as dummies.

As each corps pulled back to the German border, it sent a division staff to the *Westwall* to facilitate the military's takeover. The rapid Allied advance, however, meant that little could be done to prepare, and maps, barbed wire, mines, stores, and cabling were insufficient. Under the Inspectorate of Fortifications West, Sector Commandant Düren tried to bring these fortifications up to fighting trim. A lack of workers, and a distrust by many of the engineers of the damage or theft done by administrative personnel, hampered efforts; some even going so far as not to relinquish keys to many of the facilities.

Much of this confusion resulted from interference by the *Gauleiter* (regional leader) for the Cologne-Aachen area, Josef Grohé, and other party officials who attempted to exert their individual authorities on the military situation. Having kept the population in the dark as to the actual battlefield situation, Party officials scrambled to pass blame as the Allied advance could no longer be ignored. In reaction to the arrival of US forces before Aachen, the head of the German Labor Front, Robert Ley, even went so far as to start a rumor that the generals were purposely sabotaging German efforts.

To the north, the Canadians captured Antwerp, but were unable to force crossings over the main canal that led 80km to the English Channel. The city's considerable, and largely intact, port facilities would remain closed to the Allies as long as *Fifteenth Army* stood along the heavily mined Schelde Estuary. Allied ground forces would have to wait until November 28 before the area finally reopened to shipping. Until then, with northwest Europe quickly being cleared of *Wehrmacht* forces, Eisenhower finally accepted Montgomery's proposal for a narrow thrust to bypass the *Westwall*. Operation Market Garden was to involve a series of airborne assaults to capture bridges in Holland as a launch pad for a rapid ground advance to the Rhine River and beyond.

By early September, Model believed that if *Seventh Army* did not receive immediate support the Allies would arrive first at the *Westwall* and be able to push through with minimal effort. On the 8th he had only 100 serviceable tanks, and although the withdrawing *Nineteenth Army* from southern France and *LXIV Corps* from the Biscay coast were steadily strengthening *Army Group G*, immediate reinforcement would not be available.[12] The Dijon sector remained a candidate from which to carry out Hitler's ongoing design to strike for Third Army's lengthy southern flank, but sufficient German forces and fuel could not be organized in time. After a nearly month-long offensive through the Rhône River Valley, Patch's Seventh Army linked up with Patton near Dijon on September 11 to unify the Allied front in Western Europe. Although thousands of German military, administrative personnel, and collaborators managed to extricate themselves from southwestern France before the constricting corridor to Germany closed, many more were trapped with scant options save surrender.

To the north, at 1805, five soldiers from the Second Platoon, Troop B, 85th Cavalry Reconnaissance Squadron, 5th U.S. Armored ("Victory") Division forded the Our River near Stolzembourg to claim credit as the first Allied formation to reach German soil.[13] Forays from other formations soon followed, but with logistics in disarray and enemy opposition stiffening, strategic movement ground to a halt all along the Allied line. The retreating enemy had finally achieved a stabilized defensive line.

Footnotes

[1.] The German Declaration of War against the United States, December 11, 1941.

[2.] Roland G. Ruppenthal, *Logistical Support of the Armies*, Vols. I and II, United States Army in World War II (Washington, 1953).

[3.] May 3 draft of post-Overlord plans.

[4.] Montgomery to Eisenhower, M-160, 4 Sep 44.

[5.] Ibid.

[6.] Department of the Army, Field manual 100-5, *Field Service Regulations, Operations* (Washington, DC: Government Printing Office, 1944), para. 580: The object of the pursuit is the annihilation of the hostile forces . . . *Direct pressure* against the retreating forces must be combined with an *enveloping or encircling maneuver* to place troops across the enemy's lines of retreat. *Encirclement of both flanks* of the retreating forces or of their separate elements is attempted wherever conditions permit. By the coordinated employment of every available agency of destruction and terrorization, the shaken morale of the defeated enemy is converted into panic. The incipient dissolution of his organization is transformed into rout.

[7.] Memo for record, 2 Sep 44, sub: "Notes on meeting of Supreme Commander with subordinate commanders, 12th A Gp files, Military Objectives," 371.3.

[8.] Diary, Office of the Commander in Chief, under date of 5 Sep 44.

[9.] *Oberkommando der Wehrmacht, Organisations Abiedung* (hereafter cited as *OKW/Org. Abt.); OKH/Org. Abt.; OKW/Allgemeines Wehrmachts Amt, "Verluste der Wehrmacht bis 1944,"* 1 Dec 44; and *OKH/Generalquartiermeister, der Heeresarzt KTB* and Anlagen; MSS *#T-121, T-122, Geschichte des Oberbefehlshaber West* (Zimmermann et *al.*).

[10.] Lucian Heichler, *Germans Opposite VII Corps in September 1944*, pp. 84–86. As the Germans defined combat strength as the number of frontline combat troops; it did not include non-combat elements, such as with an average full-strength infantry division of 14,800 men would be listed 3,800 combat effectives.

[11.] Message from von Rundstedt to C-in-C Army Group B, September 7, 1944.

[12.] Teletype, Model to Jodl, 4 Sep 44; Teletype, Rundstedt to Keitel, 7 Sep 44. Both in *Army Group B, Ia Lagebeurteilungen 2O.V.-11.X.44.*

[13.] Charles B. MacDonald. *Breaching the Siegfried Line* (Washington, DC: Office of the Chief of Military History Dept. of the Army, 1963), p. 3.

Chapter 3

Breaching the *Westwall*
(September 12–30)

After a 700km, three-month advance from the Normandy beachhead, the soldiers of First Army, like those in the other US, British, and Canadian armies, were exhausted but also exhilarated by their success. The German Army in northwest Europe appeared to have disintegrated, and showed no indication that it could effectively resist a final push by Allied forces to win the war within the next few months. Between June 6 and September 11 some 2,168,307 men and 460,745 Allied vehicles had landed in Normandy, and Eisenhower now directly controlled 35 infantry, 14 armored, and 4 airborne divisions, along with numerous independent commands.[1] Whether the growing Allied logistic problems could be corrected to enable these units to achieve their upcoming goals was another matter.

As the US First Army crossed the German border north of the Ardennes-Eifel region, its overextended, 130km front line, and an extremely short supply of ammunition, necessitated a temporary halt. Courtney Hodges needed to replenish his forces and stockpile supplies before attempting the next stage of operations against the Ruhr via Aachen and Cologne. Given the circumstances, he optimistically stated that, "given ten good days of weather the war might well be over as far as organized resistance was concerned."[2] Unlike the extroverted Patton, Hodges was a placid figure, but one gifted in tactics and administration. His rigid daily routine promoted a centralized command style of consultation with his immediate subordinates and delegation to his staff. Visits to the front or interacting with those manning the positions were rare.

As the headlong rush across France wound down, Allied commanders all along the line undoubtedly wished to retain their momentum, at least until they were through the rugged terrain and bunker-infested *Westwall*. With supplies being allocated to certain units in an effort to continue operations, the overall effectiveness of the Allied offensive was unsustainable. The commander of VII Corps, Major General Joseph "Lightning Joe" Collins, however, felt he could not let an opportunity to penetrate the opposing defenses slip, considering he was so close to enemy fortifications that seemed lightly defended. As one of only three European Theater of Operations (ETO) commanders to have also led combat forces in the Pacific, he had special insight into the virtues of infiltration tactics and using momentum and maneuver to keep an enemy off balance. Already, a German attempt to defend the area between Verviers and Eupen had failed due to the speed of VII Corps' lead units, and he felt confident his formation had one last effort to give.

Hodges had been told on September 10 that ammunition sufficient for another five days of combat would not be available for nearly a week. With time a priority, Collins, the Army's youngest corps commander, conqueror of Cherbourg, and designer of the Cobra breakout, successfully lobbied his superior to conduct a "reconnaissance in force" along his 56km front. VII Corps was quickly organized to push through the *Westwall* and establish positions along the Roer River before the enemy could organize what few forces were available to *Seventh Army* following its recent losses at Mons.[3] With his goal a mere 32km distant, Collins felt that the mission offered a good chance of success; especially in view of the record Allied advances of the previous weeks.

As VII Corps approached Germany's ancient imperial capital of Aachen along the narrow road from Gemmenich, Collins had few choices between how to quickly and efficiently reach the Roer. His broad frontage, better suited to a fluid battlefield, resulted in few reserves in order to plug gaps in his increasingly vacant and static front line. Routes north and east of the city were generally open, but were conversely vulnerable to German long-range artillery atop the nearby Lousberg Heights. The southern approach, although restricted by rugged terrain and dense forests, seemed a better choice due to the two concealed avenues it offered.

The first of these corridors skirted along the north of the Hürtgen Forest and extended to the town of Stolberg. While this presented reasonable tank terrain, it was uncomfortably close to the urbanized region around Aachen, much of which had been integrated into the Scharnhorst section of the *Westwall*. The second route, along the south edge of the dark, seemingly impenetrable Hürtgen Forest, offered adequate roads around Monschau. The area's physical isolation, and the

Iron antitank obstacles and concrete "dragon's teeth" near Weissenburg on March 3, 1940. (NARA)

fact that if it were to be used as a main route risked shifting support away from British efforts along Hodge's left, relegated it to peripheral status.

The region's seven pre-war dams, and the potential problem they presented should they be destroyed by the Germans to flood the region and trap any Allied units that managed to cross the Roer River, were meantime noted by Allied intelligence. According to Bradley, "As long as he [the Germans] held the huge Roer Dams containing the headwaters of that river, he could unleash a flash flood that would sweep away our bridges and jeopardize our isolated bridgeheads on the plains of Cologne. Destruction of the 180-foot-high Schwammenauel Dam, engineers said, would swell the Roer at Düren by 25 feet and create a raging torrent one and a half miles wide. Clearly we dared not venture beyond the Roer until first we had captured or destroyed those dams."[4]

Allied intelligence believed that the Germans would present their greatest resistance east (or behind) of the Rhine River. Fighting along the *Westwall* would likely be little more than a delaying action. It was also estimated that the Aachen sector was defended by a few depleted divisional battlegroups totaling some 7,000 soldiers, with up to 18,000 remnants available as potential reinforcements.[5] With this in mind

Collins hoped to quickly pass Aachen "on the bounce" and continue to the Roer River with as little resistance as possible. As for the dams, Collins later stated, "No terrain analysis or intelligence estimate of this danger had been made by Supreme Headquarters, Allied Expeditionary Force (SHAEF), XII Army Group, or First Army, and for the first and only time my able G-2 and Corps Engineer failed to provide me with such an analysis or estimate."[6] The RAF 's Second Tactical Air Force, and the US Ninth Air Force's IX and XIX Tactical Air Commands would provide air support.

Because the strength of the enemy defenses within Aachen was largely unknown, the 1st Infantry ("The Big Red One") Division was to avoid potentially costly urban fighting. Instead it was simply to probe south and east of the city, and capture the area's high ground from which to disrupt German reinforcements. With VII Corps' left thus covered, the 3rd Armored ("Spearhead") Division would act as the assault formation, penetrating the enemy's defenses around Eschweiler and Stolberg and breaking into the open terrain beyond. On the right, the 9th Infantry ("Old Reliables") Division was to perform a similar, albeit slower thrust through the Rötgen and Hürtgen Forests, where it was to secure the road network to Düren. The 4th Cavalry Group, having covered VII Corps' flank since Mortain, would maintain contact with V Corps to the south while it continued reconnaissance and infiltration duties, and as necessary, participated in combat.

German Response

After weeks of organizing ad hoc formations to effect a fighting withdrawal across northwest Europe, the ebbing Allied offensive finally allowed *OB West*, Field Marshal von Rundstedt, to carry out Hitler's frequent calls to man a new line that was to be held "under any conditions."[7] From the Schelde Estuary in Belgium to Switzerland, his two theater commands were put in positions to hold the enemy at the German border. While *Generaloberst* Johannes Blaskowitz's *Army Group G* anchored the *Westheer's* southern strategic front, *Army Group B*, under Walther Model, operated against the British 21st and US 12th Army Groups. The "Führer's Fireman," whom von Rundstedt had recently replaced as *OB West*, controlled the *Fifteenth, First Parachute*, and *Seventh Armies*, while what remained of *Fifth Panzer Army* replenished itself behind the German border.

Model knew he needed to hold the Roer River valley, not only to keep the enemy from penetrating into the Cologne Plain to threaten the Ruhr, but to also to secure the assembly positions for the Germans' planned Ardennes offensive. To protect this sector, *Seventh Army's* Brandenberger readied *LXXXI, LXXIV, I SS Panzer*, and *XXV Corps*, while *LXXXI Corps* held responsibility for defending the anticipated main enemy approach at the "Aachen Gap." Headquartered in Hitler's former command post at Bad Münstereifel (codenamed *Felsennest*) southeast of Aachen, Brandenberger resorted to harsh discipline to restore order throughout late August and early September. As "a typical product of the general staff system," according to Model, Brandenberger took advantage of the diminishing Allied offensive by removing the battered *1st, 2nd*, and *12th SS Panzer Divisions*, as well as the Army's *116th* ("Greyhound") and *9th Panzer Divisions*, from the front line to rest and refit. At present, only the relatively fresh *183rd Volksgrenadier Division*, with seven attached, virtually worthless militia battalions of about 450 men each, was in position to contest an enemy advance between Geilenkirchen and Rimburg.

While German strength in general had increased steadily over the last few days, *LXXXI Corps* remained a polyglot of regimental-strength battlegroups where quality ranged from experienced combat veterans to poor-quality militia. Inferior signal, engineer, and tank recovery capabilities compounded problems, but while German front-line formations had taken a beating in recent months, rear echelon and support services remained largely intact. Recognizing the weakness, *Generalleutnant* Friedrich A. Schack reinforced the Aachen sector with his best, but still reforming, unit, the *116th Panzer Division*. A mix of headquarters personnel and the sub-par *8th, 12th*, and *19th Luftwaffe Fortress Battalions* were thrown in to help, along with the corps artillery.

Major Heinrich Volker's *105th Panzer Brigade* was also brought to the front, but with only a handful of tanks and a severely depleted *panzergrenadier* battalion, it would be of little use. Like the nine other *panzer* brigades that had been created following the devastating summer losses on the Eastern Front for use as rapid reaction forces, Volker's unit featured an armored and mechanized infantry battalion, as well as engineers and a considerable number of antiaircraft weapons. The philosophy behind *panzer* brigades was that smaller but stronger armored units could maneuver and react more swiftly than traditional *panzer* divisions. Numbered 101–110, each was to include a *panzer* battalion (each of three companies of 11 Panthers and a *panzer* antitank company with 11 75mm *Jagdpanzer* IV/70(V) assault guns).[8] In practice, however, the initiative produced poor results, as crew training on Germany's new 75mm-gunned Panthers was generally rushed and there were no organic reconnaissance or maintenance elements.

To the north of Aachen, the *49th* and *275th Grenadier Divisions* moved to contest XIX Corps, while south of the city the *526th Grenadier Division* was reinforced with local defense and ad hoc emergency units. The very weak *353rd Grenadier Division* was assigned east of the city in the second belt where it organized the various police, Hitler Youth, and *Landesschütz* detachments defending the *Westwall*. It also acted as a liaison between the *116th* and *9th Panzer Divisions*, and *LXXXI Corps'* rear area. Unarmed, essentially administrative *Festungsdienstellen* (fortress staffs) served little military purpose, but could be put to work constructing fortifications and roadblocks.

Although the city of Aachen was of little military value, and had been largely destroyed by Allied bombing, the symbolism and psychological value it represented to the German cause was considerable. Besides being the birthplace of Charlemagne (*Karl der Grosse*), the founder of the "First Reich," it risked being the first major German city to fall into enemy hands since Napoleon in 1801. The mindset of many of the city's *Vaterlandsverteidigen* ("Fatherland defenders") was further steeled now that they were fighting on their home territory. As one German officer commented, "Suddenly we were no longer the Nazis, we were German soldiers."[9]

September 12

US

3rd Armored Division[10]
Commander: Major General Maurice Rose
Div HHC, HQ CCR/CCC, CCA HHC, CCB HHC
Armor: 32nd, 33rd Armored Regiments (M-4 Sherman (medium), M-5 Stuart (light))
Infantry: 36th Armored Infantry Regiment
Field Artillery: HQ & HQ Battery, 54th, 67th, 391st Armored FA Battalions (M-7 Priest 105mm SP Howitzer)
Other: 83rd Armored Reconnaissance Squadron, 143rd Armored Signal Company,

23rd Armored Engineer Battalion, Service Company, 503rd Counter Intelligence Corps Detachment
Trains: HHC, 3rd Ordnance Maintenance Battalion, Supply Battalion, 45th Armored Medical Battalion, Military Police Platoon

Attached
486th AAA Automatic Weapons Battalion (SP)
703rd TD Battalion
991st FA Battalion (155mm Gun)
58th Armored FA Battalion
1st Battalion, 26th Infantry (from 1ID)

1st Infantry Division
Commander: Major General Clarence R. Huebner
Div HHC
Infantry: 16th, 18th, 26th Infantry Regiments
Field Artillery: HQ & HQ Battery, 7th, 32nd, 33rd FA Battalions (105mm Howitzer), 5th FA Battalion (155mm Howitzer)
Other: HQ Special Troops, 1st Reconnaissance Troop (Mechanized), 1st Signal Company, 1st Engineer Combat Battalion, 1st Counter Intelligence Corps Detachment
Trains: 701st Ordnance Light Maintenance Company, 1st Quartermaster Company, 1st Military Police Platoon, 1st Medical Battalion

Attached
745th Tank Battalion
A & D Companies, 87th Chemical Battalion
188th FA Battalion (155mm Howitzer)
957th FA Battalion (155mm Howitzer)
985th FA Battalion
B Battery, 15th FA Observation Battalion
HQ & HQ Battery, 18th FA Group
635th Tank Destroyer Battalion
634th Tank Destroyer Battalion (less C Company)
103rd AAA Auto-Weapons Battalion

Detached
1st Battalion, 26th Infantry Regiment (with 3AD)

9th Infantry Division
Commander: Major General Louis A. Craig
Div HHC
Infantry: 39th, 47th, 60th Infantry Regiments
Field Artillery: HQ & HQ Battery, 26th, 60th, 84th FA Battalions
(105mm Howitzer), 34th FA Battalion (155mm Howitzer)
Other: HQ Special Troops, 9th Reconnaissance Troop (Mechanized),
9th Signal Company, 15th Engineer Combat Battalion, 9th Counter
Intelligence Corps Detachment
Trains: 709th Ordnance Light Maintenance Company, 9th
Quartermaster Company, Military Police Platoon, 9th Medical Battalion

Attached
746th Tank Battalion
C, D Company, 87th Chemical Battalion
A Battery, 13th FA Observation Battalion
981st FA Battalion (155mm Gun)
Headquarters & Headquarters Battery, 188th FA Group
376th AAA Automatic Weapons Battalion

4th Cavalry Group (Mechanized)
HQ & HQ Troop
4th Cavalry Reconnaissance Squadron
24th Cavalry Squadron (Mechanized)

German

LXXXI Corps
Kampfgruppe 116th Panzer Division[11]
Commander: Generalleutnant Gerhard Graf von Schwerin
Div HQ
Armor: 16th Panzer Regiment (Panzer IV (medium), Panther
(medium))
Infantry: 60th, 156th Panzergrenadier Regiments
Field Artillery: HQ, 146th Panzer Artillery Regiment (20mm, 105mm,
150mm)
Other: 116th Panzer Reconnaissance Battalion, 281st Army

Antiaircraft Battalion (20mm, 88mm), 228th Antitank Battalion (75mm), 675th Panzer Engineer Battalion, 228th Panzer Signal Battalion, 146th Feldersatz (Replacement Training) Battalion, Services

Attached
Kampfkommandant (Aachen) (Oberst von Osterroth)
Sector elements of 353rd Grenadier and 526th Reserve Divisions
8th, 12th, 19th Luftwaffe, 453rd Grenadier Training Battalions

Kampfgruppe 9th Panzer Division
Commander: Generalmajor Gerhard Müller
Div HQ
Armor: 33rd Panzer Regiment (Panzer IV (medium), Panther (medium))
Infantry: 10th, 11th Panzergrenadier Regiments
Field Artillery: HQ, 102nd Panzer Artillery Regiment (20mm, 105mm, 150mm)
Other: 9th Panzer Reconnaissance Battalion, 287th Army Antiaircraft Battalion, 50th Antitank Battalion, Bridge Column K, 86th Panzer Engineer Battalion, 85th Panzer Signal Battalion, 60th Feldersatz (Replacement Training) Battalion, Services

275th Grenadier Division
Commander: Generalleutnant Hans Schmidt
Div HQ
Infantry: 983rd, 984th, 985th Grenadier Regiments
Field Artillery: HQ, 275th Artillery Regiment (105mm, 155mm Howitzers)
HHC, 275th Antitank Battalion, Füsilier Battalion, Engineer Battalion, Signal Battalion, Feldersatz (Replacement Training) Battalion, Services

49th Grenadier Division
Commander: Generalleutnant Vollrath Lübbe
Div HQ
Infantry: 148th, 149th, 150th Grenadier Regiments
Field Artillery: HQ, 149th Artillery Regiment (105mm, 150mm Howitzers)
HHC, 149th Antitank Battalion, Füsilier Battalion, Engineer Battalion, Signal Battalion, Services

81st Reconnaissance Company
Arko 117
432nd Corps Signals Battalion, 432nd Corps Supply, Field Police
Troops

353rd Grenadier Division (remnants)
Commander: Generalleutnant Paul Mahlmann
Div HQ
Infantry: 941st, 942nd, 943rd Grenadier Regiments
Field Artillery: HQ, 353rd Artillery Regiment (105mm, 150mm
Howitzers)
HHC, 353rd Antitank Battalion, Füsilier Battalion, Engineer Battalion,
Signal Battalion, Feldersatz (Replacement Training) Battalion, Services

"Reconnaissance in Force"

With the German border only a few kilometers distant, VII Corps set off
at dawn on Tuesday, September 12 between Aachen and Monschau. The
3rd Armored Division led the way, expecting another day of siphoning
gas from abandoned German vehicles to supplement its meager
allocations, during an advance east against increasing resistance. Its
commander, Major General Maurice Rose, who had previously served in
the 2nd Armored Division during the Cobra breakout, had recently been
transferred to the "Spearhead" Division where his aptitude for
controlling fast-moving armored formations, and desire to fight the
Germans had quickly become apparent. Emotionally detached and
unconcerned about sacrifices in pursuit of an objective, he was widely
admired by his subordinates, and had gained a reputation as an
aggressive battlefield leader who liked to be at the front—qualities that
made him well suited to command the "heavy" armored division of two
combat commands.

US Armored Division (Heavy)

Along with its sister formation, the 2nd Armored ("Hell on Wheels")
Division to the north, the 3rd Armored retained its "heavy" designation
with one armored-infantry and two armored regiments, of four medium
tank and two light tank battalions of three companies each. In combat

A bunker protected by barbed wire at Strasbourg on March 2, 1940. (NARA)

these were grouped between Combat Commands "A" and "B," each being organized into task forces around a reinforced tank battalion, with additional divisional resources being attached depending on the tactical situation, and a "Reserve" (often called CCR).[12] A task force might be built around a tank battalion by attaching a company each of infantry and engineers (tank-heavy force) or by placing a battery of howitzers and a platoon of tanks and tank destroyers under an infantry company (infantry-heavy force). Though combat commands were similar in structure and purpose to brigades, many US commanders remained tethered to a structured, bureaucratic mentality and did not use these formations in the way they were intended, as rapid reaction, semi-independent, forces where their commanders, with simple long-range orders would act predominantly on their own authority. The 2nd Armored Division commander, Major General Ernest N. Harmon, believed that combat commands were "a step forward but a half measure...the correct step was not organizational change but a mental change."[13]

All other US Army armored divisions had been previously stripped of one of their armored regiments and reconfigured to a more triangular structure. This reduced the number of tanks by one-third (390 medium and light) and infantry by 4,000 fewer men than the standard size of

14,620.[14] These "light" versions generally consisted of a tank, armored infantry, and self-propelled artillery battalion, as well as an attached tank destroyer battalion of 36 vehicles, an armored cavalry squadron, an engineer battalion, and divisional services. Although "independent," once these tank battalions were attached to divisions and parceled out, with each company supporting one of the three regiments, they were unlikely to operate again as individual entities.

Hitting the *Westwall*

On VII Corps' left, the 18th and 16th Infantry Regiments were organized as semi-independent, all arms "combat teams" before being sent to skirt Aachen to the south and occupy the area's high ground. Each was to advance with one battalion forward as a screening safeguard. Thirty minutes after the 1st Battalion, 16th Infantry Regiment crossed the German border, the 3rd Armored's Combat Command A (CCA/3) followed suit at 1545 against light opposition.

US commanders also developed ad hoc infantry battlegroups based on what the Germans had achieved using all-arms *Kampfgruppe*. Each regiment, with the addition of artillery, engineers, tanks, tank destroyers, and other supporting elements, became a regimental combat team (RCT). These represented a very capable combined-arms organization that could operate away from the division as needed. During mid-September they penetrated into a number of under-manned fortifications and entered the Aachen Municipal Forest near Hauset, but the efforts of the entire division lacked control and coordination.

As commander of one of the few capable German formations in the area, *Generalleutnant* Gerhard Graf von Schwerin was preparing his *116th Panzer Division* north of Aachen for combat. He knew that the Aachen Municipal Forest would not make a defensible region with the strength he had on hand. Three *Luftwaffe* groups—comprised primarily of obsolete airfield maintenance personnel—organized into battalions, were insufficiently trained, poorly armed, and had little combat value. Fortress and *Landesschütz* battalions, consisting of "soldiers" up to 60 years of age, were of similar value. Even though his "Greyhounds" had lost their *panzer* regiment in recent combat, and now had little more than 1,600 combat personnel between their *60th* and *156th Panzergrenadier Regiments*, he knew they would still willingly follow him into battle.[15] With a seemingly overwhelming enemy force threatening to capture the city, von Schwerin saw little point in sacrificing his valued soldiers in a hopeless fight. Later that night, however, he was made commander of Aachen's defenses with the typical orders from the high command to hold it to the last.

With few substantial American attacks along *LXXXI Corps'* front, German forces manning the security line were able to enter the shelter of the area's numerous pillboxes and entrenchments. In the early afternoon of September 12, 3rd Armored Division pushed back *Kampfgruppe* Mueller, took Eynatten, and advanced north and east. To Rose's left, the 1st Infantry Division made good progress and forced von Schwerin to pull back to the northwest as other routes out had been blocked by overzealous German engineers that had prematurely destroyed all crossings over Gueule Creek. A lack of hand-held antitank weapons and antitank mines hampered German efforts to contain the American attack. As the day drew on, senior officers from *LXXXI* and *LXXIV Corps* were often unsure where the front lines were at any given time.

By the evening *353rd Grenadier Division* reported American armor converging on Rötgen from the west, as well as reconnaissance and mounted infantry. US artillery and fighter-bombers attempted to clear a path, but the Germans simply withdrew into their nearby fortifications and by 1900 the attack had tapered off. To the east, the *60th* and *156th Panzergrenadier Regiments* occupied positions along Aachen's railroad line to create a defensive position incorporating a nearby tunnel and Gueule Creek. As with most German defenses, strong forward outposts were constructed ahead of the main line of resistance (MLR), with artillery providing support as close to the front as possible to reduce repositioning during combat.

Both the 1st Infantry and 3rd Armored Divisions had failed to penetrate the *Westwall's* westernmost section due to roadblocks, difficult terrain, and enemy resistance. Narrow roads and heavily wooded terrain that created problems with integrating infantry and armor contributed to their unspectacular performance. While the former could adapt to the rugged terrain, tanks and self-propelled guns were better suited for a conservative approach in open terrain. Armored tactics were to support the infantry, which, considering the constricted, urbanized terrain proved difficult. US tankers tended to have at least a few mechanical skills from civilian life, which helped with front-line maintenance. Once in combat, however, some American tanks posed a hazard to friendly troops merely by virtue of their construction. In September 1944, the 1st Infantry Division cautioned its units that extreme care should be exercised in firing the bow machine gun with which some US tanks were equipped, because the gun was mounted in a low position and was impossible to aim accurately, thereby creating a serious hazard for infantry in front of the vehicle.[16]

Advancing units were committed in a decentralized manner out of necessity, and they cleared strongpoints by a series of bounds. Frequent halts to reestablish contact with adjacent units were needed to prevent friendly fire. VII Corps was unable to seize the entrance to the "Stolberg Corridor," though it gained information on the enemy's strength and desire to contest the area. Collins subsequently decided to narrow his zone of attack, bypass Aachen, and limit the Corps' advance to the Roer's west bank.

The *9th Panzer Division* began to arrive on September 11 and was forced to send some of its *panzergrenadier* companies ahead with *105th Panzer Brigade* to delay the enemy advance until the rest of the division moved up. A half-dozen assault guns from the *394th Sturmgeschütz Brigade* was to assemble in the vicinity of Brand, as a *LXXXI Corps* reserve to assist the *116th* and *9th Panzer Divisions* as a rapid-reaction force. Schack also allocated his corps artillery to von Schwerin, consisting of the artillery regiments of the *116th Panzer* and *353rd Grenadier Divisions*, and a reserve regimental HQ, *Flak Gruppe Aachen*. Artillery Group Aachen, as the group was called, was placed under the *146th Panzer Artillery Regiment* commander, *Oberst* (colonel) Pean, and was to work closely with the *49th Grenadier*, and *116th* and *9th Panzer Divisions* in coordinating its fire with the main effort of defense.

Having been ordered to conduct a defense of Aachen on the 13th, von Schwerin entered the city the night before. As he moved toward his command post at Laurensberg, he was shocked to find that all government, police, and Party officials had fled. With no pre-existing evacuation plan, the remaining population of some 10,000 was abandoned without civic or military direction as they attempted to leave as per an official evacuation order. With confusion and panic escalating, von Schwerin countermanded the standing order and with assistance from his soldiers soon restored calm.

Before dawn, the *8th*, *12th*, and *19th Luftwaffe Fortress Battalions* were attached to the *Kampfkommandant* of Aachen for a daybreak counterattack against the American penetration of the Scharnhorst Line at Brandenberg Hill.[17] The *116th Panzer's Reconnaissance Battalion* was disengaged and recommitted at daybreak north of the Gueule with the mission of establishing contact with the *9th Panzer Division* (with *536th Replacement Training Division's* training battalion) at Eynatten. The remainder of *LXXXI Corps'* front included *Kampfgruppen* from the *275th Grenadier Division* along the Maastricht-Aachen highway, the *49th Grenadier Division* within the *Westwall*, and the *353rd Grenadier Division* (with Aachen's combat commandant) along the Eynatten-Forstbach road.

To the southeast, 3rd Armored Division's pair of combat commands approached the Scharnhorst Line. CCA/3's 1,600-man task force under Colonel Leander Doan consisted of the 2nd Battalion, 32nd Armored; 1st Battalion, 33rd Armored, and a platoon each of engineers and tank destroyers.[18] With the infantry probing ahead, engineers followed close behind to build bridges or demolish fortifications, both with tank destroyer support. Because of the generally greater firepower and protection of German medium and heavy armor over their US counterparts, the latter had developed self-propelled stop-gaps with large armaments, but with a lighter, more maneuverable chassis. As a mobile alternative to towed equivalents, tank destroyers such as the M-10, M-18, or M-36 were designed to take on enemy armor, while the tanks were to focus on supporting infantry. Independent tank destroyer battalions were allocated to divisions or corps, although in practice they were usually parceled out in smaller units.

As Doan's TF X crossed into the *Westwall* defenses near Ober Forstbach, the numerous pillboxes were found to be manned by quick-surrendering old men and teenagers, but heavy German direct artillery and anti-tank fire increasingly slowed progress—a situation that would have been more destructive had the Germans not had such a confusing variety of artillery plus a severely reduced pool of forward observers. The task force also faced dense rows of steel-reinforced concrete tank obstacles ("dragon's teeth") that obstructed progress. US tanks and tank destroyers deployed along the edge of a wood, but the terrain prohibited their support and integration with the infantry. With Doan's task force halted by pillbox machine gun and mortar fire, engineers attempted to blast a path through the "dragon's teeth" with tetrytol (2.5lbs M1 Chain demolition block explosives), but success continued to be slow and dangerous. After several hours of fruitless combat, a nearby, and apparently undefended, farm path was discovered that led through the fortifications, and 20 M-4 Shermans from 2nd Battalion, 32nd Armored Regiment were hurriedly pushed through.[19]

Unsupported by infantry, Doan's Shermans negotiated the clustered pillboxes, trenches, and bunkers only to be ambushed by *panzerfaust*-wielding German infantry teams. In concert with these short-range, disposable anti-tank weapons, three *Sturmgeschütze* from the West Prussian *394th StuG Brigade* used their 75mm guns to quickly knock out half of Doan's vehicles. CCA/3 sent additional armor, which was reinforced by 1st Battalion, 26th Infantry Regiment from divisional reserve, and the combined force proved sufficient to finally break through to Nütheim just beyond the Scharnhorst Line.

A few kilometers to the east, CCB/3 sent two task forces north from the open terrain around Rötgen into the edge of the Hürtgen Forest. Lieutenant Colonel Roswell H. King's group of just 60 men found pillboxes in considerable numbers and was halted by German fire. To its right, the task force under William B. Lovelady pushed through the area's narrow, undefended *Westwall* defenses and on to the German supply center at Rott via a forest-fringed highway near the Dreilägerbachtal Dam, one of seven in the area.

With two American penetrations of the Scharnhorst Line to the south and not directly against Aachen, *LXXXI Corps'* Schack sent as many reserves as he could spare to aid *9th Panzer Division's* efforts against the "Stolberg Corridor." He also ordered the *116th Panzer Division* to wipe out 1st Infantry Division's gains in the Aachen Municipal Forest, but the division's organic elements had earlier been removed for rest, were regrouping near Würselen, and were only available for action south of Aachen in the late afternoon. Von Schwerin reluctantly maneuvered his men in compliance with orders, and with help from the remainder of the *394th Sturmgeschütz Brigade* managed to drive off US patrols. As with the Germans and British, US recovery operations began at night to avoid enemy fire.

By noon, Aachen's combat commandant, *Oberst* von Osterroth, had achieved considerable success with limited manpower to seal off the American salient south of Aachen. He employed elements of the *176th Replacement Training Division* north of the city, a fortress machine gun battalion from Tenth Military District between Laurensberg and the Maastricht highway, two replacement training battalions in the Aachen State Forest, and a mix of antiaircraft units as artillery and antitank support. Von Osterroth next attempted to throw the assault guns of the *394th* against the American tanks as soon as the formation disembarked from at the Aachen-Nord Railway Station. *LXXXI Corps* similarly ordered the *116th Panzer Division* to counter the enemy penetration at Brandenberg Hill, and von Schwerin had to recall his *156th* and *60th Panzer Grenadier Regiments*.

As US forces approached the town of Rott, the *9th Panzer Division* under *Generalmajor* Gerhard Müller readied to counterattack from Kornelimuenster at 1430. Realizing the "Stolberg Corridor," and not the Aachen Municipal Forest, was where the main enemy attack would come, General Schack ordered the *116th Panzer Division* to transfer half the assault guns of *394th Sturmgeschütz Brigade* to *9th Panzer Division* at Kornelimuenster.[20] Within the next two hours the *116th Panzer Division* attacked the American salient at Brandenberg Hill and rebuffed an armored reconnaissance unit which had advanced to the outskirts of the city. Parts of CCB/3 had bypassed Rott to the east as the Headquarters and Headquarters Company of *9th Panzer Division* tried to counter their progress. In the early afternoon, American tanks and infantry continued their advance toward the oncoming *394th Sturmgeschütz Brigade*. The unit arrived at 1800 with three assault guns, and together with a battalion of *9th Panzer Division* and a few 75mm antitank guns, established a defensive front along the line Schleckheim-Nuetheim-Kornelimuenster. After *panzerfaust* teams had knocked out four American tanks, 15 more US armored vehicles flanked the *9th Panzer Division* and began to roll it up.

9th Panzer Division's headquarters company and the *105th Panzer Brigade* launched a counterattack from Rott to halt the American drive on Mulartshütte. German engineers were quickly demolishing crossings over the Vicht River between Stolberg and Zweifall. At *LXXXI Corps* headquarters, Scheck determined that the enemy's main point of impact was the "Stolberg Corridor" and ordered the *116th Panzer Division* to transfer the *8th Luftwaffe Fortress Battalion* and one battery of artillery to *9th Panzer Division*.[21] He also informed *353rd Grenadier Division* that "the enemy will probably launch a drive bypassing Aachen from the penetration area near Kornelimuenster and Hahn ... toward the second band of defenses," and Mahlmann promptly alerted three of his attached *Landesschütz* battalions. The *19th Luftwaffe Fortress Battalion* was committed in the area northwest of Würselen (northeast of Aachen), *3rd Landesschütz Battalion* in the area northwest of Stolberg, *12th Luftwaffe Fortress Battalion* in the vicinity of Stolberg, and *2nd Landesschütz Battalion* south of Stolberg. The *8th Luftwaffe Fortress Battalion* was designated *353rd Grenadier Division's* reserve.

By day's end over a dozen American tanks had broken through part of the *Westwall* at Oberforstbach, while American infantry advanced along the Langfeld-Nuetheim-Kornelimuenster road. Although some progress had been made, Joe Collins had let his "reconnaissance" get bogged down by trying to fight, rather than bypass, enemy resistance.

Ersatzheer

Throughout the war the German army was organized into a *Feldheer* (Field Army) and an *Ersatzheer* (Replacement Training Army). Every German regiment in the field had a battalion cadre that drew recruits from one of several *Wehrkreise* (military districts) throughout the Reich. This *Ersatz* battalion provided a replacement pool for the conscription, training, and replacement of personnel, and the organization of new units. The *Wehrkreis* was also responsible for rebuilding and refitting shattered divisions, which by December 1944 meant the employment of 2,572,000 trainees.[22] With the Allies rapidly approaching the *Westwall*, many of these partially trained recruits and cadets were organized and thrown into combat as a stopgap. Compositionally, the *Ersatzheer* provided a variety of formations, many of which were encountered in the Roer sector.

Marschbattalione ("march battalions") moved replacements from their *Wehrkreis* to the Theater of Operations, which in special cases entailed combat. Prior to front-line duties, regimental officers and NCOs trained these roughly 1,000-man divisional field replacement battalions from the parent unit, which were divided into three companies, one for each of the division's three regiments. Following basic training in the *Ersatzheer*, recruits advanced to *Ausbildung* (training) for additional instruction before duty in *Reserveeinheiten* (reserve units) in occupied territories. This in turn freed fully trained personnel for the front line. *Lehreinheiten* (instruction units) consisted of men with combat experience and were generally attached to one of the four types of German instruction schools: *Waffenschulen* (services), *Kriegsschulen* (officer candidate), *Unteroffizierschulen* (NCO), and specialist training. *Landesschütz* formations were technically under the Field Army and consisted of older personnel or those unfit for front-line service.

A number of semi-military organizations also provided personnel. The *Verstärkter Grenzaufsichtsdienst* (Reinforced Border Control Service) was an *SS* grouping of all frontier organizations under a single control that included military police and *Sicherheitsdienst* (Security

Westwall defenses with road barricades near Behweighofen on March 1, 1940. (NARA)

Service) personnel for investigation of subversive groups, among other duties. Regular police were likewise controlled by the *SS*, which emphasized marksmanship and discipline, and often served in combat. *Landwacht* was an auxiliary police organization in rural communities intended to capture downed airmen, saboteurs, escaped prisoners, and the like. The *Ersatzheer* also contained numerous auxiliary and militant party organizations, such as the *Allgemeine* (General) *SS* and Hitler Youth, which could be called upon to action in defense of Germany, often with fanatic devotion to the cause.

Into the Schill Line

Over the next few days the 3rd Armored Division pushed past the initial Scharnhorst Line and into the open terrain near Stolberg, which was firmly integrated into the *Limesstellung* (Schill Line). A string of overcast and rainy days added to the general misery, but progress remained steady. Enemy resistance varied considerably, with territorial defense battalions evaporating on contact, while small rearguards from regular army units fought tenaciously. German pillboxes were often poorly supported by artillery and manned by hastily trained soldiers with little motivation for a stand-up fight.

CCA/3 and CCB/3 continued to press for Eilendorf and Stolberg, half of which was integrated into the second, and final, fortification belt protecting Aachen. Between the 3rd Armored and 1st Infantry Divisions, German hilltop positions, reinforced with armor and antitank guns, were well emplaced through the area's numerous slag piles and quarries. Within Aachen itself, von Schwerin believed an American attack to be imminent and prepared a note with a request "to take care of the unfortunate population in a humane way"—a great risk considering the post-July 20 mood should it be discovered.

The 4th Reconnaissance Cavalry Squadron (Mechanized) entered Germany on September 14, and two days later the remainder of 4th Cavalry Group, 24th Reconnaissance Cavalry Squadron, crossed as well. The complete formation held sections along the *Westwall* until November 10, when it was moved to the Hürtgen Forest. Only a fraction of its resources were used for purely reconnaissance, while the remainder acted in mobile reserve, security, screening, and to a lesser degree direct combat roles.

Like "The Big Red One," Major General Louis Craig's 9th Infantry Division had fought in North Africa and across France, but had been considerably reduced by prolonged combat. The 60th Infantry Regiment was below half strength, while its remaining regiments, the 39th and 47th, were in only slightly better shape. This decrease in combat effectiveness was also the result of the US Army's system of replacement, where an inadequate number of divisions being fielded resulted in soldiers remaining in combat for extended periods. This increased non-battle casualties, but problems also existed in providing sufficient and timely numbers. Replacements were often unprepared for battle, especially with regard to "90 day wonders," officer candidates that arrived for front-line duty after having completed ten-weeks at Officer Training School (OCS), but had no combat experience. While physically rigorous, training tended to be short on the tactical and leadership challenges that junior officers would likely encounter. German officer candidates, in contrast, were selected from those of at least corporal rank who had first proven themselves with at least six months of front-line duty.

Against negligible resistance, the 9th Infantry Division was able to move all the way to Schevenhütte before stopping. All was quiet, and except for the frequent air raid sirens, the town's citizens went about their normal daily routines as if the war were still far away. Lieutenant Colonel Van Hugo Bond's 39th Infantry Regiment took up positions some 13km south of Schevenhütte before attacking enemy forces in the open terrain around Lamersdorf. The Germans responded with artillery fire and counterattacks from the nearby Hill 554, but these amounted to little. US forces likewise made regular assaults that suffered similarly heavy casualties. The lack of adequate forces allocated to VII Corps' right was becoming evident, but little could immediately be done, and it would take two more weeks for the 39th Infantry Regiment to finally overwhelm resistance.

To the north, the 60th Infantry Regiment fared little better as it attacked the Hüfen-Alzen ridge south of Simmerath. The *89th Grenadier ("Horseshoe") Division* attempted to block the Americans' path, but it was still refitting after nearly being destroyed during the summer. To make their stand the division took over from the poorly equipped *416th Grenadier Training Regiment.*[23] In the heavily wooded terrain visibility was extremely limited and US command and control continued to be a problem, not to mention dangerous due to the tree bursts that showered shrapnel and wood splinters on the stumbling infantry. Maps and radios were virtually useless, and the dirt-covered, steel-reinforced concrete bunkers proved very difficult to defeat, often requiring repeated hits from large caliber weapons at close range. The steel-reinforced concrete bunkers, often protected by layers of earth, were impervious to satchel charges and air attacks. Usually, guns larger than 155mm were needed to defeat them, and even then only after repeated firings.

On the morning of September 15, Task Force Y, CCA/3 advanced in parallel with TF X toward Munster-Busch, both encountering stubborn opposition as they penetrated into the Schill Line. With many of the fortifications unmanned, TF Lovelady's Shermans led the way through Mausbach and established a foothold to the north of the *Westwall*. Again the *394th Sturmgeschütz Brigade* stopped any exploitation of the breech. The rest of 3rd Armored Division likewise sputtered to a halt between Stolberg and Mausbach. Rose's command had taken heavy losses in armor around Geisberg Hill (Hill 228). His tanks and men were simply worn out. With the American attempts to penetrate into the south of Aachen effectively halted, and XIX Corps having taken Maastricht the day before, many German commanders believed the next major effort would be north of the city.

Although US intelligence had discounted the Germans' ability to bring in support, due to Soviet pressure and Allied air power seemingly having destroyed enemy railways, that night the first sizeable German reinforcements began to arrive in the form of the *12th Volksgrenadier Division* that had hastily been pulled from West Prussia.

As von Schwerin prepared to defend the city proper, some of the recently departed Party officials and police skulked back to Aachen and discovered his note about the humanitarian situation prior to its delivery. They accused the commander of the *116th Panzer Division*—a holder of the Knight's Cross with Oak Leaves and Swords—of defeatism and tried, unsuccessfully, to haul him before a "People's Court." When it appeared that their beloved commander would be arrested and likely executed, many of his men made preparations to contest the nearby *1st SS Panzer Division* should it move to intervene. Senior commanders close to Hitler managed to mitigate the situation, and von Schwerin was quietly relegated to "reserve" status, and later a position in Italy.

Concerned that the US push around Eilendorf had separated the *116th Panzer Division* from the *9th*, Schack ordered a *Kampfgruppe* from the latter's *10th Panzergrenadier Regiment* into action. Although it initially failed to make headway, a follow-up attack by the regiment, with support from other *9th Panzer* formations, finally stopped 3rd Armored Division.

Stalemate

On September 16, Hitler, with customary failure to appreciate conditions at the front, issued a directive that there was no longer room for strategic maneuver now that the enemy had reached German soil: every man was to "stand fast or die at his post." In a meeting with his most senior military and political leadership, Hitler announced his desire for a German offensive through the rugged Ardennes-Eifel region. Outwardly similar to the operation that enabled victory over France and the Low Countries four years earlier, this time the goal was to recapture Antwerp and split the Western Allies. Hitler's longing for a strategic counterattack looked to finally be a possibility.

When first informed of Hitler's plans, the *OB West*, von Rundstedt, had lamented that in the event the Allies launched large-scale attacks at Metz and Aachen, the counteroffensive would have to be called off. Hitler would entertain no such idea. The following day the British and

American launch of Operation Market-Garden (Montgomery's air and ground thrust to bypass the *Westwall* and enter Germany) in the Netherlands forced the cessation of Allied attacks along the German border. Already low on fuel and supplies, First and Third Armies would see any excess sent north to Montgomery, and for the rest of the month they would remain idle to recuperate, resupply, and plan their next strategic offensive.

For the Germans defending the Aachen sector, the battle was shifting in their favor with the arrival of badly-needed reinforcements. The fresh, full-strength *12th Volksgrenadier Division* arrived on Hitler's orders, and although Schack tried to commit it as a complete formation, circumstances necessitated that it go into battle as individual elements arrived. While this resulted in several counterattacks along the line, US forces were largely able to deal with them one at a time. Major General Leonard T. Gerow, a First World War veteran and VMI graduate, had long believed his V Corps was spread too thin, and called off offensive action. With VII Corps also overextended and running low on ammunition, Collins followed suit two days later and ordered the 1st Infantry and 3rd Armored Divisions to stop to consolidate their positions. The 9th Infantry Division, however, would continue into the "Monschau Corridor" and the Hürtgen Forest in an attempt to reach Düren and achieve something tangible.

Skirmishes continued over the next few days with little movement, as both sides tried to wrest control of key geographic features, especially the hills around Stolberg, and the towns of Verlautenheide and Schevenhütte. The Germans in the sector were pulling back through the forest, and had the commander of 47th Infantry Regiment, better understood the situation he might have adversely influenced the arriving enemy reinforcements.

The Germans succeeded in holding their positions in the area, though over the next several days the *12th Volksgrenadier* and *9th Panzer Divisions* steadily lost half and two-thirds, respectively, of their combat strength. With the fighting at Stolberg stalemated, the advance of the US 9th Infantry Division attracted the attention of Brandenberger, who scraped up a few assault guns to reinforce the patchwork *353rd Grenadier Division* holding its position. After repeated attempts to push into the clear terrain beyond Hürtgen-Kleinhau, the 9th Infantry Division, like the rest of VII Corps, was halted short of its goal.

With only 75 tanks available out of an authorized 232, the 3rd

Armored Division relied heavily on patrols and raids to make incremental gains against the high ground near Duffenter, Diepenlinchen, and Breinigerberg. To help counter these movements, Schack threw together a mix of anti-tank and artillery, five *Landesschütz* battalions, a *Luftwaffe* fortress battalion, an infantry replacement training regiment, and what little remained of *353rd Grenadier Division* into the Schill Line.

While most of the fighting by the US First Army had been concentrated in the VII Corps sector, Major General Charles ("Cowboy Pete") Corlett's XIX Corps had taken advantage of the weak German defenses in the southern Netherlands. After crossing the Meuse (Maas) River, the 30th Infantry ("Old Hickory") and 2nd Armored Divisions approached the *Westwall* at Rimburg and Geilenkirchen, respectively. IX TAC's P-47 Thunderbolts and P-38 Lightnings performed tactical attacks on Düren, Herbach, and other nearby targets to hamper enemy reinforcements. Corlett, another US commander with service experience in both the Pacific and European theaters, was galled by Hodges' greater faith in Collins, who was allowed to do largely as he wished, but for the time being XIX Corps was nearly out of fuel and unable to proceed.

With the VII Corps now occupying a 30km wide by 15km deep wedge between Aachen and the Hürtgen Forest, US civil affairs detachments moved into German territory to institute an interim military government. Initially with Rötgen, and then Monschau, the first *Landkreis* (district) capital to be captured, the procedure consisted of a posting of the Supreme Commander's proclamation and ordinances, followed by finding a local authority to act as a liaison to the population, usually a *Bürgermeister* (mayor) or the like. Weapons and communication devices such as radios were then confiscated. Few instances of civilian resistance were recorded.

A Dark and Ominous Place

The day after elements of 2nd Battalion, 47th Infantry Regiment hammered a battalion of *Oberst* Osterhold's *48th Grenadier Regiment*; Collins ordered it, as well as the 3rd Armored and 1st Infantry Divisions, to pause before seeking further action. The remainder of 9th Infantry Division would continue to clear the forest and reintegrate its three regiments. Craig's immediate goal was to secure Kleinhau and Hürtgen, but the general shortage of forces necessitated a battlegroup composed of battalions from both the 39th and 60th Infantry Regiments.

GIs examining a captured pillbox. (US Signal Corps)

Throughout the 19th, and for a few days afterward, Craig's battlegroup made progress against slight resistance, but an inability to effectively coordinate larger formations because of the dense terrain resulted in limited gains. Craig's force was halted by elements of the *1st Battalion, 942nd Grenadier Regiment* and 20th *Luftwaffe Fortress Battalion* under control of *Generalleutnant* Paul Mahlmann's *353rd Grenadier Division*. To the north the 47th Infantry Regiment's bulge around Schevenhütte was a threat to *12th Volksgrenadier Division's* left flank. Its commander, *Generalleutnant* Gerhard Engel, initiated a series of counterattacks to push back the American gains. Osterhold ordered another attack against the area, which failed to penetrate, but it did halt 9th Infantry Division's progress.

On September 21 *General der Infanterie* Friedrich J. Köchling replaced Schack as commander of *LXXXI Corps*. The relative lull along the Eilendorf-Stolberg-Mausbach line had enabled *12th Volksgrenadier Division* to rebuild some of its lost strength. The recently activated *246th Volksgrenadier Division* replaced the *116th Panzer Division*, now rated as *Kampfwert II* (conditionally capable of offensive missions), which was withdrawn into theater reserve for refitting.[24] Tactical reorganization also extended to the *275th* and *353rd Grenadier*, and *9th Panzer Divisions* (recently bolstered by the integration of the disbanded *105th Panzer Brigade*). The *panzer* brigade concept had proven unable to perform the role of a highly mobile and powerful intervention unit, and after September new units were not formed or existing ones used for offensive operations.

With Allied combat operations winding down, a glimmer of positive news arrived during the night of the 21st when intelligence received word that von Rundstedt had initiated an uprising in Cologne as a precursor to overthrowing Hitler. This was later proved to be a fabricated broadcast by the US Army's Publicity and Psychological Warfare Section. On the following day, Hodges postponed further offensive operations, much to the chagrin of Montgomery, who hoped First Army could continue to tie down German forces and keep them from interfering with Market-Garden.

North of Aachen, the left flank of the XIX Corps had become increasingly stretched as the British line lengthened to Arnhem. Eisenhower and his top commanders met at Versailles to discuss 21st Army Group's recent difficulties. To strengthen the British and thereby facilitate Montgomery's proposed thrust against the Ruhr, the commanders agreed to adjust the boundary between the British and 12th Army Group northward. This would free up at least two British divisions to participate in Market-Garden. For Hodges, XIX Corps would have to wait for the 29th Infantry ("Blue and Gray") Division to arrive on the line, while VIII Corps moved from Brittany to take over from V Corps.

The First Army, with ongoing support from the IX Tactical Air Command, would provide the main thrust into Germany, possibly in conjunction with an airborne drop beyond the Rhine. The Germans countered XIX Corps by sending the recently activated *183rd Volksgrenadier Division* to take over the Geilenkirchen sector from the battle-worn *275th Grenadier Division*. This formation was then shifted to reinforce *LXXXI Corps'* left flank in the Hürtgen Forest.

US forces took Stolberg on September 22, but the attack was halted and smoke was laid to allow CCB/3 to withdraw to Donnerberg. For the Germans, Köchling believed the next enemy attack would be south of Aachen, and he set to work strengthening its positions as well as deploying the *12th* and *246th Volksgrenadier Divisions*.

Volksgrenadier Divisions

The "Peoples' Grenadier" divisions had been created to cope with the manpower shortages which plagued the *Wehrmacht* during 1944, but also to give an organizational structure to the hastily developed divisions that were being used to stem the enemy advance. The 25 divisions that were created on Hitler's orders in September, as well as 18 raised in July and August, were bestowed *Volksgrenadier* status, a lofty title designed to awaken the soldiers' national and military pride.

Organized and trained under the SS, but not to be fielded as such, the formations were designated to receive some of Germany's latest small arms and equipment. Generally, out of a 10,000-man *Volksgrenadier* division, roughly half consisted of new recruits and convalescents, with the remainder divided between *Luftwaffe* and *Kriegsmarine* personnel, and a core of experienced soldiers. A higher number of automatic small arms were allocated to help make up for the drop in manpower, which in 1944 shrank from an official strength of 17,000 to 14,000 soldiers (6 battalions), although an engineer battalion was often added as a seventh. Company and battalion trains were merged into battalion supply platoons, thereby freeing commanders to focus on operational issues. These formations tended to be deficient in artillery and motorization, and their tactical mobility and combat effectiveness suffered accordingly. As available manpower continued to decline over the next several months, German infantry divisions were increasingly reorganized to the *volksgrenadier* structure.

Missed Opportunities

With First Army's goal of attacking the Ruhr on hold, Hodges moved to clear the region west of the Maas in preparation for an offensive in the immediate future. To provide additional forces, Bradley transferred the 7th Armored ("Lucky Seventh") Division from Third Army and the 29th Infantry Division from the coast following its successful capture of Brest, but their arrival would take time. Montgomery's plan of using a British corps along his right to attack between the Maas and the Rhine Rivers implied that there would be no need to broaden First Army's frontage to fill the gap. Hodges, however, continued to worry about the potential dispersion of his forces, and the need to secure his exposed northern flank until his expected reinforcements arrived.

On September 26, the day after Hitler, Jodl, and Keitel drafted the Ardennes offensive to split the western Allies and retake Antwerp, Hodges met with Montgomery and the British Second Army's commander, General Dempsey, to discuss First Army's dilemma. To Hodges' satisfaction, only 7th Armored Division would be employed to assist the British, along with support from the 113th Cavalry Group and 1st Belgian Brigade. First Army was allocated a 25km wide corridor that extended nearly 65km into the British zone west of the Maas. By not directly attaching US forces under British authority, Bradley reasoned that complexity would be reduced and logistics would remain essentially unchanged.

In the lead-up to action, the 30th and 1st Infantry Divisions conducted refresher training for attacking *Westwall* fortifications and coordinating with armor, although not for urban environments. The 18th Infantry Regiment would push north from Eilendorf to meet the southbound 119th Infantry Regiment near Haaren to seal off Aachen. The 26th Infantry Regiment would make the actual assault into the city, and was reinforced with two companies totaling 20 M-4 Sherman tanks from 3rd Armored Division as a mobile reserve. Throughout the end of September an increasing number of up-gunned Shermans, with high-velocity 76mm main guns, were being distributed to combat units. 2nd Armored Division's buildup near Aachen confirmed Köchling's belief that the next major enemy assault would be southeast of the city, and he responded by spending the remainder of September strengthening German defenses in the area. His *12th* and *246th Volksgrenadier Divisions* would be ready.

North of Aachen, US artillery began a systematic attempt to destroy all enemy pillboxes in 30th Infantry Division's projected assault path. For this effort the 2nd Armored and the 29th and 30th Infantry Divisions provided 26 artillery battalions that could lay down enough fire to virtually halt *LXXXI Corps'* daytime movement.[25] Following a general bombardment, these guns were to shift targets a few hours prior to the attack. During this phase, the artillery was to target enemy anti-aircraft guns to protect the planned preliminary air strikes and also to conduct counter-battery fire, with every effort made to avoid fratricide once the assault had begun.

By the end of the month Collins' "reconnaissance" to retain VII Corps' initiative and freedom of maneuver had largely failed. The few US reserves meant an inability to exploit favorable situations, and an unwillingness to skirt resistance led to frontal assaults that were costly in men and time—the latter especially so as it allowed the Germans to regain much of their lost strength and equilibrium.

Footnotes

1. SHAEF G-3 War Room Summary 99.
2. Ruppenthal, *Logistical Support, I* 583; Sylvan Diary, 6 and 10 Sep.
3. Field Manual (FM) 100-5, *Field Service Regulations, Operations* (Washington, DC: GPO, 1944) calls for an attacking battalion to occupy a frontage of no more than 1,000m; essentially 16km for a corps.
4. Omar Bradley, *A Soldier's Story*, (New York: The Modern Library 1999), pp. 442.
5. VII Corps, Annex 2 to FO 11. Colonel Carter, the VII Corps G-2.
6. General J. Lawton Collins, *Lightning Joe*, (Baton Rouge: LSU Press, 1979), p. 273.
7. *Heeresgruppe B, Lagebeurteilungen Ia.*
8. OKH/GenStdH/Org.Abt, July 11, 1944.
9. German AT battalion cmdr. Lt. Wenzel Borgert interview by Hugh Ambrose, EC.
10. US ARMY Center of Military History.
11. A-988 Order of Battle of LXXXI Corps (Sept 1944–Apr 1945).
FM 100-5, *Field Service Regulations, Operations* (Washington, DC: GPO, 1944). Chapter 1 Organization of Troops paragraph 23: To insure unity of effort or increase readiness for combat, part or all of the subordinate units of a command may be formed into one or more temporary tactical groupings (task forces), each under a designated commander. In each, the unity of tactical organizations is preserved as far as practicable.
12. Major General Harmon, quoted by Lt. Col. W. D. Smart: "Armored Divisions' Combat Commands." Cavalry Journal LV (January–February 1946).
13. A second reorganization on September 15, 1943 introduced a small Combat Command Reserve (CCR) headquarters and reduced the armored division to three tank battalions (each of three medium and one light tank company) to match the existing three armored infantry and field artillery battalions.
14. Heichler, *Germans Opposite VII Corps*, pp. 41–42.
15. AGFOB(ETO), report no. 120, "Employment of Tanks with Infantry," 2 September 1944, p. 7, MHI.
16. Mng Sitrep, 353d Inf Div, 0445 on 13 Sep 44, D-UXI Corps KTB, Kampfverlauf.
17. VII Corps Opns Memo 91, 11 Sep 44, VII Corps Opns Memos file, Sep 44; FO 11, 13 Sep 44, VII Corps G-3 FO's file, Sep 44.
18. FM 100-5, *Field Service Regulations, Operations* (Washington, DC: GPO, 1944). Chapter 1 Organization of Troops paragraph 23.
19. Tel Convs, LXXXI Corps to 9th Pz Div, 1420 on 13 Sep 44, and LXXXI Corps to 116th Pz Div, 1430 on 13 Sep 44, LXXCI Corps KTB, Kampfverlauf.
20. Tel Cony, LXXI Corps to Gen Mahlmann, 2040 on 13 Sep 44, LIXXI Corps KTB, Kampfverlauf.

[21.] Roland G. Ruppenthal, *Logistical Support of the Armies*, Vol. I and II, United States Army in World War II (Washington, 1953).

[22.] Oberst (a.D.) Hasso Neitzel, MS B-793, "89th Infantry Division, 13 Sep–1 Oct 1944" (1948).

[23.] The Bewertungen des Inneren Wertes ("evaluations of worth") was a changing label of a division's combat effectiveness, including material, steadiness, endurance, leadership, élan, training standards, dependability, and similar factors. Created in 1942 is comprised the following categories: Kampfwert I (capable of all offensive missions), II (conditionally capable of offensive missions), III (fully capable of Defensive missions), IV (conditionally capable of defensive missions).

[24.] Annex I to XIX Corps FO 27.

Chapter 4

Encircling Aachen
(October 1–7)

By the end of September, VII Corps' front line extended through Aachen's southern and eastern suburbs, and at points penetrated the second and final section of the *Westwall*. All that remained was for First Army to cut off the city's northern approaches, which continued to serve as a conduit to reinforce and resupply the determined urban fighters within. US efforts to capture Eschweiler, and seal off the area around Würselen, had been hampered by the same supply difficulties that had dogged the Allies for the last two months. German resistance, record precipitation, and low temperatures took a toll as well.

On October 1, Rose's 3rd Armored Division had for several days settled into a pattern of semi-static warfare that included patrols, artillery fire, and the reduction of pillboxes and other fortifications along the Schill Line. The 1st Infantry Division, however, continued to work its way around to the east of Aachen in preparation for a final push to link up with Major General Leland S. Hobbs' 30th Infantry Division, which would soon launch a similar attack from the north. With the 1106th Engineer Group anchoring 1st Infantry Division's left in the Aachen State Forest, Huebner's command would make for Ravels Hill (Hill 231), "Crucifix Hill" (Hill 239), and Aachen with its 18th, 16th, and 26th Infantry Regiments, respectively.

On VII Corps' other flank, the Hürtgen Forest was proving to be a considerable hindrance to 9th Infantry Division's efforts between the "Monschau Corridor" and Schevenhütte, as well as the vital road hub at Schmidt. Until Collins could secure VII Corps' right flank, enemy reinforcements would continue to flow into the area, ultimately to the detriment of any large-scale attempt to force crossings over the Roer. With the battle in First Army's southern sector to be decided, Hodges focused his attention on the encirclement of Aachen, and in particular XIX Corps' sector between it and Geilenkirchen.

As part of the northern pincer, the 29th Infantry Division was to make limited attacks along XIX Corps' left flank starting on October 1 with the intention of distracting German attention from Aachen's forthcoming encirclement. To its right the 2nd Armored ("Hell on Wheels") Division made ready to use its "heavy" designation to penetrate the *Westwall* and establish crossings over the Roer River, which was some 15km distant. The 30th Infantry Division, still officially resting, held XIX Corps' right flank. After having proved itself in the defense of Mortain, the unit was slated to attack southeast along a narrow 3km front and push past the Wurm River. Hobbs felt that this route would avoid the stronger defenses near Geilenkirchen and the urbanized areas around Aachen. Although this would add time to a proposed link-up with the VII Corps, the approach provided roads better suited for supply and movement, which would make up any lost time.

The 2nd Armored and 30th Infantry Divisions prepared to cooperate in the breaching of the *Westwall* scheduled for late September or early October 1944. Hobbs' infantry was to cross the Wurm River three miles above Aachen to penetrate the German defenses and capture Würselen. Then 2nd Armored's CCA (Colonel John H. Colier) and CCB (Brigadier General Isaac D. White) were to exploit the breach and rush ahead to force a crossing over the Roer River. Operation Cisco, as it was called, would have "the greatest concentration of planes in close support of American ground troops since the 'carpet' bombing along the Périers-St. Lô road in Normandy."[1] This air support was to involve more than 3,300 planes, including some 1,000 heavy bombers. The concept of close air support using heavy and medium bombers had only recently been revived as Allied units approached the German border, and were not available in the numbers hoped for to effectively supplement the designated tactical aircraft.

To contest US efforts against Aachen, Köchling threw in every reserve he could scrape together. The combat-depleted *183rd Volksgrenadier* and *49th Grenadier Divisions* were positioned across from XIX Corps. *246th Volksgrenadier Division* defended the city, while *12th Volksgrenadier Division* deployed to the south. The *217th Sturm (Assault) Panzer Battalion*, and *341st*, *902nd*, and *394th Sturmgeschütz Brigades* provided support, along with the corps' *117th Arko* (artillery command).[2] Köchling's roughly 20,000 men were also promised a refurbished *116th Panzer Division* and *3rd Panzergrenadier Division* totaling an additional 24,000 personnel. Although the German line had

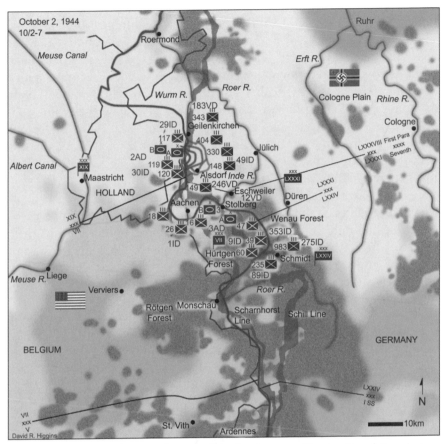

XIX Corps initiating the encirclement of Aachen between October 2 and 7 against a reinvigorated German defense.

been growing in strength for the last several weeks, the formations deploying around Aachen presented a mostly polyglot defense. Nevertheless, Hitler stressed that the defense of the city was to be a sampling of what the Allies could expect as they pushed into Germany.

Isolating Aachen from the North

On October 2 First Army launched its offensive to encircle Aachen and clear a path to the Roer River. Of the over 3,000 aircraft originally scheduled to participate, only a fraction actually arrived. Seventy B-26 Marauder (medium) bombers from the 9th Bombardment Division supported the 117th RCT's advance, while an additional 23 did the same for the 119th RCT. Seventy-one P-38 Lightnings and 88 P-47 Thunderbolts from IX TAC bombed and strafed German defenses, factories, and rail lines.[3] Heavy smoke from the 26 US artillery battalions, and intermittent cloud cover, confounded accurate aerial targeting. Many of the bomber crews, perhaps overly cautious about dropping their loads prematurely or erroneously, made their runs perpendicular to the German lines, and in accordance with an army-assigned "bomb-line" that marked an "off limits" zone. IX TAC did not want to re-earn their unwanted moniker as the "American Luftwaffe" for its perceived knack of hitting friendly ground forces.

The tactical bombers managed to hit the industrial area around Übach and Herbach, but little damage was inflicted. Napalm proved of limited value due to the damp terrain, and most bombs missed their targets, often by wide margins. Many within the German lines were unaware an attack had even occurred. Over the next several days, adverse weather would continue to ground many tactical bombing missions in support of XIX Corps. To further coordinate these operations, each infantry battalion had an air liaison officer to better manage what air support was available.

By 1055 the bombing run was over and Corlett sent his XIX Corps into the fight. 30th Infantry Division's 117th and 119th Infantry Regiments led the assault along a narrow front designed to quickly penetrate the enemy's defenses. Chemical mortar rounds concentrated at first on clearing openings through the German defenses beyond the Wurm River. The fire would then shift to a rolling barrage against the crossing areas, before preceding the infantry following several hundred meters behind. Direct support battalions of 105mm howitzers contributed to this shifting curtain of fire. With the relative lack of air support, artillery along the sector needed to increase its firing, and stocks of ammunition that were to be used to fight off the expected counterattacks were steadily depleted.

Although limited initial success was achieved, coordination between US infantry and armor was poor due to the muddy terrain hampering vehicle movement. With artillery making up the difference, the 29th Infantry Division initiated aggressive, but largely diversionary attacks against Aachen's northern suburbs. 2nd Armored Division's attempt to penetrate the *Westwall* and provide support as needed until the merger with VII Corps proved successful. With German defenses still active, US infantry was forced to organize into small assault teams to better subdue the various pillboxes and bunkers with grenades, pole charges, and flamethrowers. Many in the first wave, however, were forced to take shelter behind the Aachen-Rimburg-Geilenkirchen railway and its elevating embankment. Heavy German machine gun and mortar fire allowed few options for movement.

October 1

US

XIX Corps
2nd Armored Division
Commander: Major General Ernest N. Harmon
Div HHC, HQ CCR/CCC, CCA HHC, CCB HHC
Armor: 66th (minus G Company) 67th Armored Regiments (M-4 Sherman (medium), M-5 Stuart (light))
Infantry: 41st Armored Infantry Regiment
Field Artillery: HQ & HQ Battery, 14th, 78th, 92nd Armored FA Battalions (M-7 Priest 105mm SP Howitzer)
Other: 82nd Armored Reconnaissance Squadron, 142nd Armored Signal Company, 17th Armored Engineer Battalion, Service Company, 502nd Counter Intelligence Corps Detachment
Trains: HHC, 2nd Ordnance Maintenance Battalion, Supply Battalion, 48th Armored Medical Battalion, Military Police Platoon

Attached
195th AAA Automatic Weapons Battalion
702nd TD Battalion

29th Infantry Division
Commander: Major General Charles H. Gerhardt
Div HQ & HQ Company
Infantry: 115th, 116th (minus 1st Battalion), 175th Infantry Regiments
Field Artillery: HQ & HQ Battery, 110th, 111th, 224th FA Battalions (105mm Howitzer), 227th FA Battalion (155mm Howitzer)
Other: HQ Special Troops, 29th Reconnaissance Troop (Mechanized), 29th Signal Company, 121st Engineer Combat Battalion, 29th Counter Intelligence Corps Detachment
Trains: 729th Ordnance Light Maintenance Company, 29th Quarter-

master Company, 29th Military Police Platoon, 104th Medical Battalion

Attached
459th AAA AW Battalion (Mobile)
747th Tank Battalion
744th Tank Battalion (minus A Company)
113th Cavalry Group
246th Engineer Combat Battalion
B Company, 82nd Engineer Combat Battalion
B Company, 234th Engineer Combat Battalion

30th Infantry Division
Commander: Major General Leland S. Hobbs
Div HQ & HQ Company
Infantry: 117th, 119th, 120th Infantry Regiments
Field Artillery: HQ & HQ Battery, 118th, 197th, 230th FA Battalions (105mm Howitzer), 113th FA Battalion (155mm Howitzer)
Special: HQ Special Troops, 30th Reconnaissance Troop (Mechanized), 30th Signal Company, 105th Engineer Combat Battalion, 30th Counter Intelligence Corps Detachment
Trains: 730th Ordnance Light Maintenance Company, 30th Quartermaster Company, 30th Military Police Platoon, 105th Medical Battalion

Attached
531st AAA AW Battalion (Mobile)
4th Platoon, B Company, 602nd Engineer Combat Battalion
1st Battalion, 116th Infantry Regiment, 29th Infantry Division
823rd TD Battalion (SP)
743rd Tank Battalion
448th WWW AW Battalion

German

LXXXI Corps
12th Volksgrenadier Division
Commander: Generalleutnant Gerhard Engel
Div HQ

Infantry: 48th, 89th, Volksgrenadier Regiments
Field Artillery: HQ, 12th Artillery Regiment (75mm, 105mm, 155mm Howitzers)
12th Panzer Reconnaissance Battalion, Antitank Battalion (75mm AA and AT), Panzer Engineer Battalion, Panzer Signal, Feldersatz (Replacement Training) Battalion, Füsilier Battalion, Support Regiment

183rd Volksgrenadier Division
Commander: Generalmajor Wolfgang Lange
Div HQ
Infantry: 330th, 343rd, 351st Grenadier Regiments
Field Artillery: HQ, 219th Artillery Regiment (75mm, 105mm, 155mm Howitzers)
Panzer Reconnaissance Battalion, Antitank Battalion (75mm AA and AT), Panzer Engineer Battalion, Panzer Signal, Feldersatz (Replacement Training) Battalion, 183rd Füsilier Battalion, Support Regiment

246th Volksgrenadier Division
Commander: Oberst Gerhard Wilck
Div HQ
Infantry: 404th, 352nd, 689th Grenadier Regiments
Field Artillery: HQ, 246th Artillery Regiment (75mm, 105mm, 155mm Howitzers)
246th Panzer Reconnaissance Battalion, Antitank Battalion (75mm AA and AT), Panzer Engineer Battalion, Panzer Signal, Feldersatz (Replacement Training) Battalion, Füsilier Battalion, Support Regiment

KNA 432
319th Panzer Company (Radio-controlled) (Sturmgeschütz, Borgward IV)
902nd Sturmgeschütz Brigade
341st Army Sturmgeschütz Brigade
217th Sturmpanzer Battalion
762nd Artillery Regiment zbV (motorized)
725th Eisenbahn Artillery Battalion
117th Arko (Artillery Command) (1301st, 1310th Fortress Artillery Battalions; 1076th Army Fortress Battery; 460th, 992nd Heavy Artillery (motorized) Battalions; 63rd Observation Battalion)
432nd Corps Reconnaissance Battalion

432nd Corps Supply
432nd Field Police Troop

Across the Wurm

Excessive rains during September had washed out or reduced secondary roads to muddy quagmires, and had turned the numerous streams throughout the area into significant barriers. Because of the soft ground and need to use bridges, most wheeled transports relied on the few hard surface roads in the area. This naturally caused considerable delays in bringing forward and stockpiling supplies needed to support the assault on the city.

During October, this precipitation morphed into a continual freezing rain, with only the briefest breaks in the weather. As American ground forces tended to operate in the open they suffered from the cold, damp climate, generally more so than their adversary who could make use of the shelter offered by pillboxes and built-up areas. Living in foxholes under these conditions resulted in dehydration, immersion syndrome (i.e. trench foot), and respiratory ailments. Although this would seem to have a demoralizing effect, many found it motivating as they pushed ahead in search of the next shelter to get out of the elements.

Even though most of the German commanders remained convinced that the main US assault would be from the south of Aachen, the less heavily defended north still managed to slow 30th Infantry Division with unexpectedly strong counterattacks that caused heavy casualties. After several hours of incremental gains, lead pillbox assault teams used flamethrowers and explosive charges to steadily force a crossing over the Wurm River and penetrate the final *Westwall* fortifications in their zone. Overhead supporting fire from heavy machine guns was directed at the German fortifications, but their use of tracer ammunition to regulate their firing made them easily spotted and most were shortly put out of action.

The 1st Battalion, 117th Infantry Regiment rushed down the valley's western slope with their duckboards to make a quick crossing of the river. Originally planned as requiring assault boats, the low water level permitted footbridges. Although B Company crossed the Wurm, the follow-up company was nearly destroyed by shellfire. Faced with the possibility that his entire attack might stall, the battalion commander,

1st Patrol, 8th Infantry Division passes a tank destroyer in Düren on Feb 24, 1945. (US Signal Corps)

Lieutenant Colonel Robert E. Frankland, quickly called up A Company from its reserve position. Within 30 minutes both companies had established positions east of the river against the protective cover of the railroad embankment. With heavy enemy fire from pillboxes along the Palenberg-Rimburg road, and open ground to their front, further movement would be a slow process.

After clearing German positions around Marienberg, elements of the 2nd Battalion crossed the Wurm and entered the northern part of Palenberg. The remainder moved behind 1st Battalion in order to approach the town from the south. The *183rd Volksgrenadier Division* had worked feverishly over the last few weeks in preparation to receive an enemy attack at Geilenkirchen. When the Americans instead moved on Übach-Palenberg, the defenders were surprised by the direction and ferociousness of the enemy assault, and dissolved back to the town at around 1600. Brutal house-to-house fighting followed, while similar action was happening nearby at Rimburg and around its castle. While muddy conditions hampered infantry movement, it completely halted the armor, which proved unable to cross the Wurm until late in the day. Over the next few hours US assault teams burned and blasted their enemy into submission.

The 30th Infantry Division's other assault regiment, the 119th Infantry (Colonel Edwin M. Sutherland), had met with similar difficulties to the 117th RCT. Sutherland's regiment crossed the Wurm south of Rimburg and its lead battalion was immediately hit by German shellfire and forced to take cover along the railroad embankment. With tanks churning up the west bank of the river, and many of the infantry discarding their duckboards to gain speed with which to more quickly across the river and seek cover, improvised crossings were created using fence posts, and other nearby debris. Once beyond the Wurm, those not deployed behind the embankment received intense fire from the Rimburg Castle.

Anticipating immediate German reaction to this attack on the *Westwall*, Hobbs and his regimental commanders waited apprehensively at dusk for what was the ubiquitous enemy counterattack. The bridgehead of the 119th RCT remained tenuous, and the late arrival of tank support meant they were immediately unavailable to assist US efforts to reach the line of German pillboxes. Its inability to advance beyond the railroad had left the 117th RCT with an exposed right flank. With a bridgehead only 300m deep, Hobbs told his artillery commander to fire on German assembly positions throughout the night, including routes leading into the constricted bridgehead. By nightfall they had driven the Germans from these outpost positions.

Indirectly, help arrived as the 29th Infantry Division's demonstration drew such enemy attention as to make the Germans reconsider their idea of where the main US thrust would fall. Regiment Stoottroepen (former Dutch partisans) performed rear area security and allowed Major General Charles H. Gerhardt, 29th Infantry Division's commander, to better concentrate on front-line operations. Still concerned that his perception might be incorrect, Köchling remained unwilling to fully commit to countering a threat that might not exist. In case his initial assessment was wrong, he did send in the *902nd Sturmgeschütz Brigade* after dark to reinforce the position; however, the assault guns were soon halted by US artillery.

By the second day German resistance had proven to be unexpectedly determined and resilient. The overall US effort to encompass the region north of Aachen remained a slow process resulting in increased ammunition expenditure. The 119th RCT had managed to advance a kilometer beyond the Wurm River, but it was having better success after creating a task force to outflank German resistance in the woods around Rimburg. By 1035 enemy resistance in the area was overcome and the castle fell into American possession.

US armor had finally made its way through the muck to join the infantry in integrated attacks, and Corlett was not about to let an enemy counterattack threaten his advances. He sent in CCB/2 over the recently constructed bridges at Marienberg toward Übach. Tankdozers and assault teams led the way to seal off, or otherwise subdue, German pillboxes. CCA/2 would follow as soon as sufficient space was created on the enemy side of the river, but for the time being armored vehicles from its combat command partner were clogging the route over the Wurm. 30th Infantry Division was to yield to the armor's passage, which would expand the fledgling bridgehead. With its left flank thus protected, it could turn southward where it would attempt to link with VII Corps.

As the American bridgehead expanded, Köchling moved to counter it, and establish a new main line of resistance (MLR), by organizing the *49th Grenadier* and *183rd Volksgrenadier Divisions* under the latter's control. To support *Generalmajor* Wolfgang Lange, the *341st* and *902nd Sturmgeschütz Brigades*, and an infantry battalion of the *246th Volksgrenadier Division* were brought up from Aachen.[4] Although time was short, Köchling delayed the attack until 0215 on October 4th to better coordinate the effort. Terrain, darkness, and enemy artillery conspired to prevent most of the German force from organizing on time. With only the engineer battalion available, it achieved little when it was sent against heavy artillery fire and the 3rd Battalion, 117th Infantry Regiment in Übach.

Köchling tried to push the 119th RCT back with five infantry, an engineer, and two Sturmgeschütz battalions, but it was also stopped. Even the nearly full-strength *506th Heavy Panzer Battalion* under Major Eberhard Lange proved unable to make headway. Its complement of new Tiger IIs, with their thick armor and superior 88mm main gun, were handicapped by weight, and the soft ground further reduced maneuverability. Supporting German artillery fire prematurely lifted and only one battalion actually reached Übach, where it too ran into an equally unyielding opponent. A third German attack from north of Übach was also rebuffed when it encountered TF 1 from CCB/2 moving from the town.

Late in the afternoon of the 4th the US offensive was finally making noticeable progress. Task Forces 1 and 2 of CCB/2 attacked from Übach to seize the high ground 2km north near Hoverhof. Although the area contained numerous pillboxes, US infantry-tank cooperation forced their way through to anchor the bridgehead's northern flank.

Köchling's Counterattack

OB West, von Rundstedt, and the *Seventh Army* commander, General Brandenberger, had visited General Köchling and decided that the forces locally available were insufficient. *LXXXI Corps* was to bring together every available unit from its sector to thwart the US advance north of Aachen. In the Übach sector these included a *Landesschütz* battalion, an assault gun brigade, and a howitzer battalion (all from *12th Volksgrenadier Division*) and an antitank company with six 75mm anti-tank guns from the *246th Volksgrenadier Division*. "Remote-control robot assault guns" were also brought in, such as with the *319th Panzer Company*, but little was expected from them.[5]

Köchling felt that the magnitude of the various units would be beyond his ability to control. He broke up Lange's command and restored the boundary between the *49th* and *183rd Volksgrenadier Divisions* to run roughly from Beggendorf west to Übach.[6] Brandenberger provided additional forces from his army command, including cadets from the NCO Training Schools at Düren and Jülich, which were to relieve the *343rd Grenadier Regiment*, *183rd Volksgrenadier Division*, so that it would be able to take part in the planned German counterattack. *404th Grenadier Regiment* was ordered north from its defense of Aachen, and an infantry battalion from the *275th Grenadier Division* serving in the Hürtgen Forest was brought in along with a fortress machine gun battalion.[7] Köchling now possessed 10 batteries of 105mm howitzers and 7 batteries of 150mm howitzers, with another 27 150mm howitzers and 32 88mm antitank/antiaircraft guns arriving soon.[8]

As with Köchling's previous, and smaller, attempt to organize divergent units from different sectors, this grouping fell victim to the same difficulties with movement. Although numbers and firepower appeared impressive, these formations were to be thrown together and expected to make a coordinated effort. In a vacuum it might have been possible. US forces, however, had not remained idle and continued with their sluggish, yet inexorable offensive. On October 6 the XIX Corps finally created a corridor through the *Westwall*.

A Panzerstellung with a bolted Panzer I turret with 13mm of added armor to the face and covering the side vision ports, This Ringstände type emplacement consists of a timber-shored hole between 2 and 3 meters-deep was captured by the 30th Infantry Division just east of the Roer near Niederzier on Feb 26, 1945. (US Signal Corps)

Köchling attempted another counterattack against Übach-Palenberg, but a compromise on a speedy reaction over concentration resulted in another piecemeal effort that did not overrun US positions. German armor was unable to cope with the overwhelming fire from American Shermans, and as a last-ditch effort to halt the advance the Germans threw in all available artillery and what aircraft they could muster. Generally the latter amounted to a few sorties by Fw-190s and Bf-109s, and on rare occasions the new German Me-262 ("Swallow") jet fighter would make an appearance. Köchling's lack of adequate reserves left him largely unable to react to threatened sectors. Even the deployment of a detachment of Tiger I's did little to rebuff the enemy as they advanced around Alsdorf and into Aachen's northern suburban defenses.

For the last four days US efforts to penetrate the enemy defenses had been hampered by the weather, terrain, and enemy resistance. German reinforcements, however, were at the end of their strength. The unremitting pressure of CCB/2 and the 117th and 119th RCTs had contained every counterattack. Though Corlett had hoped originally to use only the 30th Infantry Division for the link-up while the 2nd Armored Division struck eastward for crossings over the Roer River, General Hodges made it clear that operations were to be confined to the *Westwall* until a link-up was achieved.[9] In the early afternoon Corlett told the armor to hold in place along the northeastern and eastern fringes of the bridgehead while at the same time making a main effort southeast-ward to help the 30th Infantry Division link with the VII Corps.[10]

Even before Corlett revealed his change of plan in the afternoon of the 6th, CCA/2 had gone into action in conjunction with the 117th RCT to expand the bridgehead. Part of the combat command attacked northeast toward Beggendorf, while two other columns moved southeast. One headed in the direction of Baesweiler, southeast of Beggendorf; the other advanced close along the flank of the 117th RCT in a renewal of the infantry's drive on the crossroads hamlet southeast of Übach. The weight of the armor and a clear day, which permitted six close-support missions by fighter-bombers of the IX Tactical Air Command, contributed to the ground force's success in taking Beggendorf, and CCA/2's push nearly 2km further to Baesweiler.

On October 7 the Germans prepared a counterattack at Alsdorf that was to include *Mobile (Schnelle) Regiment von Fritzschen's 503rd* (with an engineer platoon), *504th*, and *506th* bicycle battalions. Additional help came from a *Kampfgruppe* built around the *108th Panzer Brigade* totaling some 22 assault guns.[11] Von Rundstedt's reserves (*3rd Panzergrenadier* and the refitting *116th Panzer Divisions*) prepared to halt further US success, but they were held up en route due to damaged rail services. Both were attached to *I SS Panzer Corps* and tasked with keeping the northeast land corridor to Aachen open.

The *116th Panzer Division* was to capture the hills west and southwest of Verlautenheide, which dominated the city. Although the "Greyhounds" remained heavily engaged around Würselen, they were ordered to attack with an armored *Kampfgruppe* past Kohlscheid to the southeast. Again, Köchling hoped to use *3rd Panzergrenadier Division* as a whole, but the situation remained the same, and its components were thrown into battle as they arrived to counter the enemy as soon as possible.

Köchling's piecemeal commitment of heterogeneous reinforcements created command and control problems that were further disrupted by

Allied aircraft and artillery fire. Even though the Germans had shorter interior lines of communication, if they did not place their often meager supplies well forward they were often unable to receive them when under attack, which hurt their ability to mount an effective defense.

Just south of Immendorf, CCB/2's TF 1 had kept a maintenance pool of some 30–50 tanks in full view of the enemy.[12] Likely done to keep the vehicles close to the front where they could be made immediately available, their presence intimidated an enemy that could do little to intervene. As the vehicles were dug in, artillery fire would probably be ineffective, and in open terrain losses to antitank teams were often disproportionate to the damage they inflicted.

Preparations at Aachen

Cordoned off in Aachen, the German garrison found it unable to assist efforts beyond its perimeter. With roughly 5,000 German defenders, including converted naval, *Luftwaffe*, city police personnel, and a handful of tanks and assault guns, they were unable to organize a mobile reserve or mount an effective counterattack against the flanks of the forming enemy pincers.[13] Although inexperienced, and of limited strength and quality, Wilck's command would fight with several combat modifiers. With much of the city in ruins, ample cover offered not only concealment, but also protective cover. Rubble and easily fashioned man-made obstacles would confound US movement, resupply, and evacuation in an already restrictive urban environment. Upper floors and basements could also be incorporated, which added a vertical aspect for observation and snipers, while basements for grazing machine gun fire and close positions from which to use portable antitank weapons abounded within the streets.

These close battles stressed the elevation capability of direct-fire weapons and complicated their ability to aim and move. Had greater strength within Aachen been possible, the German defenders could have bolstered their fixed forces by creating a rapid response reserve with which to counter enemy attempts to penetrate the city. Barriers and fortifications positioned outside the city would provide gaps into which an attacker could be channeled, with contact to be maintained between elements actively engaged in the operations at or near the center and those in other portions of the defense zone. All German forces remained especially vigilant against airborne or air assault attacks aimed at severing contact or impeding the movement of reserves.

Footnotes

1. Charles B. MacDonald, *The Siegfried Line Campaign, U.S. Army in World War II* (Washington, DC: Office of the Chief of Military History, 1950), pp. 252–260.

2. Anlageband A (offen) zum Kriegstagebuch des Generalkommandos LXXX.

3 War Department Special Staff. *World War II A Chronology October 1944*, p. 42.

4. AAR, 183d VG Div; Tel Conv, LXXXI Corps to 183d VG Div, 1900, 3 Oct 44, in LXXXI Corps KTB, Kampfverlauf.

5. LXXXI Corps KTB, Kampfverlauf, 4 Oct 44.

6. Tel Convs, LXXXI Corps to 246th Div, 1225, 4 Oct 44, LXXXI Corps to 12th Div, 1230, 4 Oct 44, LXXXI Corps to 183d Div, 1250 and 1535, 4 Oct 44, and LXXXI Corps to 49th Div, 1530, 4 Oct 44, all in LXXXI Corps KTB, Kampfverlauf; Order, LXXXI Corps to I83d and 49th Divs, 1345, 4 Oct 44, LXXXI Corps KTB, Befehle an Div; AAR, 183d VG Div.

7. Order, Brandenberger to LXXXI Corps, 2035, 4 Oct 44, LXXXI Corps KTB, Befehle: Heeresgruppe, Armee, usw.

8. AAR 183d VG Div; Tel Convs, Seventh Army to LXXXI Corps, 2200, 2 Oct, and LXXXI Corps Arty O to aide, 2230, 4 Oct 44, LXXXI Corps KTB, Kampfverlauf; Order, LXXXI Corps to 183d and 49th Divs, 2040, 4 Oct 44, in LXXXI Corps KTB, Befehle an Div.

9. Corlett to OCMH, 20 May 56.

10. XIX Corps Ltr of Instrs 4, 1400, 6 Oct, XIX Corps Ltr of Instrs file, Oct. 44. Order, *49th Inf Div to Regt von Fritzschen*, 8 Oct 44, *LXXXI Corps KTB, Meldungen der Div.*

11. Foreign Military Studies Office, B-753.

12. Charles B. MacDonald, *The Siegfried Line Campaign, U.S. Army in World War II* (Washington, DC: Office of the Chief of Military History, 1950), p. 457.

Chapter 5

First Schmidt
(October 6–16)

Following "Lightning Joe" Collins' failure to quickly penetrate the *Westwall* en masse, First Army's commander Courtney Hodges turned his attention to securing his flanks in preparation for future operations. With XIX Corps having finally pulled even along the Wurm River south of Geilenkirchen, it could now be used as a northern pincer to complement that of VII Corps moving up from Eschweiler. Together these two commands were in a position to encircle and reduce Aachen and re-establish a solid line along their fronts. The 3rd Armored and 1st Infantry Divisions would provide the southern pincer, securing the town of Stolberg in the process. The 2nd Armored and 30th Infantry Divisions of XIX Corps would continue to serve as the northern pincer, turning to join hands with VII Corps once they were east of the city. Once completed, Hodges would be able to solidify his gains, build-up men and material, and move to regain operational momentum that would finally take his command to the Rhine River and beyond. Before this could occur, however, VII Corps' right flank would also have to be secured, and this meant that the remainder of the Hürtgen and Wenau Forests would have to be cleared.

Eisenhower's "broad front" strategy had sought to avoid allowing enemy build-ups along the Allies' operational flanks as their armies advanced. Such threats could result in disruptive attacks into the Allies' rear echelon and communication zone. While this approach worked well during the heady battles of maneuver across open terrain, the mindset persisted even as formations such as First Army became steadily bogged down by semi-static warfare along the German border. With the heavily forested region south of Aachen a logical location for the Germans to gather their strength in relative safety, bypassing the Rötgen, Hürtgen, and Wenau Forests (collectively considered the Hürtgen Forest) would not be permitted.

VII Corps' remaining division, 9th Infantry, would address this issue by attacking east through the rugged, forested terrain between Monschau and Eschweiler with the ultimate goal of reaching the Roer River. This would anchor Collins' right, as well as draw German attention away from the main US effort at Aachen. Losses through attrition were to be tolerated, as there seemed little chance that the Germans could keep pace and would more quickly be run down and demoralized.

US Tactical Plans

The lengthy frontage covered by the 9th Infantry Division forced units to deploy close to the front lines to retain a defined front. This meant there were few forces available to use as a division reserve. Because the terrain hampered communication and coordination, Major General Craig left his 47th Infantry Regiment around Schevenhütte, and placed the newly arrived 298th Engineer Combat Battalion between it and the assault elements further south. Both were to retain a defensive posture, and act as a connection to the rest of 9th Infantry Division and its HQ at Zweifall.

To penetrate the German defenses, Craig assembled the bulk of his command about a kilometer west of the Weisser Weh Creek along a 5km front. On October 5 Lieutenant Colonel Van H. Bond's 39th Infantry Regiment would initially swing clockwise around the north of Germeter in an effort to capture the town in conjunction with the 60th Infantry Regiment coming up from the south. Following the success of this effort, relatively open terrain plus the Monschau-Hürtgen-Düren highway would be within reach. The 39th RCT would then continue on to capture Vossenack, and the open ridge upon which it sits, cross the Kall River, and occupy the plateau around Schmidt. Once past Vossenack, Lieutenant Colonel Donald C. Claymen's (Van Houten's after 10/9) 60th Infantry Regiment was to take Richelskaul before turning southwest to capture Road Junction (RJ) 471 and Raffelsbrand. Should both formations achieve their goals, the 9th Infantry Division would push on for the Roer River, but also have an opportunity to strike southward to take enemy forces stubbornly fighting east of Monschau from behind.

German Tactical Plans

Having stopped the Allied air and ground offensive at Arnhem (Market Garden) by September 26, the Germans refocused their attention to the

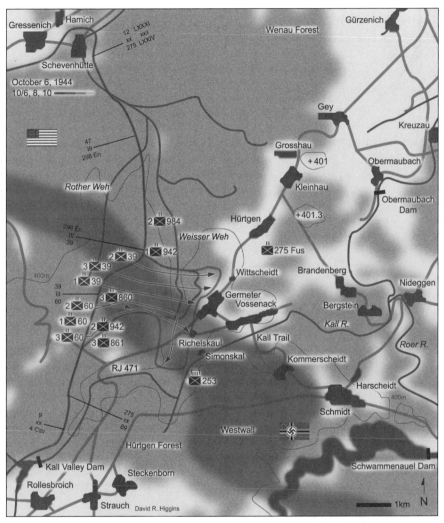

Tactical focus showing the US 9th Infantry Division's abortive attempt to capture Schmidt, and penetrate the Hürtgen Forest starting on October 6.

Aachen sector. With First Army still not adequately organized and supplied following its rush across France, and its forward units becoming increasingly cautious as they probed the outermost *Westwall* fortifications, the front west of the Roer River Valley began to solidify. The Germans attempted to make use of the unexpected time alloted them by rushing men and material to the area between Roermond and

Monschau to not only help prevent an Allied breakthrough but to secure rearward assembly positions for the coming offensive to the south in the Ardennes.

Many of the Germans defending the Hürtgen Forest were eager to inflict some punishment of their own against an enemy that had been having things his way for the past several weeks. Others had recently helped clear cities like Jülich and Düren and seen the horrific effects of Allied bombs on German civilians. The *275th Grenadier Division* was no exception. Under its commander, a veteran of the Eastern and Western Fronts in both world wars, *Generalleutnant* Hans Schmidt, the division had recently fought at Normandy and Falaise, where it had taken a considerable beating.

After an all too brief rest, the formation assumed responsibility for defending the Hürtgen Forest on October 1, followed by two days of refurbishment in the Aachen sector. Here it absorbed the combat remnants of the *353rd Grenadier Division*, as well as a mix of *Luftwaffe* and *Kriegsmarine* units, that for various reasons were of no further use to their old services and had been transferred to ground combat duties. Having numbered only 800 men when moved to the Hürtgen sector on September 22, the *275th Grenadier Division* had increased to some 5,000 soldiers and 1,500 headquarters and service personnel by October 6. Schmidt's heterogeneous formation took up positions in the close, dank environment where they hurriedly constructed numerous field fortifications, minefields, and roadblocks in preparation to defend the Aachen sector, and their homeland.[1]

Although the Germans were in a depleted state and without a completely unified defense, they realized that the densely wooded environment imparted a considerable combat modifier. The Allies' reliance on air power and artillery would be of limited use in the coming battle, causing US ground forces to fight without their customary supports. In this arena individual commanders and the strength of their personalities would make the difference in creating successful fighting forces out of the collection of demoralized soldiers running the gamut of experience and quality.

Schmidt possessed adequate and well-registered artillery, but wired and wireless communication problems were already becoming evident due to the rugged terrain. Often the first indication of a US attack was its preliminary artillery barrage. Schmidt ultimately concluded that his assaults, "...without artillery preparation were more successful, since

A German pillbox disguised as a wooden building has been converted to a command post for D Company, 120th Infantry Regiment, 30th Infantry Division on October 12, 1944. (US Signal Corps)

the enemy is alerted by preparatory artillery fire, and artillery fire had usually less effect than expected." He concluded that "Surprise is more important..."[2]

Schmidt distributed his command along the Rother Weh and Weisser Weh Creeks, as the pair's roughly parallel valleys cut through the rugged terrain to provide a good foundation on which to establish defenses. The intermittently open ground running through Hürtgen, Vossenack, and Grosshau enabled much quicker resupply, replacement, and casualty evacuation, although the continually wet weather necessitated the building of corduroy roads.

With outposts to the west of the Rother Weh, *Oberst* Joachim Heintz's *984th Grenadier Regiment*, consisting of just one battalion under Captain Bienelt, a staff, and one headquarters company, occupied the right. *Oberstleutnant* Friedrich Tröster's *942nd Grenadier Regiment* was composed of the *353rd Grenadier Division's* combat formations, while the staff and replacement units were transferred out of the sector to *LXXX Corp*. The weakest section of the line, the left, was held by additional former elements of the *353rd Grenadier Division*, now classed as the *253rd Grenadier Regiment (253rd Replacement and Training Regiment)* under *Oberst* Feind, to which a *Kampfgruppe* from the *347th Grenadier Division (Oberstleutnant* Brandes' *861st Grenadier Regiment)* was added. An assortment of *Landesschütz*, the *12th* and *20th Luftwaffe Fortress Battalions*, and a sprinkling of experienced veterans, rounded out the grouping and assisted in the feverish construction of fortifications.

As a division reserve, Schmidt established a replacement battalion of around 200 soldiers and about twice that number in the *275th Fusilier Battalion*. Six hundred additional men from *Oberst* Alexius Schmitz's *983rd Grenadier Regiment*, composed of a newly arrived and inexperienced replacement battalion of the *176th Grenadier Division* and a *Luftwaffe* battalion, could be called on. For the time being they were busily constructing defenses near Düren.[3]

Although a motley collection of mostly low-caliber soldiers, the *275th Grenadier Division* projected a certain élan, and its core had performed well in previous combat. Schmidt possessed limited artillery and armor assets to support his ground units, as only thirteen 105mm howitzers, a 210mm howitzer, and six 75mm StuG IIIs from the *902nd Sturmgeschütz Brigade* could be brought to bear.[4] Aside from man-portable, reusable *panzerschreck* and the shorter-range, predominantly disposable *panzerfaust*, these vehicles represented the division's only purpose-built antitank elements. As with the *Volksgrenadier* concept, the smaller number of infantry personnel would have their strength supplemented by a greater percentage of sub-machine guns, assault rifles, and mortars. The latter was especially effective, as its portability, high trajectory, and short range did not make demands on Schmidt's severely limited pool of artillery observers.

Much like his American counterparts, Schmidt's focus was not the dams along the Roer River Valley. He believed that VII Corps would look to expand its salient at Schevenhütte for an attack on Aachen before attempting to sever the Simmerath-Hürtgen-Düren road for an attack south of Raffelsbrand.[5] The *LXXIV Corps* commander, *Generalleutnant* Karl Püchler, likewise felt that the Americans would try to gain the high ground overlooking the Roer River Valley.[6] The fact that the town of Schmidt lay just north of the Schwammenauel Dam, however, made it an obvious sector over which both sides would eventually fight.

An American mortar squad fires an M1 81mm mortar in Aachen on Oct 13, 1944. (Note the loader about to drop an M43A1 Light HE round.) (US Signal Corps)

The Dams

Of the area's seven dams, two possessed the greatest potential for large-scale flooding should they be manipulated or destroyed by the Germans. Both were created in the 1930s to provide hydroelectric power for Düren and other cities downstream to the north. Normally the 62m high, 330m wide earthen Schwammenauel Dam near Schmidt held back a reservoir of around 22 billion gallons of water, while the concrete Urft Dam upstream created one about half that size. Throughout October, the Germans had let these levels drop to nearly half capacity, but as the Allied offensive had been slowed to a crawl the water was allowed rise once again.[7]

Within a few weeks, engineers from XIX Corps would make an official prediction based on those of Aachen's *Wasserwirtschaftsamt* (water control agency) that should the primary dams (Urft and Schwammenauel) be destroyed in one stroke, a devastating flood would result. In the first two hours a 10m high wall of water would hit Düren, and Jülich, which would then fall to some 6m after another two hours. Beyond that, the Roer River Valley would be heavily flooded and virtually impassable for nearly two weeks.[8]

Downstream, the dams at Heimbach and Obermaubach created equalizing basins to aid additional local industrial requirements. Of the remaining barriers, the Paulushof dam regulated water levels for Schwammenauel, while the Kall Valley and Dreilägerbachtal dams produced small reservoirs along the Kall and Vicht Rivers, respectively.[9] With the low water levels apparently a minimal threat, US Intelligence assessed that the destruction of all seven dams would "cause at the most local floodings for about 5 days counted from the moment the dam was blown until all the water had receded."[10] The 9th Infantry Division's G-2 (Intelligence), Major Jack A. Houston, however, had doubts. Several days before the assault on Schmidt commenced he noted that, "Bank overflows and destructive flood waves can be produced by regulating the discharge from the various dams. By demolition of some of them great destructive waves can be produced which would destroy everything in the populated industrial valley as far as the Meuse and into Holland."[11]

October 6

US

9th Infantry Division
Commander: Major General Louis A. Craig

Attached
C, D Company, 87th Chemical Battalion
C Battery, 195th FA Battalion (8inch Howitzer)
172nd FA Battalion (4.5inch Gun)
981st FA Battalion (155mm Gun)
Headquarters & Headquarters Battery, 188th FA Group
376th AAA Automatic Weapons Battalion (Mobile)
C Battery, 557th AAA AW Battalion (Mobile)
298th Engineer Combat Battalion

German

89th Grenadier Division
Commander: Generalmajor Walter Bruns

Div HQ
Infantry: 1055th, 1056th Grenadier Regiments
Field Artillery: HQ, 189th Artillery Regiment (105mm, 155mm Howitzers)
HHC, 189th Antitank Battalion, 89th Füsilier Battalion, 189th Engineer Battalion, 189th Signal Battalion, Services

Table of Organization & Equipment for late 1944[12]
US Infantry Regiment (3,118)—3 battalions, 1 HQ and HQ company, 1 cannon company (6x105mm howitzers), 1 antitank company (12x57mm and a mine-laying platoon, 1 service company for supply transport)
Infantry Battalion (871) (1-5km frontage)—3 rifle companies, 1 HQ company, 1 heavy weapons company (6x81mm mortars, 8 LMGs, 7 bazookas, 3 HMGs)
Rifle company (193)—3 rifle platoons, 1 weapons platoon (2 air-cooled .30-caliber light machine guns, 3x60mm mortars, 3 bazookas, 1 water-cooled .30 or air-cooled .50-caliber MG), 1 company HQ
Rifle Platoon (41)—3 squads and a command element
Rifle Squad (12)—(10 M1 Garand, 1 BAR, 1 M1903 Springfield sniper's rifle)

German 1944 Type Regiment (Infantry) (2,008)—2 infantry battalions, regimental HQ and HQ company, infantry howitzer company (6x75mm, 2x105mm), and antitank company (3x75mm, 18 panzerfausts)
Infantry Battalion (708)—3 rifle companies, heavy weapons company (6x81mm + 4x120mm mortars, 6 HMG (MG 34 or 42), 3 LMG (MG 34 or 42)), battalion HQ (1 LMG (MG 34 or 42))
Rifle Company (142)—3 rifle platoons, heavy MG section (2 HMG (MG 34 or 42)), Train (1 LMG (MG 34 or 42)), company HQ
Rifle Platoon (33)—3 rifle squads, platoon HQ (1 LMG (MG 34 or 42))
Rifle Squad (9)—(6 K98k, 2 SMGs (MP 40 or StuG 44), 1 LMG (MG 34 or 42))

German 1944 Type Regiment (Volksgrenadier) (1,854)—2 infantry battalions, regimental HQ and HQ company, infantry howitzer company (4x75mm, 8x120mm mortars, 5 LMG (MG 34 or 42)), and panzerfaust company (72 panzerfausts)

Infantry Battalion (642)—3 rifle companies, heavy weapons company (6x81mm mortars, 4x75mm howitzers, 8 HMG (MG 34 or 42), 1 LMG (MG 34 or 42)), support platoon, battalion HQ (1 LMG (MG 34 or 42))
Rifle Company (119)—2 SMG platoons, rifle platoon, heavy MG section (2 HMG (MG 34 or 42)), company HQ
Rifle Platoon (33)—3 rifle squads, platoon HQ/ SMG Platoon (33)—2 SMG squads, rifle squad, platoon HQ (2 LMG (MG 34 or 42))
Rifle Squad (9)—(6 K98k, 2 SMG (MP 40 or StuG 44), 1 LMG)/ SMG Squad (9)—(9 SMG (MP 40 or StuG 44)

Tactical Air Support

At the beginning of the war, US doctrine regarding direct air support of ground forces was rudimentary, and relegated behind achieving air superiority, strategic area bombing, and targeting enemy command and control assets. "Massed air action on the immediate front will pave the way for an advance. However, in the zone of contact, missions against hostile units are most difficult to control, are most expensive, and are, in general, least effective."[13] Over the last few years of combat, the British had developed a centralized system that greatly assisted the control of air assets. Their tactics and structure were increasingly adopted by US commanders, but remained under overall RAF control. Independent air support such as air transport, recon, and ground-attack were allocated to corps and division-level commands and were maintained via wireless requests. With the USAAF, tactical air support was intended to maintain a carefully considered balance of allotting aircraft to army request missions, including "immediate" requests, and attacking distant targets vital to the enemy defense. No army officer, however, could order air support directly.

The RAF, although more independent in determining targets and allocating tactical air elements, likewise focused on achieving and maintaining air superiority. The British air arm reserved the right to establish priorities and approve targets, as well as indirect support aimed at isolating the battlefield by striking communications and hindering the movement of enemy reinforcements. Direct support (arranged between impromptu and pre-arranged ground force requests) against targets of opportunity was generally provided via a "Cab-rank" system, in which several fighter-bombers (usually four RAF Typhoons) would circle the battlefield and respond to support requests.

German tactical air support was provided by the only such force in the theater, *Luftflotte 3* (Third Air Fleet). When this formation was re-designated *Luftwaffenkommando West* on September 22, it was also subordinated to *Luftflotte Reich* for homeland defense. As this would remove von Rundstedt's tactical air support, he successfully appealed the decision and Hitler ordered it placed under *Reichsmarschall* Hermann Goering's control instead. Even though the *Luftwaffe* command structure was further complicated by this move, it did return a degree of tactical support for the *Westheer*. With only some 573 serviceable aircraft of all types, overwhelming Allied air superiority largely negated this force, which placed German ground forces in a difficult defensive position considering their deficiencies in anti-aircraft weapons.[14]

Luftwaffenkommando West (10/6)
Commander: Generalleutnant Alexander Holle
HQ: Dehrn/Limburg
II Jagdkorps
3rd Fliegerdivision (Ju-87D, Fw-190A/F/G, Ar-66, Fw-58, Go-145, He-45, He-46, Hs-126)
5th Jagddivision (Fighter Division) (Fw-190A/D/R, Bf-109A/G/R, Bf-110G/R, Do-217N)
III Flakkorps (motorized)
IV Flakkorps

Clearing the Kall River Valley

With a forecast that the characteristically overcast, rainy weather would partially clear during the morning, the 9th Infantry Division's Craig would delay his ground assault no longer. On October 6 he gave the word that the preliminary tactical bombing run from IX Tactical Air Command could commence. Fog, however, persisted across much of the forest, and more importantly at many of the airfields scheduled to participate in the attack. American ground forces near the target area expected more delays, but optimistically positioned aerial identification panels to define their front line for the inbound friendly aircraft.

At around 1000 the drone of the approaching air armada informed US artillery around Aachen to fire red smoke-producing rounds to mark targets. Thereafter, 102 B-26 Marauders and 100 A-20 Havoc (light) bombers, from the 9th Bombardment Division, carpet-bombed Düren and its nearby marshalling yards. Eighty-nine P-47D and D-25-RE Thunderbolts of 365th Fighter Group (386th, 387th, 388th Fighter Squadrons) and 404th Fighter Bomber Group (506th, 507th, 508th Fighter Squadrons) arrived soon after to support 9th Infantry Division's projected push into the forests southeast of Stolberg. Primary targets included enemy positions between the Weisser Weh and Germeter (including the town itself), and the area around RJ 471.[15] In addition to strafing and bombing targets of opportunity, some planes were to drop leaflet bombs as an inducement for German ground forces to surrender.

After more than an hour the planes departed. 9th Infantry Division's artillery, with support from three artillery battalions and two corps batteries, opened up with a heavy three-minute barrage. As planned, the guns ceased firing to feign an end to the bombardment, and draw the surviving Germans from their fortifications. Five minutes later, a second, slightly shorter barrage again hammered the enemy lines.

By 1130 the 39th (Bond) and 60th (Claymen) Infantry Regiments rose up from their entrenchments and advanced toward their objectives across the post-bombing landscape. Because of 9th Infantry Division's excessive frontage, reduced to 14km by the recent arrival of Ninth Army and the corresponding shift in unit boundaries, its remaining infantry regiment, the 47th, went over to the defensive south of Schevenhütte. To cover the remaining distance between it and Bond's regiment, the recently arrived 298th Engineer Combat Battalion took up a static position behind roadblocks at four critical sections of their forward road network. Craig's attacking infantry regiments had been fighting in the Hürtgen Forest for over three weeks, and were showing signs of fatigue.

US Intelligence estimated that there were no more than 5,000 enemy combatants defending the Schmidt sector, and that these suffered from low morale and were scattered among some fourteen separate home guard and replacement battalions, none of which were organized above regimental level. Although generally accurate, the fact that the Americans were assaulting through a largely trackless, impenetrable terrain, against German defenses between Germeter and the Weisser Weh that had been progressively strengthened during the lull of the last few days, meant that numbers alone would not be a factor as much as would be the case under "normal" combat conditions. Worse, with Allied air support likely to be inconsistent due to the forest, and with poor flying weather obscuring visibility, even if Schmidt's *275th Grenadier Division* were to become physically isolated it would likely be able to resist for some time afterward.

After progressing against increasing resistance, the 2nd Battalion (Major Lawrence Decker), 60th Infantry Regiment halted about a kilometer east of its jump-off positions due to mounting casualties, mostly from enemy artillery and mortar shells spraying shrapnel from just inside the forest canopy. What had initially looked like a reasonable distance to cover on a map was in reality an arduous trek over steep hills and dense underbrush, not to mention against an entrenched, camouflaged enemy. Claymen's lead 1st and 3rd Battalions had encountered similar resistance from the combat elements of *353rd Grenadier Regiment* (now *942nd Grenadier Regiment*) soon after advancing from their dugouts.

With both US infantry regiments each dependent upon just one supply trail, moving ammunition in and casualties out became a considerable chore—one made worse by mines, booby traps, roadblocks, and enemy patrols and snipers, the latter regularly operating in the trees to increase their weapon's range. Well-trained American engineers worked around the clock to facilitate the transport of men and material, but the road and bridge repair work was slow going. To speed progress, a recon section was attached to the engineer battalion headquarters and service company, so the officer in charge could formulate his own estimates and better allocate resources. Able to fight as infantry, divisional engineer units were generally kept at full strength. For larger jobs, such as pontoon bridging, corps or army-level command could allocate heavy engineer assets.

On the following day the 39th and 60th RCTs, having only reached the Weisser Weh, pressed on, while P-47's provided tactical support during any break in the cloud cover. Exploiting the confusion of the aerial attack, part of the 1st Battalion (Colonel Oscar H. Thompson), 39th Infantry Regiment advanced past German positions, unnoticed, to gain the wooded plateau between the Weisser Weh and the forest line overlooking Germeter. While this created a potential opportunity to outflank the enemy around the town, the lack of immediate armored support, and an increasingly lengthy and exposed northern boundary, meant little could be done against the *275th Fusilier Battalion*. After pushing back German outposts, 39th RCT's efforts continued to be eroded by renewed resistance from pillboxes along the eastern slope of the Weisser Weh. What US air and artillery support was available could often do little to help, as the terrain allowed the combatants to fight at such close distances that friendly fire proved too great a concern.

Around 1100 the 1st Battalion, 60th Infantry Regiment worked its way up to within a few hundred meters of the village of Richelskaul, but Colonel Lee Chatfield was reluctant to move from his semi-protected position in the woods until armor and artillery support could be brought forward. Again, American forces remained unable to even reach Germeter and the open terrain along the Germeter-Hürtgen road.

Throughout October 8, engineers from the *275th Grenadier Division*, supported by some 600 soldiers from the *983rd Grenadier Regiment* out of Düren, counterattacked 60th RCT's positions near Richelskaul. Similar to their enemy's struggles in the woodland environment, the Germans were hit by tree-bursting artillery and mortar fire, became disorganized, and fell back. Straube subsequently ordered artillery resources from *LXXIV Corps* to support *275th Grenadier Division's* efforts. The adjacent *89th Grenadier Division's* batteries, an antiaircraft artillery regiment, and a *volks artillery* corps would provide these. *Seventh Army's* commander, Brandenberger, also contributed by sending in two fortress infantry battalions, but these sub-par formations were of little value, even if they had not been recently depleted by combat.

By the end of the third day the Germans maintained a continuous line along the west edge of the clearing around Wittscheidt, Germeter, and Richelskaul. With few reserves, however, further offensive action was not possible. To the west, US tanks and tank destroyers finally arrived after painfully negotiating narrow, muddy roads and avoiding mines, often placed in twos and threes to hamper removal by engineers. Darkness negated any further action in 60th RCT's offensive, but the infantry at least now had the support it considered essential for a breakout from its static, woodland positions.

October 9th dawned with typically cold, rainy weather, but it did little to dampen the spirits of the newly arrived *XXIV Luftwaffe Fortress Battalion*. Even at 0200 the mostly seventeen-year-old candidates from *Luftwaffe* NCO School 1 were initially very eager to fight. Some even whistled as they walked to their assembly positions in preparation for an attack on RJ 471. Temporarily attached to the *983rd Grenadier Regiment*, the attack was over almost before it began. US artillery scattered the formation, with some individuals rushing into their own minefields to escape the barrage. Schmidt asked for and received reinforcements for *275th Grenadier Division*, but the two companies he was granted from *89th Grenadier Division* would not arrive for two days.

26th Infantry Regiment, 1st Infantry Division clearing German position in Aachen on Oct 15, 1944. Help is provided by an M-10A1 (M4A3 chassis) GMC Wolverine from 634th Tank Destroyer Battalion. (Note the counter-weights on the turret's rear, the .50 cal Browning M2HB machine gun, and the M7 grenade launcher carried by the soldier to the left.) (US Signal Corps)

Chatfield's 1st Battalion attacked out of Richelskaul in a wedge formation behind a platoon of medium tanks after a 10-minute artillery barrage. The sudden appearance of this force had a demoralizing effect on the Germans, and with little opportunity to effectively resist, many soon surrendered. From the perspective of many of the German defenders, the 9th Infantry Division possessed unlimited supplies, and front-line soldiers who had been specifically trained for fighting in a forest. The arrival of two companies of Düren policemen to bolster the defense at Wittscheidt only magnified the seeming disparity between the forces, as German replacements and supplies dwindled along with quality. In reality, the Americans were also exhausted and short of experienced replacements. The 39th RCT, after capturing Wittscheidt, required a full day in which to construct a defensible position along the tree line outside the town.

At 0500 on the 10th, a mixed, company-sized group from the *73rd Engineer Battalion*, with supporting armor, emerged from near Richelskaul. Having achieved surprise, the *Kampfgruppe* first split, then overran the two forward platoons of 2nd Battalion, 39th Infantry Regiment. By noon Chatfield's battalion had driven the enemy out of the settlement and renewed its advance, which remained hampered by the dense woods and German pillboxes. As they were able to bypass these positions between Richelskaul and Raffelsbrand, the pace improved. German defenders began to surrender in sizeable numbers, and in less than three hours Chatfield's force had acquired its objectives and the wooded high ground around it. At the end of the day, Colonel John G. Van Houten's (having taken command of 60th RCT the previous day) reserve had been committed at Richelskaul, and he subsequently had no force available to prevent the Germans cutting in behind Chatfield's advanced position.

The 2nd Battalion, 60th Infantry Regiment, now commanded by Major Quentin R. Hardage after Decker was wounded, remained engaged west of the Weisser Weh. The German outpost near Wittscheidt, with which the regiment had been contending for the last four days, showed no sign of collapse, and would not do so for another five. With the 39th RCT stalled, Thompson's battalion at Germeter was forced to forgo any major push, and only reached Germeter when it was discovered that the Germans had evacuated the town. Already, after just four days of action, 9th Infantry Division's two regiments had been crippled by the loss of nearly 1,000 men. At 1645 the *XXIV Luftwaffe Fortress Battalion* was ordered onto the defensive.

Surviving in the Hürtgen

Upon entering the Hürtgen combat zone, new units on both sides had to quickly learn the often unique tactics and techniques of fighting in the dark and foreboding environment. The digging of foxholes, or other entrenchments, long second-nature to the frontline soldier, were of little use in such a forest where artillery shells would detonate high in the treetops and spew shrapnel and debris downward. Log and sod covered foxholes were mandatory, and if caught in the open, the best option was to remain upright or crouch against a tree. Night movement was extremely dangerous and best avoided. Adjusting artillery and mortar fire by sight was impossible, even with the aid of smoke shells, with sound being the best indicator of direction. Maps were of limited value, but could be used to coincide with cement survey markers distributed through the forest at intersections of the numerous, narrow firebreaks to determine an individual's location. A compass was a final resort barring maps.

High Water Mark

Having gained the first clearing a day ahead of the 39th RCT, which remained halted before heavy German resistance west of Vossenack, the 60th RCT initiated the second part of its attack. On the fifth day of the offensive, Van Houten shifted his reserve battalion to hold Richelskaul, and directed Chatfield to re-enter the woods to secure the road junctions near Raffelsbrand and RJ 471.

Before dawn on the 11th, the Germans sent in a company-sized counterattack against Chatfield's position at Raffelsbrand. Though beaten off, the colonel remained concerned about the sector, as the enemy maintained pressure here for the rest of the day. Around noon Van Houten sent the rest of his reserve battalion to attack northwest from Raffelsbrand toward the regiment's remaining objective, RJ 471.

Hopes for quick success were dashed as of two companies that headed for the road junction, one became entangled with an uncleared cluster of pillboxes along the Richelskaul-Raffelsbrand road. The other ran into similar trouble behind Raffelsbrand. Although tanks and tank destroyers were able to steadily move up along the narrow MSR to reach the village, they accomplished little more than disrupting the flow of friendly logistics and casualty evacuation.

Hardage's 2nd Battalion, still west of the Weisser Weh, noticed signs that the outpost that had thwarted his efforts for nearly a week was finally showing signs of collapse. Driving southward against its left flank, the battalion was finally able to achieve steady progress. While the 60th RCT re-entered the forest to seize the road junctions southwest of Richelskaul, the 39th RCT moved unsuccessfully into the open fields between Germeter and its objective, Vossenack. Each time, German assault guns in the village exacted a prohibitive toll against Thompson's supporting tanks. Lieutenant Colonel Richard H. Stumpf's 3rd Battalion, however, had an easier time of it and entered the woods east of Wittscheidt and advanced, apparently undetected, for nearly 2km to emerge from the woods onto an open nose of the Vossenack ridge a few hundred meters northeast of the village. From there it could cut off the objective from the rear. The 39th RCT was meanwhile to continue southeastward across the Kall gorge to the final objective of Schmidt.

Despite the encouragement provided by this battalion's success, Craig was cautious as German forces in Vossenack only had to hold their front and send in a second group from the north to hit Stumpf's battalion in the rear. To prevent this, Craig directed that Stumpf delay an attack until the next day, when Thompson's battalion in Germeter might be incorporated to hit Vossenack simultaneously from the west.

That night, Stumpf's battalion was stretched in an elongated column of companies through the woods north of Vossenack. This strained Lieutenant Colonel Frank L. Gunn's battalion, which had also been recently engaged in heavy combat as it now protected the regiment's northern flank against anticipated counterattacks from the direction of Hürtgen. Though the 298th Engineer Combat Battalion and the 9th Infantry Division's reconnaissance troop had assumed responsibility for blocking the north along the Weisser Weh, Gunn's companies remained overextended and vulnerable to enemy infiltration. After Stumpf's battalion had spread into the woods north of Vossenack, it had to defend Wittscheidt, while sending a company east of the highway to maintain contact with the rear of Stumpf's battalion.

As darkness fell, the same enemy company that had attacked earlier struck again at Chatfield's position at Raffelsbrand, only this time attempting a bayonet charge. When it too failed, the Germans pulled back about 800m, and remaining resistance along 9th Infantry Division's front seemed to decline as well.

Since mid-September the division had been fighting a largely isolated battle in the dank, depressing forest, which had only grown increasingly difficult. Tree-detonated air bursts and fire breaks caused heavy losses in the woods, while passage along the relatively open Monschau-Düren road drew considerable enfilading fire. Evacuation of the wounded and resupply was difficult or impossible. Casualties were high, evacuation, resupply, and progress was difficult, and the environment was as much an enemy as the Germans.[16]

The US Army was largely unprepared for combat in a forest environment. Army Field Manual 100-5 recommended that such areas be bypassed. If this were not possible, a frontal assault would be acceptable. As with the problems the Americans had being unprepared to fight in the hedgerows of Normandy, combat in the dense forests along the *Westwall* was not much different. Little was mentioned about how armor or engineers were to be used.

In contrast, the lengthy German experience on the Eastern Front had given them a good idea of what to expect in such a primitive environment and how best to prepare for it. One key feature was the establishment of forward outposts designed to determine the direction of an enemy advance and delay its progress enough to mount a counterattack, or in some way to be prepared. They also preferred to fall back from an overwhelming assault in stages along a series of defenses, and to position artillery and mortars close to the front to avoid having to move them frequently.[17]

Enter *Kampfgruppe Wegelein*

With the 39th and 60th RCTs protruding into German territory, it seemed logical to US Intelligence that an enemy counterattack from Hürtgen was likely. A secondary attack from the south might also be attempted either to divert US attention or to act as the second arm of a pincer, with the goal of cutting off the American bulge toward Schmidt, and re-establishing the front prior to the October 6 attack.

Wary of a potentially large enemy buildup, Hardage's 2nd Battalion, 60th Infantry Regiment, spent the rest of October 12 moving along the Weisser Weh toward Road Junction 471. The 39th RCT, however, would remain on the offensive with a coordinated, two-battalion attack against Vossenack. At this point neither of the regiments fielded battalions of more than 300 combat personnel, and reserves were negligible, yet US commanders believed the likelihood of success was good considering the apparent weakening of the German defense, and the enemy's likely diminishing resolve. This optimistic belief that just one more assault might be all that was needed to penetrate the German lines remained a prevalent theme, and one that would consistently result in the trade of men and material for limited physical gains.

To better determine the situation in the Schmidt sector, Brandenberger and Straube visited *Generalleutnant* Schmidt's headquarters to offer what help they could. With few options available it was decided that the regimental-sized independent *Kampfgruppe* under *Oberst* Helmuth Wegelein, who during the previous month had been commander of the *Heeresunteroffiziersschule* (Army NCO School) at Saarlautern, could be brought in the following day. This 2,000-strong formation, half of which consisted of NCO candidates from the school, had recently been part of *Division Jais* under *LXXX Corps*. The force was comprised of three infantry battalions, a *feldersatz* battalion, and a staff from the *352nd Grenadier Regiment*, and was well equipped with machine guns and heavy and medium mortars. Schmidt was optimistic about the German counterattack slated for the next day, although it was a considerable gamble should the formation be destroyed, thereby eliminating a resource—officer candidates—that was in very short supply.

With the 9th Infantry Division having suffered 4,500 casualties in the Hürtgen Forest from October 5 through 11, its combat elements were so exhausted that, when pulled from the line, many were unable to avoid walking on their fallen comrades.[18] Apathy and mental breakdowns had grown among many battalion commanders, and an overall depression set in following their lengthy stay in the gloomy forest. The difficult terrain nearly negated coordination, as well the option for direct artillery support, to which US forces had grown accustomed.

When Wegelein arrived later than expected on the morning of the 12th, and just before his scheduled jump-off for the attack, he asked Schmidt for additional time to expand his communications network to better coordinate the assault. With a swift German reaction paramount to eliminating the US 9th Infantry Division's gains, Schmidt declined and ordered him to adhere to the established, 0700 attack timetable.

Kampfgruppe Wegelein assembled as best they could, and after a concentrated 10-minute artillery barrage to disrupt the 39th RCT, the cadets swept southward along the wooded plateau between the Weisser Weh and the Germeter-Hürtgen highway toward Richelskaul. Quickly surprising and enveloping a part of Gunn's overextended battalion, the Germans poured through to cut the east-west trail leading into Germeter, as well as 39th RCT's MSR. Colonel Bond had few reserves to throw against the *Kampfgruppe*, and after receiving an erroneous report that the engineer roadblock on the Weisser Weh road had been overrun, he requested that the 298th Combat Engineer Battalion send what reinforcements it could spare to the threatened area. Bond also told Thompson, whose positions at Germeter were under attack, to release two platoons to Gunn, but these had become depleted and were of minimal value. Judging from the order's wording, Bond believed that Stumpf's protruding battalion north of Vossenack was also locked in combat. In reality, Stumpf had experienced no enemy action and knew virtually nothing about what was occurring behind him.

By 1100 Wegelein had achieved considerable success, and he halted the attack to reorganize for a renewed push in the afternoon. Nearly two hours later, the *14th Luftwaffe Fortress Battalion* was made aware of Wegelein's counterattack, and for the rest of the day the battalion helped

The 9th Infantry Division's 39th and 60th Infantry Regiments fighting around Vossenack between October 12 and 16.

contain localized attacks by the withdrawing US forces.[19] Several days later, after having been strafed, bombed, and mortared in pillbox fighting, some in the fatigued unit would incorrectly report American engineers as paratroopers that had recently dropped into the area.

To stabilize the situation, Craig alerted the 47th Infantry Regiment for a possible move south to support 9th Infantry Division's hard-pressed right. He also notified the division reserve, consisting of part of the division reconnaissance troop and a platoon of M-5 light tanks. This meant that 9th Infantry Division had no remaining units that could be used to address unforeseen circumstances, or to support success. In early afternoon Craig sought to remedy the situation by directing that the 47th Infantry at Schevenhütte withdraw two companies to create a motorized reserve.

Although *Kampfgruppe Wegelein* made a renewed effort to move south during the afternoon, it steadily succumbed to poor communications and coordination, and could not advance beyond the western trail out of Germeter. The 39th RCT was spared a catastrophe, which Schmidt attributed to a lack of aggressiveness on the part of Wegelein's subordinate commanders. In fact, the fighting was brutal and at close quarters. American artillery fire had quickly dealt a deathblow to a communications system that was shaky from the start. Tenacious resistance by Gunn's Ammunition and Engineer Platoon, and another from G Company, encircled earlier in the day, bloodied the attackers, as the US units held out in small pockets that hampered enemy movement through the area and contributed to Wegelein's lack of success.

Unaware of German problems with keeping the counterattack going, Bond ordered Stumpf to withdraw from his salient in the woods north of Vossenack. Around noon, the battalion left one company east of the Hürtgen highway to strengthen the defense of Wittscheidt, while the remainder was positioned to assault the eastern flank of Wegelein's bulge the next morning.

Schmidt planned to use Wegelein's force for a renewed assault the next morning, but having lost some 500 men during the day, the *Kampfgruppe* was in no shape for the effort. To make better use of the cadets, *LXXIV Corps* reallocated them to other duties, and Schmidt integrated the remainder into the *275th Grenadier Division*.

Stalemate

While the 39th RCT continued to deal with the after-effects of their pre-empted attack against Vossenack, the 60th Infantry Regiment had already turned southward toward RJ 471. Unable to effectively redirect 180 degrees to help stem Wegelein's attack, it continued on its present heading, pushing south along the Weisser Weh. Hardage's battalion encountered a force of about 300 soldiers working in conjunction with Wegelein's attack from the north. A fight developed, but with the Americans already in position around RJ 471, the supplementary German counterattack steadily dissolved. By the late afternoon the regiment had reorganized, and Hardage's 2nd Battalion captured the intersection. Soon after, two companies from 1st Battalion, 47th Infantry, and a tank company from the 3rd Armored moved down from Schevenhütte as reinforcements.[20]

After establishing a relatively firm line against *Kampfgruppe Wegelein's* penetration on the 13th, the worn-out 39th RCT required another three days to reestablish its original flank positions, which ran from the engineer roadblock astride the Weisser Weh highway to the wooded plateau near Wittscheidt. The next morning, while watching the Americans reoccupy the territory that had devoured a third of his force, Wegelein was shot and killed.

By October 16, Craig's 9th Infantry Division was thoroughly spent. Still far from its objectives, it would be unable to renew offensive action until rested and refitted. With the encirclement of Aachen progressing at a slow but satisfactory pace, VII Corps' priority would again turn to throwing bridgeheads across the Roer River. Although the capture of Schmidt remained a prerequisite to such an effort, pulling badly needed units from the main effort to take Schmidt would not do. Hodges solved the problem by establishing a temporary boundary adjustment between

VII and V Corps, with the latter taking responsibility for securing Schmidt. This was to become effective on the 25th and encompass 9th Division, minus its 47th Infantry, at Schevenhütte.

The recently refitted 28th Infantry ("Keystone") Division, one of 18 National Guard infantry divisions in the US Army, was brought up as the 9th Infantry's replacement. Similarly untrained for combat operations in wooded areas, the 28th Infantry Division would soon be thrust into an environment that had extracted 4,500 casualties from the previous division over the course of ten days. Allied estimates of German losses approached 3,300, though General Schmidt claimed only half that number.[21]

Footnotes

[1.] MS# B-810.

[2] MS# B-804.

[3.] MS# B-373.

[4.] MS# B-411, 353rd Div. in the Hürtgen.

[5.] Schmidt, MS B-308.

[6.] General der Infanterie Karl Püchler, MS B-118, "The Rhineland—74 Armee-Korps—The Period from 2 to 27 October 1944 and Dec. 1944 to Mar. 1945 (1946)."

[7] Ltr, FUSA to 12th A Gp, 29 Oct, FUSA G-3 Ltrs and Inds file, Oct 44.

[8] XIXth Corps special G-2 Report—"Rur & Urft Valley Dams," November 14, 1944.

[9.] Annex 2 to 5th Armd Div G-2 Per Rpt 85, 24 Oct, 5th Armd Div G-2 file, Oct 44. See also FUSA Rpt of Opns, Vol. 1, p. 95; VII Corps Engrs, "Study of Possible Flooding of the Rur (Roer) River," 17 Nov, 1st Div G-2 Jnl file, 19–20 Nov 44.

[10.] Record of tel conv between G-2, MASTER Command, and G-2 FUSA (Tac), 3 Oct, FUSA G-2 Tac Jnl file, 1–3 Oct 44.

[11.] Annex 1 to 9th Div G-2 Per Rpt 78, 2 Oct, 9th Div G-2 file, Oct 44. The first recorded references to the dams were contained in reports by Belgian officers on 23 and 30 September. See Memo to Col Dickson (G-2 FUSA), 23 Sep, FUSA G-2 Tac Jul file, Sep 44; Memo to CofS from 1st Div, 23 Sep, VII Corps G-3 file, Sep 44. FUSA repeated the report of 30 Sep in its G-2 Per Rpt 113, 1 Oct, FUSA G-2 Tac Jnl file, 1–3 Oct 44.

[12] The following are given as official, full-strength regimental formations.

[13.] War Department Field manual FM 100-20, *Command and Employment of Air Power.* Section III Tactical Air Force, 16.b.3. 1944.

[14.] British Historical Section's Luftwaffe Records.

[15] *Leap Off, 404th Fighter Group Combat History,* p. 80.

[16.] 9th Inf Div RO, Oct 44, Annex 3, "Lessons Learned."

[17] U.S. Army War Department, Military Intelligence Division, "German Forest Fighting," Tactical and Technical Trends, no. 54 (January 1945), pp. 70–77.

18. Charles B. MacDonald, *The Battle of the Huertgen Forest* (Philadelphia: J. B. Lippincott, 1963), p. 86.

19. Onderwerp: "Battle Report XXIV LFB," p. 7.

20. 9th Inf. Div. RO.

21. MS# B-810, General Schmidt estimated German losses through 12 October at a seemingly low 1,600. US figures ranged from 2,800 to 3,300 German casualties.

Chapter 6

The Fall of Aachen
(October 8–31)

While VII Corps' effort to secure its right flank remained tangled in the Hürtgen Forest, the encirclement of Aachen neared its conclusion. At dawn on October 8, the 117th RCT pushed beyond Alsdorf only to run head-on into *Oberstleutnant* von Fritschen's counterattack to retake the town. Although the assault was hindered by American artillery, the left wing of the attack managed to cut off an entire American platoon, while the *246th Volksgrenadier Division*, with support from the *217th Sturm Panzer Abteilung* (with its *Sturmpanzer IVs*) along the right, reached a road junction north of the town of Alsdorf. After several armor duels the Germans were forced to withdraw back to their starting points.

Meantime, the *3rd Panzergrenadier Division* was transferred to Aachen in a bid to reinforce the city's defenses. This division was followed by the *I SS Panzer Corps*, sent in the previous day, along with the *116th Panzer Division* and the *101st SS Heavy Panzer Battalion* (tank ace Michael Wittmann's former unit), an element of the *1st SS Panzer Division*. The *246th Volksgrenadier Division* replaced *116th Panzer* in Aachen proper after Hitler became suspicious of its allegiance following von Schwerin's removal from command. A "mobile defense" of several *panzer* and *panzergrenadier* formations was held 10–20km behind the line

The *246th Volksgrenadier Division* now fought against the 18th RCT to the south, as well as XIX Corps' attack from Alsdorf. Forces could not be released for a mobile reserve, which meant that little could be done proactively. With the Aachen sector retaining priority over any other section of the Western Front, it naturally drew the attention of political, as well as military elements. The Reich Minister of Public Enlightenment and Propaganda, Paul Joseph Goebbels, visited Köchling during the day and stressed the seriousness of holding the line.

The Germans managed to close the gap in *49th Grenadier Division's* lines, with large caliber assistance from the *723rd Railway Artillery Battery*, whose rounds panicked many US soldiers who believed it to be a new "wonder" weapon. That night Köchling told Lange to push the US forces back across the Wurm River and eradicate their small bridgehead. Lange used the last German-occupied pillbox east of Herbach as a headquarters from which to coordinate his counterattack. One battalion on either side of the bunker advanced against an American front that quickly pulled back. US infantry sought shelter in the previously taken fortifications, where many were isolated or became casualties. What Shermans were in the area were unavailable due to maintenance problems, and the Germans held sway for several hours. In readying for their final assault to clear the area, friendly artillery lifted prematurely and the Germans were then hit hard by US artillery and small arms fire.

A frustrated Köchling ordered all available artillery to fire into the US lines to stifle their response, but time and ammunition were running out. Soon the Americans had retaken the lost territory, even as Field Marshal Model arrived to get an appraisal of the deteriorating situation north of Aachen.

German

3rd Panzergrenadier Division
Commander: Generalleutnant Hans-Günther von Rost
Div HQ
Armor: 103rd Panzer Battalion
Infantry: 8th, 29th Panzergrenadier Regiments
Field Artillery: HQ, 3rd Artillery Regiment (105mm, 155mm Howitzers)
103rd Panzer Reconnaissance Battalion, 3rd Antitank Battalion (75mm), 312th Army Antiaircraft Battalion (20mm, 88mm), 3rd Engineer Battalion, 3rd Signal Battalion, Services

South of the City
The city of Aachen was surrounded by generally higher ground, but observation and fields of fire were limited by the wooded areas to its

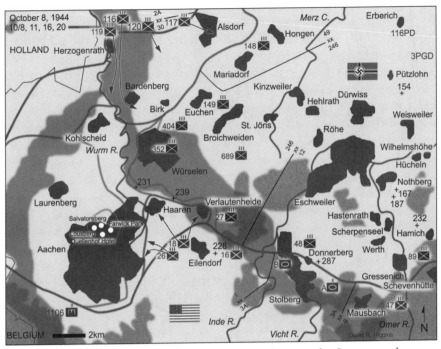

XIX and VII Corps' efforts to encircle Aachen and eliminate the German pocket starting on October 8.

south and west. The remaining terrain was more open where three hills towered over the city, collectively called the Lousberg Heights. The largest and northernmost feature, "Observatory Hill," was adjacent to a lower cathedral-topped hill called the Salvatorberg. Farwick Park and the Quellenhof Hotel occupied the final hill, with the latter serving as the German command post for Aachen's defense. Generally free of heavy vegetation, these three hills provided poor cover and concealment, but were scattered with numerous bunkers and pillboxes. Whoever possessed these features would be able to effectively cover the northern and northeastern approaches to the city.

Holding double its dictated frontage, the 1st Infantry Division renewed its assault along a 20km stretch southeast and east of Aachen to capture the remaining roads out of the city. The 26th Infantry Regiment, with two battalions (the third having been allocated to 3rd Armored Division), postured as if to attack the city as well, but this distraction was to draw attention from XIX Corps' efforts to take Würselen and complete its enveloping action. The 18th RCT seized

Verlautenheide and its surrounding high ground to gain observation positions from which to call in artillery fire to interdict the remaining routes northeast of Aachen.

Here, and to the east, von Rundstedt struggled to keep open the corridor's two remaining roads into the city. The 18th RCT retaliated with a ferocious assault that secured "Crucifix Hill" (Hill 239), the commanding ground northeast of the city. Here, as in other sectors, flamethrowers, close-range artillery, and explosives were needed to subdue the German defenders. As was typical of Collins' style, his artillery was often made to fire within 200m of his forward positions. Even though 600m was the doctrinally established minimum, the Germans had learned to draw close to Allied lines prior to a bombardment to avoid casualties. Nearby, the 26th Infantry Regiment moved into Forst and Beverau Wood, which, combined with the previous capture of Verlautenheide and Hill 239, brought the final route into Aachen under direct US artillery fire.

In an effort to regain Hill 231, the *I SS Panzer Corps* was ordered to proceed with its counterattack. The *3rd Panzergrenadier Division*, as well as a rejuvenated *116th Panzer*, were not to be committed until they could be used in a coordinated attack. Von Rundstedt reasoned that such a large force, if used in this manner, would provide enough mass to do considerable damage to XIX and VII Corps' inner wings. As with previous German efforts, such concentrations could not easily be affected due to continual US pressure, and Brandenberger was concerned that the German position would be compromised if something were not done immediately. Model was similarly troubled that Aachen would fall before the full weight of *I SS Panzer Corps* could be brought together, and assented to individual units of *116th Panzer Division* being employed as soon as they arrived on the scene, provided an emergency existed and the fall of Aachen seemed imminent.

Brandenberger needed little prodding after waiting nervously for the last few days for reinforcements to arrive. Finding emergencies everywhere, he acted on his superior's recommendation, with the result that no more than two battalions were in action at any one time during the counterattack. Elements of the *116th Panzer Division* moved against the 18th and 16th RCTs, as well as the 116th and 119th RCTs of 30th Infantry Division moving to seal the Aachen corridor near Eilendorf.

On the morning of the 10th, Hodges ordered the 26th Infantry Regiment to send envoys into Aachen to deliver an ultimatum to the

German *Kampfkommandant* (combat commander), *Oberst* von Osterroth, stating, "Aachen was surrounded; the city was to be surrendered within 24 hours, or the Americans would pulverize it, then assault into the rubble." Although the supply route through Würselen remained open, it looked to be only a matter of time before that too was closed.

As the 30th Infantry Division approached its expected link-up with the waiting 1st Infantry Division, enemy counterattacks again proved unable to halt their progress near Hill 231, and were eventually forced to withdraw. US forces took the Aachen suburb of Haaren to sever one of the two remaining supply routes into the city. With just 3km separating the advance elements of VII and XIX Corps, *116th Panzer* and *3rd Panzergrenadier Divisions* counterattacked into the gap.

The Last Corridor

After 24 hours with no response from the acting regimental commander of the besieged *246th Volksgrenadier Division* inside Aachen, four groups totaling 300 P-38s and P-47s from the US IX Tactical Air Force commenced a nearly five-hour bombardment to cut rail lines and support the US VII and XIX Corps around the city.[1] Twelve artillery battalions from the 1st Infantry Division followed up by firing for the next two days while selecting targets closest to the American lines. The 2nd and 3rd Battalions from the 26th RCT advanced into northeast Aachen with each rifle company supported by three tanks or tank destroyers, two 57mm antitank guns, as well as a flamethrower and two bazooka teams.[2] As the "Big Red One" rebuffed several determined counterattacks to the east, its 26th RCT was ordered not to get "inextricably engaged in the city."[3] Since laying siege to Aachen would require more forces than the Americans were willing to commit, instead, it was decided to have 26th RCT assault the city directly.

The *246th Volksgrenadier Division* had been formed only three months before the Battle of Aachen, and comprised a very heterogeneous group. On the day after the American surrender ultimatum had been rejected, the actual commander, Colonel Gerhard Wilck, arrived to take charge of all military and civilian forces in the city, with orders to defend Aachen to the last man. In preparing for an urban defense, Wilck and his staff came to the incorrect conclusion that the 1st Infantry Division would attack from the south, and correspondingly positioned the bulk of his command to deal with it.

The 26th RCT had been in nearly continuous combat since the

initial Normandy landing, and although well trained, they were handicapped by minimal experience in urban operations, and numerically inferior to the enemy. As a result the regiment improvised many of its assault techniques and expanded on what little doctrine was available. Small, decentralized teams up to platoon size contained anti-tank elements and were partnered with tanks and tank destroyers in a direct fire role, which provided over-watch and target suppression as the infantry moved up. To reduce casualties these teams would use 155mm howitzers to blast holes in interior walls. These "mouse holes" allowed assaulting infantry to fight from building to building, using small arms and hand grenades, while avoiding have to move outside.

I SS Panzer Corps's counterattack attempted to disrupt 30th Infantry Division's efforts, but it was disrupted by incessant Allied artillery and anti-tank and armored elements. An escalating tank battle at Birk was similarly swayed by portions of the 2nd Armored Division. The 30th Infantry Division remained in a precarious position, however, and despite its appeal for reinforcements, it was ordered to continue south to seal the city. Two infantry battalions from the 29th Infantry Division were subsequently attached to the 30th, but were unable to prevent a pair of German infantry regiments from retaking "Crucifix Hill." By day's end the German force was effectively repelled from the heights.

German Defensive Tactics along the *Westwall*

Though the concept of static defenses and fortifications had little place on the modern, mobile battlefield, such strategic emplacements, especially in the Aachen sector, provided a considerable degree of protection and security for its defenders. As such the Germans felt that fortified zones were a tactical defensive option from which to conserve their strength and cohesion for counterattacks following a heavy and prolonged bombardment. These defenses were often connected by a system of tunnels that tended to give the defender an advantage in coordination, observation, and communication, and permitted the storing of large amounts of supplies and ammunition.

During combat, the *Westwall's* pillboxes and bunkers were designed to be mutually supporting, preferably with heavy infantry weapons and artillery. When individual bunkers were captured, organized resistance from the remaining works continued until mobile forces could be brought forward to eject the new occupants. German doctrine stressed that the most favorable time for a large-scale counterattack was just as the enemy artillery and antitank weapons were en route to new positions, especially during the afternoon, as once an objective was reached it could then be consolidated that night. Enemy penetrations through a fortified position were to be ignored by the flanking German positions. These breeches would instead be countered by prepared reserves, flank installations, and heavy infantry weapons not otherwise employed toward preventing any consolidation of the gains. The Germans reinforced this last measure by unleashing a steady artillery and mortar barrage behind the penetration to delay enemy reinforcements from moving up.

Close combat actions were brought under the controlled fire of neighboring light and heavy infantry weapons as well as light artillery. Heavy infantry guns, however, were not used due to the risk of friendly fire. To coordinate the variety of artillery and mortars, the Germans employed gapless firing charts to provide complete coverage over a particular area. Any decision to open fire was made by the battalion commander, or by the commander of a fortification or group of fortifications, initially at as long a range as was permissible.

Allied Countering Tactics

To subdue the *Westwall's* integrated static defenses, Allied soldiers developed a number of new tactics that expanded on often out-of-date official doctrine. Because much of the rugged terrain in the Aachen sector was unsuited for armor, infantry/engineer formations up to company size were found to be the best able to achieve success. As decentralized groups they employed a variety of close support weapons including the flamethrower, grenade, bazooka, and explosive charges. Each man in the assault team was also expected to be proficient with each weapon. Sometimes each rifle platoon was assigned a fixed zone of responsibility where each pillbox becomes a phase line for coordination and reorganization.

During an attack against pillboxes the Allies would lay down suppressing fire not only against the target structure, but also to negate localized enemy flanking fire. The distance between pillboxes averaged

100m with each being of three possible configurations: single aperture, double aperture (with mounted machine guns), and small personnel shelters. When fighting, these would be "buttoned up" with the occupants returning fire through small slits in the embrasures. Although most pillboxes were designed to provide long-range fire, the rough terrain in which they were constructed offered numerous dead spaces that could be exploited by an enemy.

Previous observation and detailed mapping of suitable approach routes was paramount. Additionally, Allied soldiers found it beneficial to approach an enemy position during the hour before daylight in order to achieve surprise. The use of smoke and white phosphorous, while not desirable for every mission, reduced visibility and placed the pillbox defenders at a considerable disadvantage during an attack. Should armor be available they were used in the direct fire role, in particular against the apertures, but only until friendly forces got within 25m of the target.

Two teams would take up positions in the rear of the pillbox, with suppressing fire if need be, while the remainder of the assault group moved past to secure the ground beyond. Assault team members were not to move into the rear prior to the pillbox being cleared or otherwise subdued. As anti-personnel mines were commonly placed at a fortification's entrance, and die-hards might attempt an ambush, no one was allowed to enter the pillbox to take prisoners. Surrendering occupants had to leave on their own or be neutralized by measures such as demolition charges, mines (often remote controlled), point-blank armor or artillery fire, grenades, flamethrowers, or simply having a tank dozer cover the exits with dirt. As the Germans continually tried to infiltrate bypassed or previously occupied fortifications, US forces needed to virtually destroy them to prevent their re-use by the enemy.

Once a pillbox was secured the assault team would establish a perimeter to the front and flanks to counter the expected German counterattack, and supporting artillery and mortars. Assault teams tried to halt attacks before nightfall so as to have enough time to establish adequate defenses around a newly conquered area, since many such attacks occurred after dark. German combat patrols would often precede these assaults by infiltrating a few soldiers into the American rear to focus on their machine guns and serve as a distraction. The main counterattack involved much shouting and talking, as the advancing Germans calmed each other's nerves and, hopefully, panicked the enemy.

A 3rd Armored Division Tank Recovery Vehicle T-2 (M31) with a Gar Wood power boom crane, two .30 cal M1919 machine guns, and dummy 75mm gun moves past Stolberg on Oct 24, 1944. What appears to be an M3A1 halftrack, with its attached M-49 pulpit mount for the .50 cal Browning M2HB machine gun, follows behind. (US Signal Corps)

60mm illuminating shells were found to be very useful in helping the US coordinate an effective defense, followed by a limited pursuit should the German attack fail.

Urban Fighting

By October 13 the weather had again turned overcast, cold, and damp, and would remain so for the next two days. Because of continued efforts to stave off German counterattacks while trying to close the encirclement of Aachen, the 1st Infantry Division could only afford to give the task of taking the city to its 26th RCT, which only had two of its three battalions on hand. The combat team captured most of the factory district between Aachen and Haaren, and after heavy fighting had taken most of "Observatory Hill," but German counterattacks halted further advances. The 30th Infantry Division, with elements of the 29th Infantry and 2nd Armored Divisions, continued its push southwards near

Würselen, where the Germans covered the narrow front with artillery and positioned armor within buildings to better spring an ambush. Despite heavy air support they were still unable to break through the German defenses and link up with VII Corps.

To contest the US assault into Aachen, 6,500 defenders from four German infantry divisions and two understrength tank formations dug in beyond.[4] Reinforcements for the *246th Volksgrenadier Division*, if needed, were to come from the theater reserve, specifically the *3rd Panzergrenadier* and *116th Panzer Divisions*. Within the city, observation and fields of fire were poor, being restricted to major streets and avenues. German defenders had constructed several bunkers and pillboxes at key intersections, maximizing what fields of fire and weapons were available. Wilck's objective was to hold the line with infantry and withdraw his tanks to the rear to be used as something of a fire brigade—a situation not aided by the roughly 9,300 artillery rounds landing in the city each day from VII and XIX Corps' 25 artillery battalions. In response, the Germans averaged 4,500 rounds.[5] Eventually, the overall plan failed because German forces participating in the counterattack had become cut off and surrounded.

26th RCT's recent urban experience had provided important insight on how to improve combat tactics in such an environment. M-4 Sherman tanks found it difficult to maneuver and suppress enemy fire in anything save the most open avenues. Many fell victim to German antitank teams that hid in basements and rubble to get as close as possible before using their shape-charged weapons. As a counter they resorted to cautious movement and firing on buildings to guarantee they were free of German defenders.

While armor could operate in the open, infantry was subjected to a number of hazards and looked for ways to minimize casualties. The Germans initially used Aachen's sewer system to deploy behind enemy positions, and US soldiers were forced to clear every such opening before continuing. This allowed the infantry to advance under cover while in parallel to the street, but the progress was slow and substantial amounts of explosives were needed. Because of the extreme thickness of some of the ancient city's structures, the 26th Infantry Regiment brought up heavy howitzers in a direct fire role.

To the east and northeast, the 3rd Armored Division continued to maintain defensive positions and patrol along the Diepenlinchen-Mausbach line, where enemy activity on their sector consisted of intermittent artillery and mortar fire. Along its left flank, the 1st Infantry Division fought off elements of the *3rd Panzergrenadier Division* as it moved to keep open the narrow land corridor into Aachen. Over the next two days the Germans threw tanks and infantry against the dominating ridge of "Observatory Hill" on the northern edge of the city. Although a number of heavy German tanks broke through US lines, the attack was eventually halted by artillery, air support, and close-quarter fighting.

Into the Closing Vice

The *3rd Panzergrenadier Division* finally began its assault in the late afternoon of October 5 to avoid enemy aircraft, and to be ready to defend their new positions by morning. The *506th Antitank Battalion*, with upwards of 20 supporting tanks, was attached to von Rost's command, as was a *Volkswerfer* brigade, and an independent collection of depleted artillery brigades, collectively a *Volks Artillery* corps comprised of around six battalions of 75mm antitank guns, and 105mm and 150mm howitzers. All artillery slated to support the *3rd Panzergrenadier Division* was under the control of *Seventh Army's Arko* (senior artillery commander). This resulted in a softening of American positions along *3rd Panzergrenadier Division's* projected path, and helped it make initially good progress.

The *8th* and *29th Panzergrenadier Regiments* were committed side by side in the sector, which was limited on one side by the railroad. The pair was to thrust past the outpost line of the *12th Volksgrenadier Division* (with attached elements from the *246th Volksgrenadier Division*) to capture the hills south and southwest of Verlautenheide. The *12th Volksgrenadiers* would engage in defensive fighting, disengage, and follow behind *3rd Panzergrenadier Division* to exploit any favorable situation. After reaching its first objective, the regiment on the right would thrust for the top of "Crucifix Hill." As part of this main effort, 15 Tiger IIs from the *506th Heavy Panzer Battalion* were committed. The attack was opened by a combined artillery fire, during which the regiments approached their objectives. US infantry and artillery steadily forced the Germans to halt, pull back to more concealed ground, and dig in for the night. Their armor had difficulty traversing the rugged terrain east of Aachen, and coordination with infantry suffered.

At 0600 on the 16th, the *3rd Panzergrenadier Division* continued toward its objective, but without preemptive artillery. Surprise was gained, and a greater advance was achieved than on the previous day. Small groups supported by a few tanks probed 1st Infantry Division's defenses for an opening. US counterattacks inflicted considerable casualties on the *I SS Panzer Corps'* uninspiring assault, especially from mortars. German armor failed to penetrate the northern part of Verlautenheide, mainly because the open terrain provided little concealment. Without armor support the infantry had to remain east of Verlautenheide

With much of *3rd Panzergrenadier Division's* attack having originated from the Reichswald, the distance to their jump off positions was too great. German infantry were unable to advance close behind their artillery, and when their supporting fire stopped the infantry would lag behind and be caught by enemy artillery. Too much time was wasted that allowed the Allies to organize an all-arms attack against the German armor, which could not account for the volume of defensive fire and could not greatly influence the battle. *I SS Panzer Corps'* counterattack was further impeded in that it was not used against the weakened 18th RCT, but against the solid left flank of the 16th RCT.

The Vice Closes

Throughout the next few days, clear skies allowed US tactical bombers to provide support for the remainder of the battle. The 1st Infantry Division's Huebner needed to follow closely the actions to his north, not only because he might have to commit his reserve there, but because the outcome of that fighting would fundamentally affect his operation in the city, not to mention the projected linkup occurring on the seam between XIX and VII Corps. At 1615, a patrol from the 30th Infantry Division's 119th RCT reached the positions of 1st Infantry Division's 18th RCT near Ravels Hill to complete the encirclement of Aachen. A second attack, the next morning, by the *3rd Panzergrenadier Division* was also unsuccessful, and the division withdrew at nightfall. With the German defenders outside the city halted and the garrison reliant solely on air drops, the end could not be far off.

US air activity continued the next day at dawn, with many planes spotting for US artillery. With *3rd Panzergrenadier Division's* heavy losses, especially in infantry, their attack steadily lost momentum. That night von Rost abandoned the counterattack that was intended to keep open the last ground supply corridor into Aachen.

The *3rd Panzergrenadier Division* was next ordered to take

The 899th Tank Destroyer Battalion passes a knocked-out 88mm Jagdpanther southeast of Düren. (Note the penetrations in the glacis and right track.) (US Signal Corps)

Ravelsberg, and the nearby hill, before regrouping south of Würselen. In an effort to add more weight to its drive, the division was echeloned in depth along a narrow sector. A *Kampfgruppe* was created around a battalion from the *8th Panzergrenadier Regiment*. Additional infantry was held back for a second wave in order to support the main thrust, and to deal with pockets of enemy resistance. Heavy weapons, especially antitank, were brought up immediately after. All were to build a defensive line to stop an expected Allied counterattack.

An evening artillery barrage preceded the attack in an attempt to make use of the limited daylight and reduce the effectiveness of enemy ground and air observation. Allied resistance was rather weak, and a surprised *3rd Panzergrenadier Division* repossessed the hill and the surrounding pillboxes. US artillery fire between the hill and Würselen dispersed German infantry, however, and forced many into the security of the recaptured pillboxes. Others had to dig in amidst uncovered terrain. German morale quickly dropped, and bringing up heavy weapons became impossible.

American armor led a counterattack as artillery provided covering fire. The tanks countered the pillboxes and opened a path for their infantry, which followed close behind. Like before, enemy artillery was a contributing factor. The Allied artillery was quickly repositioned against the German assault group atop the hill, while its screening fire up to Würselen isolated the *Kampfgruppe* and prevented reinforcements.

Considering the chaotic state of the German command, control, and communication structure, resistance within Aachen became considerably degraded. The *246th Volksgrenadier Division* had been organized a mere two weeks prior to its baptism of fire against the US in September. Training as a division had been beyond current abilities and the time available, and staffs were understandably hard pressed to mount a cohesive defense. Wilck had established his CP in the west of the city at the Quellenhof Hotel, where it would be one of the last German positions to be assaulted, and thus remain in contact with his withdrawing combat units until the very end.

In contrast, US staffs had been operating with their units for some time, and controlled a functioning, intact chain of command. With overwhelming air power and extensive artillery, American forces preferred to fight during the day, and evacuate wounded and resupply at night. Assaulting infantry teams also developed a "Measles System," in which structures and intersections that had been searched and cleared were numbered, or otherwise marked. This facilitated movement through an extremely dangerous environment, and limited casualties.

Communications

Behind the advancing American front line, large amounts of telephone wire were laid behind the advancing platoons, which were then interconnected laterally at the company and battalion level. Although this network provided reliable communications, it was also very susceptible to artillery fire unless the wires were deeply buried. Fortunately, Aachen's sophisticated underground telephone system had been left essentially untouched and supplemented that of the US ground forces.

Portable radios supplemented the hardwired set-up, but these were often unreliable considering the vast amount of environmental debris and clutter. During combat, radios were the workhorse, and the US held an advantage with a good intra-company radio system using an AM set, the SCR-536, or handie-talkie. The SCR-300 (walkie-talkie), an FM set, was generally used at battalion and company level. German wireless systems were AM, and as these suffered from interference by other AM signals, they had to rely more on visual signals and flares than their American counterparts.

Planning for Operation Queen

To determine their next course of action, an Allied strategic conference was convened in Brussels on October 18. Eisenhower and his staff commanders planned a major assault to take the west bank of the Roer River and press on for Cologne and the Rhine. SHAEF believed that with winter approaching, the best policy might be to hold in place, then to launch a final victorious offensive in the early spring; but several concerns ruled out such a delayed offensive.

Allied intelligence had learned that German jet aircraft production was on the threshold of a large increase in output, and that they were nearing development of a proximity-fused antiaircraft projectile. That spelled trouble for the ongoing Allied strategic bombing campaign to ruin the German war economy. At present the Germans were taking considerable casualties in the battle of attrition, and the longer the delay the greater German strength and organization would become. Eisenhower later commented that, "We were certain that by continuing an unremitting offensive we would, in spite of hardship and privation, shorten the war and save 'thousands' of Allied lives."[6]

Following the failure of Market Garden, Courtney Hodges' First Army was to initiate the main Allied offensive to penetrate the German border. Hodges' First Army would lead the offensive scheduled to begin in less than ten days, with Ninth Air Force providing aerial support. VII Corps was again chosen to make the tactical push, and to help this effort Hodges redrew its boundary with V Corps, which would attack the Hürtgen Forest to finally capture Schmidt. The fact that Antwerp remained blocked to Allied shipping did not seem much of an issue, as *Fifteenth Army's* position in the Scheldt Estuary seemed increasingly untenable, and the opening of the port appeared imminent. Even if it were not operational within sufficient time, however, Allied commanders could still re-ignite their offensive to strategically breach the German border. Although not designed to be a war-winning offensive due to the present logistical situation, it would at least establish a framework by which to accomplish it.

Eisenhower's "broad front" strategy would remain in effect as Allied forces embarked on achieving three primary objectives. Following a buildup along the west bank of the Rhine River (optimistically scheduled between November 1 and 5), First Army would cross over south of Cologne. Ninth Army would also drive to the Rhine before turning northward to support First Army by clearing the region between the Rhine and the Maas Rivers along the western fringe of the Ruhr. Because Antwerp remained closed to Allied shipping, Montgomery's 21st Army Group was not to participate until around November 10, when Second British Army would drive southeast from Nijmegen to meet the Ninth Army. Depending upon the logistical situation, the Third Army was to drive northeastward from the vicinity of Metz to protect First Army's right flank.

The conference concluded with the decision to resume the offensive, codenamed "Queen," using the US First and Ninth Armies. Using a relatively narrow frontage to maintain overwhelming numbers at the point of impact, the Allies felt a breakthrough could be achieved. If the weather cooperated, Queen would begin on November 5 after a preliminary bombardment by 4,500 aircraft—3,000 more planes than were used to support Operation Cobra and the Normandy breakout. In the Aachen sector, this force, half of which were bombers, would pulverize German defenses between Geilenkirchen and the Hürtgen Forest. In support, First Army would use 40 battalions of field artillery to attack along a mere 13km of front.[7] With such firepower and resources the Allies looked to accomplish another strategic breakout.

Endgame

After a third failed counterattack to resecure Hill 231, the *3rd Panzergrenadier Division* was withdrawn. The Germans had been unable to mount a significant, coordinated counterattack to save Aachen, and those inside were driven into an ever-constricting cordon. The 3rd Battalion, 26th Infantry Regiment prepared to assault one of the last areas of resistance in the city around the Hotel Quellenhof. American tanks and other guns were soon firing on Wilck's headquarters at pointblank range, but the thick walls proved surprisingly resilient. That night, Köchling slipped the 300-man *1st SS Battalion* into Aachen to reinforce the German defense, as well as to pressure Wilck to continue resistance.[8] Although they rebuffed several attacks made against the German headquarters, and managed to overrun a number of American

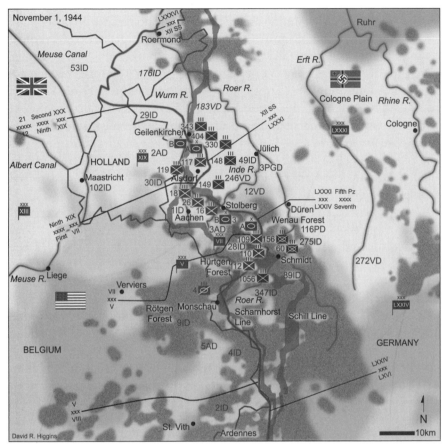

Campaign view for November 1 illustrating the front line following the elimination of the Aachen pocket.

infantry companies in the surrounding area, the SS men were eventually driven off by enemy mortar fire.

While most of the 3rd Armored Division maintained static defensive positions, Task Force Hogan was attached to the 1st Infantry Division and became the armored division's only element to fight inside Aachen. It was responsible for the city's western perimeter where it seized the strategic Lousberg Hill on October 19. Fighting continued throughout the city's western fringe for the next two days, specifically against the Technical High School and the Hotel Quellenhof. On the morning of the 21st, with German defenses now limited to a small cordon, a 155mm gun from the 3rd Battalion, 26th Infantry Regiment was brought up to finish the job with a decisive, intimidating pointblank bombardment.

Hodges, following an October 31 meeting among Bradley, Montgomery, and Eisenhower, told Collins to prepare two plans to reach the Roer's west bank: one based on a target date of November 5 with three divisions, and another between November 10 and 15 with four. Collins and his staff responded with plans that were little different except in strength and in position of various divisions within the line. Both plans were predicated upon the objective of seizing crossings over the river at its closest point, not quite 11km away. From there, supplemental orders were to be issued for renewing the drive across the Cologne plain to the Rhine.

Both plans also named the same three initial objectives as prerequisites for breaking the German containment of VII Corps' *Westwall* penetration and subsequently reaching the Roer. These were: (1) the Eschweiler-Weisweiler industrial area northeast of Stolberg, the capture of which would spell access to a more open portion of the Roer plain, and firm contact with the Ninth Army on the north; (2) the Hamich ridge, one of the more prominent terrain features along a sixteen mile corps front, and one that denied egress from the Stolberg Corridor between the industrial complex and the Hürtgen and Wenau Forests; and (3) in the south of the corps zone, the long sought Hürtgen Kleinhau Gey road net, capture of which would end the miserable confinement of US units within the Hürtgen Forest.

After Hodges heard from Bradley on November 1 of the decision to postpone the offensive for five days, he notified Collins that he sanctioned his second contingency plan based on a later start date, and four divisions instead of three. The revised target date was November 10 with a deadline date of November 15, and Collins used the added time to reorganize his divisions. During this period, in the Hürtgen to the south, however, the 28th Infantry Division suffered defeat around Vossenack, Kommerscheidt, and Schmidt.

Inexperienced in combat except for a brief commitment near Antwerp, the incoming 104th Infantry ("Timberwolf") Division was to relieve the 1st Infantry Division on the corps left wing northwest of Stolberg. The veteran 1st Infantry Division then was to move to the center of the corps zone to carry the weight of the corps' main effort. Discovering three days before the target date that the 104th Infantry Division would not arrive in time for this regrouping, the First Army G-3 (Operations), General Thorson, recommended another postponement of twenty-four hours, and Hodges concurred. As finally determined, First Army was to attack on November 11, or on the first day thereafter that weather permitted large-scale air support. The absolute deadline date was November 16.

Always accompanied by an active propaganda campaign designed to exhort the workers to do more with less, Hitler had sought to establish his concept of *Volksgemeinschaft* ("people's community"), a national sense of solidarity within Germany. The fact that the army at Aachen did not fight to the last bullet, and the civilians attempted to evacuate the city against the expressed orders of Hitler, and did not actively resist once occupied, illustrated the great failure of the policy upon which the Party so heavily depended.

With the Germans constricted into a small section of western Aachen, further resistance would achieve few, if any, military successes. Wilck, like other *"Festung"* commanders, had signed an oath that forfeited his family's lives back home should he surrender. Unwilling to sacrifice his soldiers or cause further damage to the city, at 1205 Wilck hoped his family would be spared and unconditionally surrendered what remained of the *246th Volksgrenadier Division* and the defending garrison.

Footnotes

[1] Hq, USAF in Europe, *The Contribution of Air Power to the Defeat of Germany*, Vol. 2, Western Front Campaign, p. 170.

[2] Dr. Christopher R. Gabel, Historian, Combat Studies Institute, USACGSC. "Military Operations on Urbanized Terrain: The 2d Battalion, 26th Infantry, at Aachen, October 1944."

[3] Monte M. Parrish. "The Battle of Aachen: City Fighting Tactics." *Field Artillery Journal* XLIV (September–October 1976), pp. 25–30.

[4] MacDonald, *Siegfried Line*, page 308.

[5] Eisenhower, *Crusade in Europe*, p. 323; SHAEF G 2 Weekly Intel Summary, 15 Oct 44.

[6] Ibid.

[7] Decisions reached at Supreme Commander's Conf, 18 Oct 44, dtd 22 Oct 44, and SCAF 114.

[8] Whiting, Charles. *Bloody Aachen*, p. 115.

Chapter 7

Second Schmidt
(October 21–November 9)

In the aftermath of the German debacle at Falaise, the "Miracle of the West" came as quite a shock to the Allies bent on achieving victory in Europe by Christmas. Named as a twist on the phrase "Miracle of the Marne," when in the First World War the French had halted a seemingly inexorable German advance on Paris, the Germans considered it no less a miracle that the Wehrmacht had somehow pulled itself together in order to stop the Allies at the borders of the Reich. Much of the credit for filling "the void" in September and October 1944 belonged to the gifted, energetic, and fanatical Walther Model. His skill and experience at waging an effective strategic defense, while outnumbered and outgunned, was well known throughout the German Army. This talent was most recently demonstrated at Arnhem and then Aachen where he pulled reserves from seemingly nowhere, organized them, and sent them against an enemy teetering at the end of a potentially extensive, yet over-stretched supply tail.

After having failed to quickly penetrate the *Westwall* and force crossings over the Roer River, US senior commanders prepared to renew the offensive to finally accomplish their original mission. With Aachen now under American control, and the sector front straightened and shortened, all that remained was to secure VII Corps' right flank at Schmidt. For the last six weeks the Hürtgen Forest had served as a formidable, and frustrating, physical barrier between VII and V Corps. The 9th Infantry Division had already taken considerable casualties in its abortive assault on Schmidt the previous month. The combination of limited forces and an increasingly resilient enemy had a cumulative effect, which left Craig's command severely depleted.

As the use of aerial carpet-bombing to pave the way for a ground penetration of a stubborn enemy defense had proven successful in breaking the Normandy stalemate, Bradley was eager to repeat the tactic to regain the strategic initiative. For two months First Army had been restricted to the Aachen sector where it was hampered by enemy resistance, difficult terrain, and limited logistical support. By the end of October Hodges' command had grown to some 311,000 soldiers, and was largely rested and well supplied.[1] As additional support, the 99th and 104th Infantry Divisions were assigned to V and VII Corps, respectively. VIII Corps was brought forward as well, but it would not take part in the forthcoming offensive's initial stage until its redeployment was completed. Hodges had concentrated the bulk of his strength in V and VII Corps, and as with the previous battles along the *Westwall*, the importance of manning front line positions at the expense of adequate reserves was again practiced.

To finally clear the Schmidt sector and its surrounding forest, V Corps commander Gerow looked to his one armored and four infantry divisions to address the weakness, and on October 21 decided to rely the oldest division in the US armed forces. The 28th Infantry Division, having suffered heavy casualties throughout the late summer, had since been relegated to the rear to recoup. Far from enjoying a quiet zone, however, the division had suffered an additional 993 casualties due to combat.[2] Four days later Major General Norman Cota established his division command post at Rott and began coordination with the V Corps staff. To help complete his task Cota was given the 5th Armored Division.

The 28th Infantry Division's G-2 (Intelligence) estimated that in his immediate front the Germans had a predominantly infantry force numbering 3,350 soldiers. Two thousand more were believed to be in close reserve, with 3,000 potentially available from nearby quiet fronts.[3] As had largely been the case since September, Intelligence did not address the enemy's possession of the remaining dams, especially at Schwammenauel, and the threat of flooding the Roer River and further hampering an Allied push to the Rhine.

The US 4th Infantry ("Ivy") Division was tasked with clearing the northern half of the forest between Schevenhütte and Hürtgen, and then advance to the Roer River south of Düren. Its 12th Infantry Regiment had been badly depleted following action at Schmidt, which left just two fully effective regiments to achieve the divisional objectives. In the Hürtgen Forest, the *275th Grenadier Division* waited in its entrenched and fortified positions, with 150 pieces of artillery as support.[4] Because the permanent boundary between V Corps and VII Corps intersected the planned zone of operations, First Army established a temporary boundary between Kleinhau and Hürtgen on the 25th in order to place the Schmidt operation under the control of V Corps.

As the target date for the First and Ninth Armies approached, Montgomery proposed a change in the British role. A surprise German counterattack in the Peel Marshes on October 27 had necessitated a quick response from available British forces. Instead of a planned attack southeast from Nijmegen, which Montgomery felt would unnecessarily expose the British flank and rear, he allocated Second Army to counter the German spoiling attack. With the 104th Infantry and 7th Armored Divisions still fighting under British authority, neither would be returned to the Americans in time for their planned November 5 offensive. Ostensibly because First and Ninth Armies needed these two divisions before jump-off, but also because of the support a British drive close along the Ninth Army's left flank would provide, Bradley pushed out the jump-off date once more, but even November 10 remained questionable subject to the weather.

US Tactical Planning

Along V Corps' left flank, Hodges stressed that the 28th Infantry Division was to initially capture Vossenack and the tree line facing the village of Hürtgen as a prelude to moving on Schmidt. To this, Gerow added very detailed instructions on how the individual regiments were to be employed. The 109th Infantry Regiment (Lieutenant Colonel Daniel B. Strickler) was to attack north along the western ridge and seize the village of Hürtgen. This would pre-empt an expected German counterattack through the village, as had been done previously against 9th Infantry Division's left. The 110th Infantry Regiment (Lieutenant Colonel Theodore A. Seeley) was to provide similar flank protection along the division's right where it was to capture Simonskall, Steckenborn, and Rafflesbrand.

With both wings thus anchored, the 112th Infantry Regiment (Lieutenant Colonel Carl L. Peterson) would conduct the main effort, which was to push up the center and capture Vossenack, cross the Kall River gorge, and secure Schmidt and the surrounding high ground and road network. The 28th Division's commander, Cota, would have preferred to have at least two regiments attack Schmidt, but he was not given that option. Instead the 112th would have to cover 5km of extremely rugged and wooded terrain to reach its objective.

Perhaps the most important goal of the operation was keeping

119

German armor out of the immediate area. In addition to targeting enemy transportation and communications, the IX Tactical Air Command would assist 28th Infantry Division in this goal. The air plan involved the use of five fighter-bomber groups (the 365th, 366th, and 368th (P-47's), and the 370th and 474th (P-38's), as well as the 422nd Night Fighter Group (P61's)). On the first day of 28th Infantry Division's attack, a third of the IX TAC aircraft were to perform armed reconnaissance on all roads leading out of Schmidt to a limit of 40km. Another third were to distribute leaflet bombs.

The 28th Infantry Division was to conduct a preliminary attack to reinforce the 4th Infantry Division (now under VII Corps), with one regiment moving on Schmidt and the high ground overlooking the Roer River Valley, before pushing southwest to secure a front stretching from Lamersdorf to Steckenborn. From there, the 28th Infantry Division would go over to the defensive after replacing the 5th Armored Division between Kesternich and Simmerath, while maintaining the security of the Schmidt-Vossenack-Steckenborn position.

Whatever pause Bradley, Hodges, and other US commanders may have had about attacking a forested area, Eisenhower remained convinced that should tactics and maneuver fail, a frontal assault was a viable option. As evidenced by his telegram to the 12th Army Group commander, "Combat units are authorized to base daily replacement requisitions on anticipated losses forty-eight hours in advance to expedite delivery of replacements. To avoid building up over strength, estimates should be made with care." While intended to more quickly replace combat losses, and apply pressure on a retreating enemy via the resulting momentum, in practice many US senior commanders viewed the order as a license to incur heavy losses in the accomplishment of a mission. Because replacement personnel remained in critically short supply, this policy would be temporarily halted on November 22.

German Tactical Planning

The LXXXI Corps remained in its position between Geilenkirchen and Schmidt, and Köchling prepared his harried formations for additional combat. Pre-planned American artillery fire and reports and observation of American troop movements in the rear of Rötgen indicated an imminent US offensive. In anticipation of another US attempt to secure the Schmidt sector, in particular Vossenack, no specific precautions had been taken in movement of troops, as the timing and direction of the attack

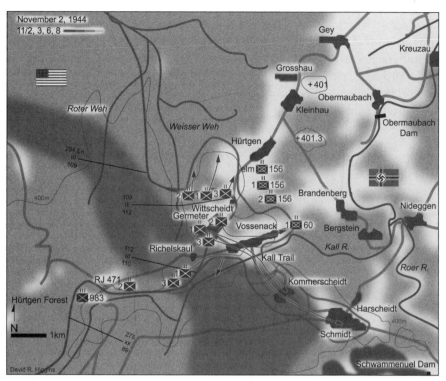

Starting on November 2, the 109th and 112th Infantry Regiments (28th Infantry Division) captured Schmidt, but were soon forced back to the Kall River Valley.

were still unknown. Köchling positioned the *12th Volksgrenadier Division* north of the *275th Grenadier Division*. The *89th Grenadier Division* moved to the south, where it was soon to be relieved by the *272nd Volksgrenadier Division* and re-equipped. The *116th Panzer Division* was pulled back to München-Gladbach as an *Army Group B* reserve.

Delays

28th Infantry Division's attack was to begin on October 31, but rain, fog, and poor visibility necessitated a two-day postponement. This would avoid the possibility of delaying the subsequent VII Corps attack. After Hodges heard from Bradley on November 1 of the decision to postpone the offensive for five days, he sanctioned Collins' second operational plan. With the extra time, a fourth division would be incorporated into the renewed assault on Schmidt. Scheduled for November 10, the jump-off date could be extended to November 15 should weather or other

121

conditions warrant. It looked like Third Army's Patton would subsequently initiate the strategic offensive, instead of Hodges, but overcast, rainy weather predominated along both Third and First Army's fronts.

Although senior US leadership was finally seeing the threat posed by the Roer dams remaining in German hands, their almost pathological unwillingness to bypass strong enemy resistance meant that the fighting in the Hürtgen would continue until the area was completely secured. Hodges retained Collins' VII Corps as the spear tip of First Army's renewed effort to drive on Cologne, set to commence on November 5. Gerow's V Corps and Middleton's VIII Corps were to provide support, with the ultimate intent of advancing to Bonn and Koblenz, respectively. To draw enemy reserves and disrupt reinforcements, Gerow was to initiate an operation no later than November 2 to take Schmidt and protect First Army's southern flank by securing firm positions along the Roer River.

November 2

US

28th Infantry Division
Commander: Major General Norman D. Cota
HHC
Infantry: 109th, 110th, 112th Infantry Regiments
Field Artillery: HHB, 107th, 109th, 229th (105mm Howitzer), 108th Field Artillery Battalions (155mm Howitzer)
Special: HQ & HQ Company, 728th Reconnaissance Troop (Mechanized), 28th Quartermaster Company, 28th Signal Company, 726th Ordnance Light Maintenance Company, Military Police Platoon
Other: HQ & HQ Company, 103rd Engineer Battalion, 103rd Medical Battalion, Band

Attached
707th Tank Battalion
D Company, 87th Chemical Battalion
C Company, 86th Chemical Mortar Battalion
20th, 146th (less B Company), 1340th Engineer Combat Battalions, 1171st Engineer Combat Group
A Battery, 987th FA Battalion (155mm SP)

76th Field Artillery Battalion (105mm Howitzer)
893rd Tank Destroyer Battalion (SP) (less A Company)

Second Schmidt (November 1–9)

On November 1, Hodges made a rare visit to the front to discuss the following day's offensive with Cota, and to make sure all was in order. The 28th Infantry Division's commander outwardly professed confidence in the operation, but privately harbored doubt. The plan was overly detailed and left little flexibility to adapt to unforeseen circumstances. Hodges, however, came away from the meeting believing the chances were very good, and that, "they are feinting to the north in hopes of fooling the Boche into the belief that this is the main effort, and then whacking him with everything in the direction of the town of Schmidt."[5] The 28th Infantry Division was thus to be used in an uncreative operation that had divergent regimental objectives, and varied little in its planning from the disaster that had befallen 9th Infantry Division the previous month.

Cota voiced his concerns to his immediate superior, but Gerow would not yield on his overly structured plan. Instead, he tried to mollify his division commander with additional support. Because the division was the only sizeable US formation in offensive action along the front, considerable artillery was available for support. V Corps provided two 155mm howitzer battalions from the 187th Field Artillery Group, and a battalion of 4.5-inch guns for general support. One 155mm gun battalion and one 8-inch howitzer battalion from the 190th Field Artillery Group were also added, as was VII Corps' 188th Field Artillery Group, consisting of one 155mm gun battalion and one battalion (less one battery) of 4.5-inch guns.[6]

US Tank Destroyers (1944)

The American concept of a tank destroyer came in response to the large German armored forces fielded during the early months of the war. As US doctrine designated tanks to be used in an infantry support role, the tank destroyer was introduced to counter enemy armor. In addressing the trinity of armament, mobility, and protection, it was decided that the latter could be reduced. This allowed for the added weight of a large main gun, and compensated for the limited armor by relying on speed. Organizationally, tank destroyer battalions were used as a corps or army-level reserve to exploit a battlefield situation with aggressive movement and action. In practice, US commanders routinely deviated from doctrine to better adapt to a less numerous, but heavier and more powerful enemy armor.

Since September, US tank destroyer battalions had been receiving the M-36 Jackson with its potent 90mm main gun. Intended as a replacement for the 3-inch M-10 Wolverine, limited production meant that even as late as December 20, 1944, only 236 M-36s were in service.[7]

Vossenack (11/2)

After two more days of weather delays, November 2 dawned cool and foggy, but clearing skies were expected. At 0800, US artillery opened up a barrage along 28th Infantry Division's projected attack path. After 45 minutes the fire shifted to targets just in front of immediate ground objectives, and was joined by the 112th Infantry Regiment's half dozen 105mm howitzers.

Exactly 11,313 rounds and an hour later, the 28th Infantry Division emerged from its positions and attacked. The 1st Battalion (Major James C. Ford, Jr.), 109th Infantry Regiment led the advance on the left up to about 2,300m, meeting only light enemy resistance. The 3rd Battalion (Major Howard L. Topping) advanced along its right to some 1,300m where it encountered heavy artillery, mortar, machine gun, and small arms fire.[8] As the 109th Infantry Regiment pushed north along the Germeter-Hürtgen road, German artillery on the Brandenberg-Bergstein Ridge disrupted unit cohesion and its three battalions became intermixed.

German tanks followed up by moving through the town of Hürtgen and into the US right rear to help halt the drive along the Germeter-Hürtgen road. German defenses along the Weisser Weh constrained 3rd Battalion along its parent regiment's left, while the 2nd Battalion (Lieutenant Colonel Ross C. Henbest) had stumbled into an extensive minefield along the Germeter plateau near Wittscheidt, and was of no further use on the right. These positions would remain largely unchanged until the 12th Infantry Regiment, 4th Infantry Division, relieved the 109th on November 7, when it was 1,275 fewer in number.[9] With 28th Infantry Division's left firmly fixed, the Germans were able to move units to more threatened sectors to the south.

The Germans had been steadily building this defensive barrier

An abandoned German foxhole near Beeck is occupied by 333rd Infantry Regiment, 84th Infantry Division in preparation for an attack on November 11, 1944. (US Signal Corps)

(known as the "Wild Pig") since the end of October into what was perhaps the largest of its kind on the Western Front, being some 150m deep and stretching for a kilometer in front of Hürtgen. Combined with barbed wire and other impediments were every type of booby trap and mine imaginable. Thousands of teller anti-tank mines, S-mines ("bouncing betties") and the small wood and glass *shümeinen*, designed to avoid metal detectors, had been laid. German engineers booby-trapped felled trees, added anti-lifting triggers to mines, and even rigged shell holes in an attempt to catch those unwarily seeking shelter. As anti-personnel mines were intended to maim rather than kill, additional uninjured soldiers would subsequently be put in danger as they tried to rescue and evacuate their injured comrades.

From the opening bombardment until noon, the 229th Field Artillery Battalion provided direct support for the 112th Infantry Regiment as it moved on Vossenack. In addition to the preparation fires, missions were harassing, counter-battery, and targets of opportunity. Company B, 86th Chemical Battalion, fired 274 high explosive and 225 white phosphorous rounds with its 4.2-inch mortars, and at various times during the day Vossenack was reported burning and covered with a haze of smoke. D Company, 86th Chemical Battalion, did not fire, having pulled out of its position to be prepared to follow the 1st (Major Robert T. Hazlett) and 3rd Battalions (Lieutenant Colonel Albert Flood), 112th Infantry, to Schmidt.[10]

The 2nd Battalion (Lieutenant Colonel Theodore S. Hatzfeld), 112th Regiment, and an attached tank company from the 707th Tank Battalion (Lieutenant Colonel Richard W. Ripple), attacked east from Germeter. By early afternoon, and with German resistance remaining light, Hatzfeld's battalion followed up on its success and pushed beyond the southern slope of Vossenack ridge and up to the Kall River. As with the 109th Infantry Regiment, increasing German resistance and difficult terrain eventually degraded the advance. The 1st and 3rd Battalions attacked from Richelskaul into the woods, but were stopped just west of the gorge by enemy infantry and artillery and would remain so for the rest of the day.

The 110th Infantry Regiment started its offensive at noon, but achieved even less success than 28th Infantry Division's other two regiments. With the 1st Battalion allocated as a division reserve, the 3rd Battalion moved southeast toward Simonskall. To its right the 2nd Battalion ran into a string of pillboxes along the Rollesbroich-Richelskaul road known as the Raffelsbrand strongpoint. Both assaulting battalions were subsequently stopped almost before they started. Minefields, muddy roads, and dense terrain finished whatever the strong German defenses could not. Over the next several days, the 110th Infantry Regiment repeatedly tried to gain their objective of the Strauch-Schmidt road, but to no avail.

After having been grounded by poor midday weather, only three of the five planned air support missions arrived on the scene. At 1445, twelve P-38 Lightnings (474th Fighter Bomber Group) attacked Bergstein, barges on the Roer River, a bridge at Heimbach, and two factories east of Nideggen. The 28th Infantry Division's air control officer reported that one squadron mistakenly bombed an American artillery position near Rötgen and caused several casualties before attacking German positions at Schmidt. Two other groups likewise flew beyond the immediate battle zone to attack targets of opportunity. The missions did little to assist US forces in retaining the momentum they had achieved earlier in the day. The lack of success did not seem to bother Cota, however, who felt it was too soon to consider his division's efforts a failure.

At Schlenderhan Castle, west of Cologne, the commanders and staffs of German *Army Group B*, *Fifth Panzer* and *Seventh Army*, and subordinate corps and divisions had been conducting a map study concerning the possibility of an enemy attack along the above army boundaries. Coincidentally, this scenario was actually unfolding in the Hürtgen Forest. When word arrived from the front opposite the 28th Infantry Division's offensive, *LXXIV Corps'* chief of staff frantically called for army reserves to throw at the enemy penetrations around Vossenack. The message stressed a critical situation, and that with negligible reserves to close the gaps opened by the American attacks, *Seventh Army* would need to compensate. Model ordered *LXXIV Corps'* commander, Straube, to return to the front and form a *Kampfgruppe* from the *116th Panzer Division* to be sent to counter the 109th Infantry Regiment. The remainder of the division would follow suit from around München-Gladbach and Jülich to take part in a dawn counterattack intended to carry as far as Vossenack.

While the map study continued until noon, *116th Panzer Division* was attached to *LXXXVI Corps* as it moved from München-Gladbach to Kreusen, Kufferath, Untermanbach, and Winden. Straube wanted a quick resolution and sent a 20–30 *panzer Kampfgruppe* ahead.[11] Other corps elements were added to clean up the Schmidt situation. During the night the remainder of the *116th Panzer Division* arrived in the Schmidt area. The *89th Grenadier Division's* *1st* and *3rd Battalions* deployed on either side of the Harscheidt-Schmidt road, while the *2nd* moved near the Strauch-Schmidt road. The *341st Sturmgeschütz Brigade* entered Harscheidt. None of this activity was picked up by US intelligence.

The next day, heavy cloud cover returned to prevent anything save intermittent air support. With the 109th Infantry Regiment's flanks fixed, its 1st Battalion forged up the middle. German artillery along the Brandenberg-Bergstein Ridge continued to take a toll of men while ripping up phone lines. The Germans responded to the thrust by ordering the *253rd Engineer Battalion*, with support from the recently arrived *60th Panzergrenadier Regiment*, to counterattack Cota's northern flank as soon as possible.

At 0700, the 112th Infantry Regiment's 1st and 3rd Battalions were finally able to push through German defenses along the Germeter-Richelskaul road. In columns both moved across Vossenack and along the narrow "Kall Trail" and up the steep gorge, both with an eye on reaching Steckenborn. Flood's 3rd Battalion pushed on through the Kall Gorge and up the muddy, narrow trail to Kommerscheidt at 1300. Leaving the 1st Battalion to hold the town, he pushed on after overcoming a very surprised and negligible German force.

Armored support would not be immediately forthcoming. The status of the bridge at the base of the gorge was originally listed as destroyed, but after an eight-hour delay engineers deemed it intact and fit for traffic. When tanks from A Company, 707th Tank Battalion, attempted to negotiate the pass, however, they found it too slick and steep for a safe crossing. The 20th Engineer Combat Battalion worked through the night to correct the problem, but no tanks crossed until the following morning.

In reaction to the 112th Infantry Regiment's penetration, the Germans moved up reinforcements from the Monschau sector. Two battalions from the *1055th Regiment* passed through Schmidt to the northeast and halted around Harscheidt. Flood's 3rd Battalion, however, occupied Schmidt and cut off the *1055th's* remaining battalion, which dug in to the west of the town.

With Schmidt captured and the 28th Infantry Division apparently making good progress, the division staff at Rott was understandably delighted. Feeling like "a little Napoleon," Cota believed that the road network around Steckenborn was vital to supporting his position at Schmidt.[12] He committed the 1st Battalion (Lieutenant Colonel Floyd A. Davison), 110th Regiment to subdue the pillboxes near Raffelsbrand. Davison decided the best way to accomplish this was with a flanking move around Richelskaul and into the enemy's right as the 3rd Battalion acted as the anvil.

Peterson recommended to an agreeable Cota that the 112th Infantry Regiment distribute each of its battalions in Vossenack, Kommerscheidt, and Schmidt. As a precaution against a German coun-terattack, 1st Battalion was moved up to make contact with the forces at Schmidt. As the 28th Infantry Division's commander never saw the situation personally, the precarious, projecting deployment remained in effect. Schmidt was too big for 3rd Battalion to defend effectively, a situation made worse as its men were exhausted and did not take the time to construct proper defenses. In most cases they sought shelter from the rain and cold in the town's buildings. Even a shipment of antitank mines was simply laid atop the three roads into the town without an effort to mask their presence. Patrols were not sent out, and Peterson remained unaware that German forces were gathering for a counterattack a mere kilometer to the east at Harscheidt.

Schmidt and Kommerscheidt (11/4–6)

At 0700 on November 4, a German artillery barrage suddenly hit 3rd Battalion's position at Schmidt. A half-hour later, armor and infantry from the *16th Panzer Regiment*, teaming up with the *1055th Grenadier Regiment*, struck the surprised Americans from three directions. Additional infantry, with eight tanks and four *Sturmgeschütze*, arrived from Strauch as support.

By 0830 the nearly surrounded 3rd Battalion was attempting to hold on, but heavy fire took a toll on the exhausted soldiers. Ever-increasing groups broke under the strain and began withdrawing the way they had come the previous day. Bazooka teams tried to counter a trio of *Sturmgeschütze* from the gardens and buildings north and east of Schmidt, but were of little effect against their frontal armor. German armor overran the shallow American foxholes and kept going. US artillery was slow to respond to calls for support, and by the time it arrived, 3rd Battalion's unfolding disaster could not be averted. Even though V Corps allocated as much ammunition as possible to the 28th Infantry Division, getting it across the intermittently secure and difficult-to-negotiate "Kall Trail" proved extremely difficult. The Americans fought stubbornly, but their position was compromised. Units progressively lost contact with their higher commands, as ever-greater numbers joined the retreat, believing they had missed the order to pull back. The battalion quickly ceased to exist as a cohesive fighting unit.

A similar situation was unfolding southwest of Kommerscheidt, where the Germans continued their counterattack. With only sporadic US artillery support, the enemy was able to effectively coordinate their assault, even in the case of the *275th Grenadier Division*, whose mix of unit types was inherently difficult to organize. Inversely, even though German artillery remained effective during this stage of the battle, it was difficult to manage in large numbers. Poor communications meant that these assets often waited until they heard the enemy's guns before moving to respond.

As 3rd Battalion survivors streamed into Kommerscheidt, chaos reigned east of the Kall River. Officers and staffs tried with minimal success to stem the rout and integrate remnants of units into 1st Battalion's defences. Even 2nd Battalion, 112th Regiment's position north of the river was subjected to intense enemy artillery fire.

Cota received word that Schmidt was under attack, but he was unaware of its magnitude. He directed his Assistant G3, Lieutenant Colonel Trapani, to go to the town and let him know what was happening. Trapani was unable to get through the "Kall Trail," and reported back to receive the full wrath of his division commander. In mid-morning Cota was given erroneous reports that the 3rd Battalion was holding its position, and he ordered it to continue its attack eastward as soon as they had defeated the enemy foray into the village.

Army doctrine stated that a commander should place himself where he can best influence an operation's progress. On the division level this was at the command post, as it enabled better dissemination of information from which to plan and issue orders. Complete isolation from the battlefield, however, would prevent a commander from being able to feel the pulse of operations. It also gave the impression that he was not weathering the same dangers that he expected of his subordinates.

By 1000 the rout was on, as 3rd Battalion's position at Schmidt was untenable. German counterattacks drove the GIs back to Kommerscheidt, and American artillery did not immediately respond to try to correct the development. In fact, the seventeen artillery battalions from V Corps and 28th Infantry Division had failed to suppress or destroy enemy ground forces to any great degree. Collins believed that this was the major reason for the 28th's failure in the Hürtgen: "My personal judgment was that the reason for not taking Schmidt was they didn't use their artillery fire as well as it could have been used."[13]

Poor radio or wire communication between the infantry, forward observers, and the artillery headquarters coordinating the fire support, was found to have broken down during several critical periods of the battle. With his three regiments attacking in three different directions, communication had been poor at best. The terrain, including both the numerous valleys and thick fir trees, especially in and around the "Kall Trail," had severely impacted radio transmissions. This hampered the forward units' efforts to keep the "Kall Trail" open, and interrupted their efforts to keep their higher headquarters informed of what they were encountering at Schmidt and Kommerscheidt.

By 1130 the Germans had recaptured Schmidt, and the 3rd Battalion, 112th Infantry no longer existed as a cohesive unit. The staffs of both the 1st and 3rd Battalions had been captured, along with more than 130 other men from the 3rd Battalion. Peterson, at his command post at Vossenack, was finally made aware that Schmidt, and his regiment, was under attack.

13th Infantry Regiment, 8th Infantry Division pass through the Hürtgen Forest on Dec 9, 1944. (US Signal Corps)

Cota received updated information around noon that led him to believe that the Germans had recaptured the village. He then directed his Assistant Division Commander, Brigadier General George A. Davis, to gain information to make informed decisions and to serve as his eyes and ears. Cota then turned his attention to his Main Supply Route (MSR) and directed the 1171st Engineer Combat Group commander, Colonel Edmund Daley, to find out what was happening on the "Kall Trail."

After relieving Flood, Cota handed the 3rd Battalion over to Hazlett, the 1st Battalion commander, who took charge of the remnants and incorporated the 3rd Battalion survivors into his own unit. Along the "Kall Trail" the situation had deteriorated considerably in a short time, as German units cut the American MSR to Kommerscheidt.

At 1400, eight Panzer IVs from the *16th Panzer Regiment* and 200 soldiers from the *1055th Grenadier Regiment* attacked Kommerscheidt. The *panzers* remained out of bazooka range as they fired into the US positions. Three tanks from A Company, 707th Tank Battalion moved up to counter the enemy armor, and with help from artillery largely succeeded. German tanks engaged in a close-range fight with the recently arrived M-4 Shermans, only to lose three vehicles the effort. With a disabled fourth destroyed by its crew, and with improving weather, American fighter-bombers arrived and destroyed a fifth tank and the Germans withdrew.

Meantime, five disabled Shermans blocking the trail held up further US armor support. Cota sent in engineers to correct the situation by the next morning at the latest. With the MSR closed to traffic, the 112th Infantry Regiment's efforts east of the Kall River would be unsustainable, and endanger 28th Infantry Division's chance of salvaging the situation.

With the 109th and 110th Infantry Regiments halted well short of their objectives at Hürtgen and Steckenborn, respectively, Cota's hope for his remaining regiment's success was quickly fading. Out of contact with his subordinates at the front, Cota's staff continued to send reports to Gerow that 28th Infantry Division's offensive was going well. Apparently, Cota hoped to correct the situation before word got out that he had lost control of the situation, and that much of his command had ceased to be an effective fighting force.

Just after dawn on November 5, nine self-propelled tank destroyers and the six remaining tanks from A Company, 707th Tank Battalion crossed the recently opened "Kall Trail" and moved toward Kommerscheidt. At dawn the *16th Panzer Regiment* and *1055th Grenadier Regiment* attacked Kommerscheidt, but were rebuffed.

Within the hour, Gerow visited 28th Infantry Division's headquarters at Rott to assess a situation that was quite different from the one described by Cota's staff. He voiced his displeasure at Cota, left, and returned at 1030 with Hodges, his chief of staff, and Collins in tow. Hodges informed Cota that he had postponed VII Corps's attack (scheduled for the 5th) and wanted Cota to explain how his division had allowed the Germans to recapture Schmidt. When Hodges and his retinue left, the 28th's commander had assured him that a plan was being drafted to retake Schmidt the following day. A tall order considering that the Germans would now be able to concentrate their forces on the lone enemy division trying to take Schmidt.

German artillery observers on the Brandenberg-Bergstein Ridge had a clear view of their enemy's exposed foxholes, which had received nearly constant fire since the advance had started out on the 2nd. Just before dark, the Germans began concentrating their fire on individual foxholes by shooting 20–30 rounds into one before moving to the next.

In this manner they destroyed three fighting positions, which the troops refused to reoccupy. On the next morning, the Germans stopped the shelling temporarily. Aware of the gap in their lines and the exposed nature of their positions, the GIs began individually to leave their foxholes during the pause. After about 30 minutes the Germans resumed their shelling, and the defenders started to break. First one company, then another, began to shuffle to the rear.

That night, elements of the 707th Tank Battalion integrated with 3rd Battalion (Lieutenant Colonel William S. Tait), 110th Infantry Regiment as a battlegroup. Under the tank battalion commander, Task Force Ripple prepared to move out the following day. In its present, combat-depleted state, however, it seemed unlikely to salvage the situation east of the Kall River. The fact that it was sent to complete a job that an entire infantry regiment, with armor support, could not, perhaps best reflects the gap between Cota's understanding of the battle and its reality.

TF Ripple linked up with his infantry support just before daylight on November 6. On receiving word that the "Kall Trail" was occupied by the Germans, Ripple ordered his men to make their way along a firebreak that paralleled the trail. Minutes later, after much exertion, Ripple and his 300 infantrymen entered the woods, and a meeting engagement occurred with the reconnaissance battalion of the *116th Panzer Regiment.*

No maneuvering force was available to attempt to regain the original objectives, so VII Corps had hurriedly attached the 12th Infantry Regiment to 28th Infantry Division. By the morning the 109th Infantry had been relieved for action to the south, and the 12th Infantry Regiment had again begun offensive action. With this attack began the hardest fighting that this regiment had ever been through. Added to the natural obstacles of tall, closely knit woods, steep hillsides, and lack of roads were mine fields, wire entanglements, and booby traps planted by the enemy during the weeks of inactivity in this sector.

The *156th Panzergrenadier Regiment* attacked Vossenack from the wooded terrain south of Hürtgen, while the *60th Panzergrenadier Regiment* advanced southwest and south of Brandenburg. The *116th Panzer Reconnaissance Battalion*, with engineers and some armor, rushed along the Kall River to cut in behind the American penetration at Schmidt. Upon cutting the "Kall Trail," the *Kampfgruppe* laid mines. After heavy fighting, the *60th Panzergrenadier Regiment* took half of Vossenack.

Peterson met with Ripple, and both agreed there was no chance of success given the condition of the men. Peterson canceled the attack and ordered the infantry battalion to dig in along the tree line behind Kommerscheidt. While Task Force Ripple was encountering the *116th Panzer Reconnaissance Battalion* along the "Kall Trail," a furious barrage struck Hatzfeld's battalion. Intense small arms fire was then intermixed with the barrage, coming from the opposite tree line. Word spread through the American positions that German infantry was attacking through a gap between two companies of the 2nd Battalion. The cumulative effect of the artillery and small arms fire shattered nerves, and within minutes a mass of US soldiers abandoned their fighting positions and went streaming for the rear. Officers and non-coms officers tried to stop the rout but were unable to do so. Chaos ensued. Several company commanders and platoon leaders, seeing men on their flanks withdrawing, gave the order for their formations to likewise withdraw. The tanks and tank destroyers supporting the 2nd Battalion, seeing the infantry retreat, started their engines and withdrew as well.

German artillery pounded the 2nd Battalion's positions, causing even more casualties with men in the open. American artillery began to shell the German positions, but several rounds fell short, landing near the command post, killing and wounding several of Pruden's group. When the 28th Infantry Division's G3 reported this incident to V Corps, the report read that 2nd Battalion pulled back under heavy artillery fire before rallying to regain the lost position. In reality they had been routed and were no longer a cohesive combat unit. With only one battalion still possessing the will and ability to fight, the 112th Infantry Regiment was in no shape for continued operations.

At around 1200, German infantry began to occupy the northeast portion of Vossenack, in part to get shelter from enemy artillery. With only about 70 infantrymen left in the 112th Infantry's 2nd Battalion, a continued defense of the town seemed impossible. Davis stepped in and allocated the 146th Engineer Combat Battalion to reinforce the position, and sent part of the 1340th and 20th Engineers to the "Kall Trail" to maintain its ability to flow traffic.

Cota notified Gerow that with the *156th* and parts of the *60th Panzergrenadier Regiments* arriving at Vossenack, the Germans were close to splitting the 28th Infantry Division in half. At 1410, the 12th RCT was notified to immediately move to the vicinity of Zweifall, over 70km distant. Once there it was to be attached to the 28th Infantry Division as its reserve. When notified he would be receiving the 12th Infantry

Regiment, 4th Infantry Division, Cota planned to keep the 1st Battalion, 109th Infantry Regiment in Germeter, move the 2nd Battalion into Vossenack to relieve the remnants of 112th Infantry Regiment, and then push the German forces out of the village and move on and capture the ridge. The 3rd Battalion would take up positions on the southern slope of Vossenack ridge where it could protect the MSR along the "Kall Trail."

The Germans Retake Kommerscheidt (11/7)

The 12th Regimental Combat Team had a difficult approach march, as muddy, narrow roads caused vehicles to slide into ditches. The blackness of the night hampered operations, but around 0200, 12th RCT arrived at an assembly point behind the front lines, where it was met by guides, and relieved the 109th Infantry Regiment, unit for unit.

As Cota realized that Task Force Ripple would not be able to recapture Schmidt alone, he had Davis create an additional battlegroup. TF Davis was to consist of the recently relieved 1st Battalion, 109th Infantry Regiment, which although strengthened by 200 new replacements, remained in disarray and considerably depleted from heavy fighting near Hürtgen. The 1st and 3rd Battalions of 112th Infantry Regiment had likewise been hammered over the last few days, and along with them 3rd Battalion, 110th Infantry. A and C Companies, 707th Tank Battalion; B and C Companies of 893rd Tank Destroyer Battalion would also be included.

While Cota and Davis were planning the latter's task force, the 146th Engineer Combat Battalion, supported by the 70th Tank Battalion, advanced behind an intense artillery barrage, fighting house to house to clear the *156th Panzer Grenadier Regiment, 116th Panzer Division* out of Vossenack. After nearly eight hours of intense street fighting, the Germans were forced to retreat, leaving behind more than 150 killed and wounded.

Davis pushed, prodded, and yelled, but to little avail. There was no way his task force would be able to traverse the Kall Valley, maneuver and fight through Vossenack and Kommerscheidt, and then recapture Schmidt. The attack planned for Task Force Davis was canceled when the infantry battalion became lost in the forest and could not link up with the other elements in a timely manner. The 28th Infantry Division withdrew from the Kall Ravine.

In Kommerscheidt, the Americans huddled in their foxholes while a cold rain fell. A fierce artillery barrage began to sweep through the village for more than an hour, setting many of the houses on fire and stunning the American defenders with its intensity. Then, through the mist, a battalion of German infantry, supported by 15 tanks, appeared moving down the road from Schmidt. An intense tank battle ensued in which the Germans had five tanks destroyed and the Americans lost two Shermans and three tank destroyers. At 1125 Peterson radioed Cota from Kommerscheidt to say the situation east of the Kall was becoming untenable. Cota directed him to hold the village and his positions "at all costs."

German infantry supported by ten tanks stormed into the village and began to overrun the American fighting positions, inflicting many casualties. Individually and then as groups, the Americans began to pull back. Unlike the panic stricken routs at Schmidt and Vossenack, it was an organized withdrawal back to their reserve positions in the tree line behind the village. American forces in Kommerscheidt now had only two tank destroyers and three tanks operational. The five armored vehicles provided support while the infantry pulled back, and then they too withdrew into the trees. Cota was then notified the 112th had lost Kommerscheidt and had occupied a defensive line west of the village.

On 7 November, when the soldiers began to run in the face of the enemy, quick action by junior officers and NCOs stopped the potential rout. This type of forward dynamic leadership differed markedly from the situations in the other two battalions. Ultimately, neither the reinforcements from division nor the bravery of the junior leaders was enough to stop the Germans. The overwhelming superiority of the German forces attacking the defenders of Kommerscheidt eventually defeated them with extremely high losses to the defenders. Nonetheless, this collection of Americans maintained their cohesion and withdrew in a relatively orderly fashion under the leadership of their officers and NCO.

Cota and Davis met late in the day to discuss the situation. Kommerscheidt was in German hands, and the enemy was still attempting to push the engineers out of Vossenack. Davis agreed with his division commander when Cota recommended he pull all units forward of the "Kall Trail" back to the west side of the river. Cota contacted the corps commander and requested he be allowed to pull his units forward of the trail back to a defensive line west of the Kall River. Gerow stated he would contact First Army and discuss the situation with Hodges.

Just before midnight, Gerow contacted Cota to tell him Hodges "was very dissatisfied with the situation. It seemed that over the last

Antitank (teller) mines: Model 29 (discontinued due to a small pressure plate); Models 35 and 35 "steel" (the latter with its corrugated top was used predominantly in North Africa) are essentially the same; Models 42 and 43 (a simplified variation of the Model 42). (US Signal Corps)

three days the only thing the 28th was doing was losing ground."[14] Grudgingly, Hodges authorized Cota to pull back to the west bank of the Kall. The 28th Infantry Division must continue to hold the Vossenack Ridge's southern slope, and Cota needed to provide a unit to reinforce the 12th Infantry Regiment as it prepared to attack around Hürtgen. As the 1st Battalion, 109th Infantry Regiment had suffered the least number of casualties in the division to date, its 190 remaining soldiers would get the job.

Shortly after dawn on the 8th, Eisenhower and Bradley arrived at Cota's command post, followed soon after by Hodges and Gerow. The Supreme Allied Commander and Bradley did not stay long, probably sensing that the First Army commander wanted to talk to Cota alone. Again Cota was reprimanded, but Gerow's inability to implement Hodge's directions brought him under scrutiny as well.

That night, Cota called all of his regimental and battalion commanders to a briefing at the division command post. He directed that a minefield be established east of Vossenack to separate the American and German forces. 5,000 mines were subsequently laid the following day, and with German engineers having destroyed the bridge over the Kall River, both sides were effectively separated. After November 9, the 28th Infantry Division continued with patrols and local attacks, but its offensive operations were essentially concluded. Five days later, the division would be relegated to the still quiet sector in the Ardennes.

Footnotes

[1] Table IX, Annex 11: Medical, in Vol 3: Annexes 9–14, "First United States Army, Report of Operations, 23 February–8 May 1945," p. 141.

[2] Headquarters 28th Infantry Division, "Unit Report No. 4 From 010001 October to 312400 October 1944," (14 November 1944), p. 3.

[3] FUSA Rpt; V Corps Opns in the ETO, 6 Jan 42 to 9 May 45; V Corps Study; V Corps FO 30, 21 Oct 44, and V Corps Ltrs of Instn, 23 Ocf 44 and 30 Oct 44, V Corps G-3 Jnl and File, Oct 44; 28th Div G-3 Jnl and File, 26 Oct–2 Nov 44; Combat Interv 77 with Cota.

[4] 21 A Gp Gen Opnl Sit and Dir, M 534, 2 Nov 44, 12th A GP 371.3 Military Objectives, II.

[5] William C. Sylvan and John T. Greenwood. *Normandy to Victory: The War Diary of General Courtney H. Hodges*, p. 161.

[6] Combat Interv 77 with Cota. This dictation by V Corps was apparently based on the limitations of terrain, number of troops involved, and missions of the attack as originally decided by First Army and 12th Army Group. (All combat interviews on the Schmidt operation are by the 2d Information and Historical Service and were conducted in November 1944 or early December 1944).

[7] Charles M. Baily, *Faint Praise: American Tanks and The Tank Destroyers during World War II* (Hamden, CT: Archon Books, 1983), p. 117.

[8] 28th Infantry Division G-3 "Periodic Report. 020001 November to 022400 November 1944."

[9] Cecil B. Curry. *Follow Me and Die. The Destruction of an American Division in World War II*. New York, New York: Stein & Day Publishing 1984, p 41.

[10] 28th Div Arty Jnl, 2 Nov 44; 28th Div G-3 Jnl, 2 Nov 44; Hq and Hq Co, 28th Div Arty, AAR, Nov 44; 86th Cml Bn AAR, Nov 44.

[11] Generalmajor a.D. Siegfried von Waldenberg, MS A-905, "116th Panzer Division, 1–9 Nov 1944" (n.d.).; Generalmajor Alfred Toppe, MS C-089, "Units Opposing Our 28th Div. in the Hurtgen Forest" (n.d.).

[12] Interv with Gen Cota, 15 Sep 48.

[13] Gerald Astor. *The Bloody Forest: Battle of the Huertgen September 1944–January 1945* (Novato, CA: Presidio Press, Inc, 2000), p. 147.

[14] James Gavin, *On To Berlin*, p 221.

Chapter 8

Operation Queen (Third Aachen)
(November 16–18)

Ever since the October 18th meeting between Eisenhower and his command chiefs at Brussels, plans had progressed for the major assault to reach the west bank of the Roer River. At the time Antwerp still remained closed to Allied shipping, but it looked as if it would soon be delivering vast amounts of supplies to Montgomery's 21st and Bradley's 12th Army Group.

By November, the Allies had largely cleared the German coastal garrisons from their "fortresses" that had been bypassed the previous summer. This not only opened new channels for resupply but made more Allied forces available to reinforce the main front. In the lead-up to the final campaign before the Rhine River, 12th Army Group steadily received these freed-up forces, and underwent a considerable reorganization.

The 99th Infantry ("Battle Babies") Division reinforced V Corps. Major General Alvan Gillem, Jr.'s XIII Corps was also brought up, having completed its operations in Brittany. Subordinated to First Army on October 22, its combat units were to be parceled off to other formations for the time being. The inexperienced 104th Infantry Division went to VII Corps to relieve the "Big Red One" at Stolberg. The 7th Armored and 84th Infantry ("Railsplitters") Divisions would temporarily stay under British control, while the 102nd Infantry Division lacked organic transport and artillery.

Gerow's V Corps, with the 99th Infantry Division, and Middleton's VIII Corps were to provide support, with the ultimate intent of advancing to Bonn and Koblenz, respectively. Hodges' front extended approximately 200km, with some 130km belonging to VIII Corps, which was not slated for immediate offensive operations, while V and VII Corps covered the remainder. Even with its increased strength, however, First Army would soon find itself spread among numerous responsibilities that would negate it forming anything more than a nominal army reserve.[1]

Although William Hood Simpson's recently arrived Ninth Army was in an area favorable to large maneuvers, the British forces along its left were still reorganizing after their failed Market Garden operation. With Simpson lacking sufficient flank protection to the north, he was given the duty of protecting First Army, whose staff and soldiers represented the more experienced American force. The lanky, pleasant son of a Confederate veteran of the Tennessee Cavalry, Simpson got on well with Montgomery, often to the irritation of his Army peers. As a WWI vet, he had knowledge of the terrain over which he now fought. The Ninth Army, still involved during the early days of November in assembling sufficient formations to undertake offensive operations, was "relatively untried," and suffered from a lack of combat units. Of the two corps headquarters and six divisions that were assigned to the army, only General McLain's 113th Cavalry Group, the 2nd Armored, and the 29th, and 30th Infantry Divisions of XIX Corps were available for operations.

Allied Planning

Since the beginning of November, Ninth Army had been establishing its presence between the British Second Army and First Army to its south. As 12th Army Group needed these units before commencing renewed hostilities, Bradley moved the start-date of his offensive five days to November 10, but even this date remained subject to weather conditions to ensure air support. Sunny skies at this time of year were a rare occurrence, and official word to commence the offensive would be day-to-day.

North of Aachen, General McLain's XIX Corps would attempt to effect a bridgehead over the Roer River at Jülich and Linnich. Until the issue of the remaining German-held dams was resolved, and the Allied forces could cross the river without facing a flooded battlezone, there was to be no advance beyond this boundary "except on Army order."[2]

Oddly, the elimination of the strong German presence around Geilenkirchen was not considered, possibly because it was nearly astride the Army Group boundary between the British and the Americans. Only after XIX Corps had made sufficient progress were the British to "develop offensive operations," relieve the XIII Corps, and eliminate this threat.[3] With substantial German resistance from Geilenkirchen, XIX Corps would have to initially advance along a constricted, 15km frontage between the town and Würselen. Its expanding northern flank would be shored-up by the 113th Cavalry Group and the 102nd Infantry Division. Upon relief by the British, the XIII Corps was to be prepared to drive northeast along the left of the XIX Corps to the Rhine.

After the British had relieved XIII Corps, and with XIX Corps having acquired sufficient ground along its left flank between Geilenkirchen and the Roer, XIII Corps was to be committed along the left of XIX Corps to seize a Roer bridgehead at Linnich. XIX Corps was naturally slated as Ninth Army's offensive component, where its position between Geilenkirchen and Aachen dictated its goal of establishing a bridgehead over the Roer River at Jülich.

Collins and his staff developed plans to seize crossings of the Roer at its closest point, some 11km away. The first would call for three divisions based on a November 5 jump-off date. This force would capture the Eschweiler-Weisweiler industrial area northeast of Stolberg to provide room to maneuver, while retaining contact with Ninth Army to the north. The prominent Hamich Ridge, and especially Hill 232, would also be taken to ensure safe passage beyond the Stolberg Corridor and the Wenau Forest. Finally, seizing the long sought-after Hürtgen-Kleinhau-Gey road network would then conclude the fighting in the Hürtgen. A follow-up assault, between five and ten days later, would clear the middle and northern part of the forest, and open the way to the Roer River. In this way, when the dams were eventually captured, the Americans would be in a position to quickly move into the Cologne Plain, and beyond.

Over 300 armored vehicles and 32 battalions of field artillery would support VII Corps, and its commander, "Lightning Joe" Collins, not to mention the normally reserved Hodges and Bradley, felt the chances for success were good. Besides, intelligence estimated that US strength outnumbered the enemy by up to 5:1 west of the Roer.[4] With a repeat of the summer's headlong advances unlikely, maintaining close contact on the flanks would be necessary as the offensive progressed. This would be relatively simple given the more accessible terrain bordering Ninth Army, but to the south, the Hürtgen Forest remained a considerable obstacle, and would remain so until the Kleinhau-Gey road network was occupied. This final task was allocated to the 4th Infantry Division, which would then make for the Roer River at Düren as a springboard to securing the remaining, and highest priority dams.

US intelligence estimated that in addition to the German forces in front-line positions, there were an additional 31,000 troops available west of the Rhine River (mostly the *9th Panzer* and *15th Panzergrenadier*

Divisions). These could reinforce enemy defenses west of the Roer River, but could also be used to launch a sizeable counterattack. Further back, the *2nd*, *5th*, and *7th Fallschirmjäger Divisions* were refitting around Cologne, and the *1st*, *2nd*, and *10th SS* and the *130th Panzer (Panzer Lehr) Divisions* were doing the same near Arnaberg-Paderburn.

With overcast skies repeatedly postponing the operation's start, responsibility switched to Hodges for the last two days before the absolute commencement on November 16. Because of the weather's uncertainty, three contingency plans were created to best utilize Allied air assets: one for fighter-bombers, one mixing tactical elements (fighter-bombers and medium bombers), and one adding heavy bombers to the second option. Even though poor weather continued, on the 15th Hodges had little choice but to greenlight the attack for the following day, regardless of conditions in the sky. Whether air support would be available remained to be seen. Should adverse weather prevent any type of aircraft from operating between the target date of 11 November and the deadline date of 16 November, the attack would begin no later than the latter, with or without air support.

Aerial Support

Considering the example at St. Lo that had solved the Normandy deadlock, Bradley was still eager to employ a massive aerial bombardment to pave the way for ground forces and thus regain the strategic initiative. To ensure the success of the new offensive, Bradley requested air support of unprecedented magnitude. After close coordination in early planning, top air commanders and representatives of the ground forces met on November 7 at Ninth Air Force headquarters to discuss and approve a final plan. Out of this conference emerged a blueprint for the combined British and American aerial contingent for Operation Queen.

Because of the importance of aerial support Eisenhower's air commander, Lieutenant General Carl Spaatz, had responsibility for designating the attack's start-time during the period of November 10–13. Under this most comprehensive plan, the bulk of the air effort was to be centered in front of the First Army, but resources were also allocated to Simpson's Ninth. Three divisions (more than 1,200 planes) of Eighth Air Force heavy bombers were to participate in the attack. The RAF would provide a similar sized force, in addition to Ninth Air Force (600 medium bombers), IX and XXIX Tactical Air Commands (750

Soldiers from I Coy, 3rd Infantry Battalion, 8th Infantry Regiment, 4th Infantry Division enter the Hürtgen Forest on Nov. 18, 1944. (US Signal Corps)

fighter-bombers total), and 800 escort fighters for the heavy bombers.[5] The heavies would concentrate on destroying personnel and field installations in two major target areas: the Eschweiler-Weisweiler industrial complex and the Langerwehe-Jüngersdorf area, an urban obstacle at the northeastern tip of the Wenau Forest lying squarely astride the projected route of the VII Corps main effort.

In general, the fighter-bombers were to operate on call from the ground troops for targets of opportunity, although some squadrons were to perform normal tasks of column cover and reconnaissance. The rest of the mediums were to concentrate on personnel and field installations in front of First Army. The target areas were around three villages representing likely sites for enemy command posts and local reserves: Luchem, Echtz, and Mariaweiler. With over 4,500 aircraft slated to participate, Operation Queen would be the largest air attack in direct support of ground troops to that date in World War II.

Like the First Army, Simpson desired assistance from the coming air armada. Instead of the target bombing approach his peer was promoting, he favored carpet-bombing as the best way to open a path through the various village strongpoints in Ninth Army's path. Air operations against the villages close to the army's forward positions would be confined to the four groups of fighter-bombers available from the newly operational XXIX Tactical Air Command. Medium and heavy bombers were to concentrate on communication centers, including Aldenhoven, Jülich, Linnich, and Heinsberg.

If there was any weakness in the Allies' air supremacy over the battlefield, it was a lack of aircraft suitable for operations at night. With most German movement being conducted at night, US tactical air assets were largely unable to interdict it. To aid targeting in poor weather and at night, Allied pilots relied on radar systems such as the very advanced mobile Signal Corps Radio (SCR)-584, which vectored aircraft to their objective.

German Buildup and Deception

Although Allied intelligence had detected German strategic reserves between the Roer and Rhine Rivers, neither the massive buildup for the coming Ardennes assault, nor the quiet transfer of *Fifth Panzer Army's* headquarters to *Army Group B* (where it took responsibility for *XII SS Corps* and *LXXXI Corps* under the deceptive name, *Military Police Command for Special Assignment*) were discovered. This formation added a badly needed armor element to the sector, and helped to shorten *Seventh Army's* lengthy frontage. *Fifteenth Army* headquarters was similarly shifted into the Aachen sector under the designation *Gruppe von Manteuffel*, and the Allies remained unaware of its absence or that the headquarters of the *Armed Forces Commander Netherlands* (General Christiansen), which took over the sector, then called itself *Fifteenth Army*. If anything, they believed that the Germans were resting and refitting a *panzer* reserve consisting of "the key to the enemy's essential capabilities and intentions," which would likely be used as the core of a counterattack force along the Roer River.[6]

Senior German commanders in the West logically deduced that in November the Allies would make a concentrated thrust to finish their two-month effort to push beyond the *Westwall* in November, most probably along the "Stolberg Corridor." The Germans reacted by stripping forces from other fronts to improve the defenses in this area. They were also stripping workers from factories and farms within Germany and replacing them with lower quality substitutes, lowering admission standards for military service, and combing out the *Kriegsmarine*, *Luftwaffe*, and rear echelon units.

Senior commanders in *Army Group B* knew they would be unable to regain the lost territory between Aachen and the Hürtgen, and would have to resort to localized counterattacks. They had expected an enemy attack either against the Roer Plain to the north or against the dams, and not the push through the comparatively less significant Hürtgen Forest. *12th Volksgrenadier Division* commander, *Generalmajor* (as of November 1) Engel believed the Americans would move on Langerwehe and Merode in preparation for a follow-up attack south to secure the Schwammenauel Dam.

While the fight raged about Aachen and on the approaches to the Roer River, some thirty divisions were massed behind the Roer and in the Eifel Mountains, ammunition and fuel were stockpiled, and new *volks* artillery corps and *Volkswerfer* brigades were assembled. Of the titanic German mobilization and production effort in the West, the lion's share went to the buildup for the counteroffensive. All forces and materiel set aside for the Ardennes were designated *OKW* Reserves, where not even *OB West* could use them without Hitler's authorization.

German Planning

Model's *Army Group B* now commanded two armies: *Gruppe von Manteuffel (Fifth Panzer)* and the *Seventh* under Brandenberger. The army group's northern boundary ran south of Roermond, thus corresponding roughly to that between the Americans and the British. The southern boundary remained unchanged, in effect a prolongation of the boundary between the US First and Third Armies. Within *Army Group B*, the boundary between Manteuffel and Brandenberger cut through the northern edge of the Hürtgen Forest. Thus the *Fifth Panzer Army* faced the US Ninth Army and part of VII Corps under Hodges. *Seventh Army* confronted the remainder of VII Corps, as well as V and VIII Corps, also under First Army.

Gruppe von Manteuffel possessed roughly 1,000 artillery pieces, and above average ammunition stockpiles. The *3rd Panzergrenadier*

Division, for example, was fully motorized and had an arsenal of 24 105mm and 13 150mm howitzers, seven 150mm rocket launchers, two 100mm cannons, 11 88mm antiaircraft guns, and 35 *Sturmgeschütze*. *LXXXI Corps* artillery consisted of an artillery regiment of two 240mm railway guns, nine French 220mm howitzers, two 240mm guns, 24 76.2mm fortress antitank guns, and several fully motorized Soviet 152mm and 122mm howitzers. Both it, and *XXII SS Corps* each possessed a motorized *volks* artillery corps (75mm and 210mm guns) and a *Volkswerfer* brigade (150mm, 210mm, and 280mm rocket projectors).[7] *Gruppe von Manteuffel* gained considerable ground forces after the November offensive began, especially *XLVII Panzer Corps* (*General* von Lüttwitz). Its *15th Panzergrenadier* and *9th Panzer Divisions* included a combined 66 tanks, five *Sturmgeschütze*, and 65 105mm and 150mm howitzers.[8]

On November 9, Hitler ordered *OB West* von Rundstedt to hold the line without any reinforcement from those units arrayed for the offensive in the Ardennes. Ground, however, could be relinquished if needed, but not in the Aachen sector under any circumstance. In particular, the Germans were to maintain "at all cost" bridgeheads west of the Roer at Jülich and Düren. Six days later, as planned, *General der Infanterie* Gustav von Zangen's *Fifteenth Army* took control of *XII SS, LXXXI*, and (*Army Group B* reserve) *XLVII Corps*. *Gruppe von Manteuffel*, in turn, was sent south to prepare for action in the Ardennes.

November 16

US

104th Infantry Division
Commander: Major General Terry de la Mesa Allen
Div HHC
Infantry: 413th, 414th, 415th Infantry Regiments
Field Artillery: HHB, 385th, 386th, 929th FA Battalions (105mm Howitzer), 387th FA Battalion (155mm Howitzer)
Other: HQ Special Troops, 104th Reconnaissance Troop (Mechanized), 104th Signal Company, 329th Engineer Combat Battalion, 104th Counter Intelligence Corps Detachment
Trains: 804th Ordnance Light Maintenance Company, 104th Quartermaster Company, Military Police Platoon, 329th Medical Battalion

Attached
555th AAA AW Battalion
750th Tank Battalion
692nd Tank Destroyer Battalion

4th Infantry Division
Commander: Major General Raymond O. Barton
Div HHC
Infantry: 8th, 12th, 22nd Infantry Regiments
Field Artillery: HHB, 29th, 42nd, 44th FA Battalions (105mm Howitzer), 20th FA Battalion (155mm Howitzer)
Other: HQ Special Troops, 4th Reconnaissance Troop (Mechanized), 4th Signal Company, 4th Engineer Combat Battalion, 4th Counter Intelligence Corps Detachment
Trains: 704th Ordnance Light Maintenance Company, 4th Quartermaster Company, Military Police Platoon, 4th Medical Battalion

Attached
377th ADA AW Battalion
70th Tank Battalion
24th Cavalry Reconnaissance Squadron
C Company, 87th Chemical Mortar Battalion
951st FA Battalion (155mm Howitzer)
196th FA Battalion (105mm Howitzer)
172nd FA Battalion (4.5-inch Gun)
981st FA Battalion (155mm Gun)
B Battery, 285th FA Observation Battalion
803rd TD Battalion (SP)

German

LXXXI Corps
275th Grenadier Division (Generalleutnant Hans Schmidt)

Attached
18th Fortress Battalion
20th Fortress Battalion

1031st Security Battalion
481st Arko (1310th Fortress Artillery, 63rd Observation Battalions)
432nd Corps Signals Battalion, 432nd Corps Supply, Field Police Troops
762nd Engineer Regiment Staff
506th, 301st Heavy Panzer Battalions
319th Panzer Company

Hastenrath, Gressenich, and Hamich

Having decided to continue with the scheduled offensive regardless of the weather, Hodges watched the skies on the morning of November 16 for any change in the ongoing string of rainy, cold days. By 1100 a ceiling of broken clouds hovered between 1,000m and 8,000m over the target area, and within a half hour had improved enough to allow the approaching British and US aircraft a reasonable chance of success. Many of the scheduled aircraft, however, were unable to take off due to lingering fog around their bases, especially at IX and XXIX Tactical Air Commands.

As the 1st Infantry Division moved into its jump-off positions, Allied aircraft dropped "Christmas Trees" (parachute flares) to mark targets for the tight carpets of heavy bombers that followed. As the planes approached they were aided by several devices on the ground, including large white panel markers near Liege, north of Aachen, and four kilometers behind friendly lines that illustrated First Army's left boundary. Orange panels were placed parallel some 500m behind friendly lines, and spaced about half a kilometer apart. Low-altitude barrage balloons from the 104th RAF Balloon Command, backed by the 413th AAA Gun Battalion, performed a similar function some 4,000m behind their front line.[9]

The Eighth Air Force also employed a system of radio beacons close to the front lines, and an SCS-51 fan marker transmitting a thin vertical signal over the row of balloons, in addition to prescribing that bomb bay doors would be opened and locked over the English Channel to prevent any damage should bombs be released accidentally in the process. While there was some slight apprehension that the enemy might attempt to fire a counter line of bursts to confuse the bombers, it was felt that the counter-flak artillery fire and the lucrative bomber targets presented to the Eighth Air Force would account for any remaining enemy AAA fire capabilities.

The new marking systems proved satisfactory, and pilots had no trouble in identifying the locations of friendly troops. Where at Normandy the bomb line had been some 1,200m from the Allied front, for Operation Queen the distance was to be increased nearly threefold. The new safety aids demonstrated that visual bombing by heavy and medium bombers was possible with a 2,000m safety zone without damage to friendly forces. From 1113 to 1248 the aerial attack repeatedly bombed its targets and obliterated towns such as Düren and Jülich.

Air Missions[10]

RAF Bomber Command: 1,119 heavy bombers dropped 5,437 tons on Düren, Jülich, and Heinsberg to pulverize the cities and block roads and intersections.

8th Air Force: 1,204 heavy bombers dropped 4,120 tons of fragmentation bombs on Eschweiler, Langerwehe, Weisweiler, Dürwiss, and Hehlrath.

1st (490 B-17s), 2nd (228 B-24s) Bombardment Divisions (Eschweiler) 3rd (486 B-17s) Bombardment Division (Düren)

VIII Fighter Command: 2 escort groups (98 P-51s) to strafe transportation targets

9th Air Force: 80 (of 119) B-26s from 9th Bombardment Division dropped 15 tons on 4 targets. A portion of eleven groups (approximately 600 planes) of Ninth Air Force medium bombers drew a similar mission of devastating the towns of Linnich and Aldenhoven in the Ninth Army zone.

IX TAC: 3 groups of about 221 planes were to support VII Corps by attacking the Hürtgen-Kleinhau sector, the southeastern end of the Hamich Ridge near Hamich, and a built up area around Hastenrath and Scherpenseel.

XXIX TAC: four groups of 137 fighters and fighter-bombers to support Ninth Army

German antiaircraft defenses had few successes, bringing down just four fighter-bombers and eight heavy bombers, and the four *Luftwaffe* aircraft that were in the area refrained from combat. Even with the largely inaccurate antiaircraft fire, the bombing was not as successful as expected. Clouds and smoke hampered visibility, and many planes had to rely on targeting by radar. Although there were virtually no friendly casualties, actual damage to German positions was limited and did not produce the same psychological effects as had happened in former large bombing operations.

Ground Offensive

As the heavy bombers finished their runs, US ground forces, having been held well back from the targeted areas, now had to move a considerable distance to make contact with the enemy lines before the Germans regained their senses. Operation Queen clearly demonstrated that the effectiveness of close air support was contingent upon the confidence of ground forces. Commanders needed to accept the necessary risk of short bombing in order to more quickly capitalize on the effects of an aerial bombardment.

At 1245, Ninth Army initiated its offensive between Geilenkirchen and Würselen to finally secure crossings over the Roer River. Simpson's command started out from the line it had secured the previous month, which was now completely east of the *Westwall* (only a single belt in this sector) and the Wurm River.

While providing lengthy fields of fire, the area's numerous villages had been turned into German strongpoints that could be supported by an extensive road network. With Simpson to cover the northern flank of the primary offensive launched by First Army, Major General Raymond S McLain's XIX Corps led the way. It would not at first contest the urbanized areas of Würselen, Stolberg, and the Inde River, which had confounded US efforts in October. Instead, the corps initially moved through the more rural area to the north before turning against the German strongholds.

A regiment of the newly arrived 84th Infantry Division bolstered 30th Infantry Division, which was to act as a reserve. All three regiments of the former were subsequently made available for action, to which McLain added three battalions of corps artillery as support. Each regiment advanced with two battalions abreast and one in reserve. Extensive mines, especially non-metallic antipersonnel *Schuh* and antitank *Topf* varieties, soon hampered progress. Once stopped, American ground forces were often pinned down by enemy artillery and

An 8th Armored Division 76mm M4A3 passes a forward command post at Linne en-route to clear the German pocket around Roermond as part of Operation Grenade on Feb 26, 1945. (Note that it has an M1A1 main gun, HVSS suspension, and an apparent armor plate field modification behind the turret hatches.) (US Signal Corps)

mortar fire, and were only able to extricate themselves after dark. So thick were antitank mines around Würselen that supporting Sherman tanks and tank destroyers were forced into a static support role.

By nightfall the 117th and 120th Infantry Regiments had made modest progress to capture Mariadorf and Euchen, respectively. Würselen, as expected, presented considerable resistance. To the north, only half of CCB/2 was committed. With no preliminary artillery bombardment, surprise was initially achieved, but mud and mines hampered movement. What vehicles that were damaged were quickly repaired and returned to the fight. By mid-afternoon the northernmost of CCB/2's three task forces had captured Immendorf. A second threatened Puffendorf, but German resistance from Apweiler presented a more difficult obstacle. Here the center task force confronted heavy antitank fire that knocked out 14 out of its 16 Shermans and forced the operation to halt for the night.[11] The 2nd Armored Division had advanced up to 2,500m into the enemy positions. Along its right, the 29th and 30th Infantry Divisions managed 3,000m, and 1,600m, respectively.

Köchling's *LXXXI Corps* occupied a central position that extended from just north of Jülich down to Düren. *246th Volksgrenadier Division*, though reinforced with elements of the defunct *49th Grenadier Division*, remained weak after its stint in Aachen. To its left, *3rd Panzergrenadier Division* occupied the corps' center, while *12th*

Volksgrenadier Division buttressed up against *275th Grenadier Division* in the Hürtgen Forest. What remained of *Mobile Regiment von Fritzschen* was reconstituted as the *404th Grenadier Regiment*. *Gruppe von Manteuffel* also made a *Kampfgruppe* from *116th Panzer Division* available to Köchling that consisted of a tank battalion, a *volksgrenadier* battalion, an artillery battery, and an engineer company.[12]

South of Aachen, VII Corps led the main push for First Army. On the far left, Major General Terry de la Mesa Allen, the friendly, relaxed commander of the 104th Infantry Division, moved on Eschweiler. CCB/3 was to capture several villages including Werth, Köttenich, and Hastenrath. Task Force 1 secured its objective by early afternoon after skirting minefields, while TF 2 advanced rapidly along the left. US artillery of all sizes provided support.

1st Infantry Division spearheaded the attack through Langerwehe and Jüngersdorf with its 16th Infantry Regiment moving on Hamich and Hill 232, while maintaining contact with the 26th and 47th Infantry Regiments on the right and left, respectively. Hill 232, as well as Hills 207 and 203, were used by the Germans to provide excellent observation of much of the surrounding terrain. The attached 47th Infantry Regiment, 9th Infantry Division would take Gressenich, while 26th Infantry Regiment would sweep the northern reaches of the forest and maintain contact with 4th Infantry Division along its right.

German artillery took a toll on A Company, 745th Tank Battalion, and mud hampered its progress. Like most of *Fifteenth Army's* artillery, positions were dug in and camouflaged so well that the effect of enemy air and counter-battery fire was greatly diminished. For once the Germans were capable of laying down really massive fires. As 28th Infantry Division proved unable to secure the area around Schmidt, the remainder of VII Corps would have to keep its right along the Kall River.

When the aerial bombing subsided, five battalions of US artillery totaling 60 guns fired a nearly simultaneous bombardment against Gressenich. This "Time on Target" technique was designed to inflict heavy casualties through concentrated surprise.[13] 47th Infantry Regiment (recently allocated to 1st Infantry Division) fought among Gressenich's houses for the remainder of the day.

47th Volksgrenadier Division was to replace *12th Volksgrenadier Division* as it was slated, like many other formations, to participate in the coming Ardennes Offensive. Köchling appeared to be reluctant to use the new division as long as the US effort was being made well north of the Hürtgen Forest, but events on the 16th changed these plans. Von Zangen responded to the enemy offensive by keeping *12th Volksgrenadier Division* in place, and using its intended replacement as a reserve for *LXXXI Corps*. When Köchling refrained from following up with a counterattack, Model stepped in to correct what he saw as a lack of decisive effort against the enemy's perceived main thrust north and east of Aachen. *47th Volksgrenadier Division* subsequently was moved to the Schevenhütte-Eschweiler sector.

Eliminating the Triangle

At 0420 on the 17th, the *9th Panzer Division* initiated a two-part counterattack to retake Immendorf. By 1000 about 45 Tiger IIs (*506th Heavy Panzer Battalions*) and Panthers (organic), combined with a battalion of infantry, ran into the 2nd Armored Division near Gereonsweiler.[14] Tanks, artillery, and antitank guns fought an attritional battle that steadily forced the Germans back.

As *3rd Panzergrenadier Division* pulled back from Euchen to Broichweiden just before dawn, the 120th Infantry Regiment maintained its advance and kept the Germans from establishing an effective defense. Nearly an entire *panzergrenadier* battalion was wiped out, and the Americans massed strong artillery assets to hold off a noon counterattack from seven tanks and assault guns. Along 30th Infantry Division's left, 117th Infantry Regiment kept pace. To the south German resistance around Würselen remained strong, due primarily to extensive minefields. By late afternoon, however, 119th Infantry Regiment's effort paid off and they captured the town. At 1010 CCB/3 secured Hastenrath, and three hours later Scherpenseel fell as well.

The commander of the *3rd Panzergrenadier Division* could have entertained no more hope of holding this line than he had of holding the two he had occupied earlier. As seen by the corps and army commanders, the focal point of danger was not here but farther north, in the sector of the *246th Volksgrenadier Division* and even farther north outside the zone of the *LXXXI Corps*. When General Köchling on November 18 had introduced the *47th Volksgrenadier Division* opposite the US VII Corps and directed a general shift of division boundaries northward, he had done it so that the *246th Volksgrenadier Division* might achieve greater concentration. The *3rd Panzergrenadier Division* thus became responsible for the entire sector opposite the US 30th Infantry Division and part of the 104th as well.

Because the 30th Infantry Division was nearing the extremity of the triangle it had been assigned to clear, General Hobbs could concentrate almost unrestricted fire support against one short segment of the new line—at the villages of St. Jöris and Kinzweiler. Virtually all the divisional artillery, two companies of the 743rd Tank Battalion, as many tank destroyers, and the heavy weapons of an adjacent regiment were available to support an attack by the 117th Infantry Regiment.

1st Battalion, 33rd Armored Regiment was counterattacked by infantry at 1745. A heavy artillery concentration was placed on the attacking force, and by 1900 hours the attack had completely died out. Clear skies allowed 352 fighter-bomber sorties from IX TAC.[15] Enemy activity consisted of constant pressure on CCB/3 including heavy artillery and mortar fire, though at 2125 Hamich finally fell.

Footnotes

[1] 12th A Gp G-1 Daily Summary, 11 Nov, 12th A Gp G-1 Daily Summaries file, Nov 44; FUSA G-1 Daily Summaries, 12 Sep and 11 Nov 44; FUSA Rpt, Annexes 1, 5, 6, and 7, Vol. 2; FUSA AAR, Nov 44; V Corps Opns in the ETO, p. 326.

[2] 83d Div G-2-G-3 Jnl, 18 Dec 44, and AAR.

[3] 21 A Gp Gen Opn1 Sit and Dir, M 534, 2 Nov 44.

[4] VII Corps FO 12, 8 Nov 44.

[5] Air Chief Marshal Sir Trafford LeighMallory, Air Commander in Chief: Allied Expeditionary Air Force, "Despatch, Air Operations by the Allied Expeditionary Air Force in N. W. Europe," Nov 44.

[6] 12th A Gp Weekly Intel Summary 14 for week ending 11 Nov, dtd 13 Nov, 12th A Cp G 2 AAR, Nov 44; subsequent 12th A Gp rpts until mid Dec.

[7] *LXXXI Corps Arty Sit as of 10 Nov 44, LXXXI Corps KTB, Art Lage u. Art. Gliederungen; LXXXI Corps KTB, Zustandsberichte; Kampf um Aachen: Maps;* MS # B 290, *Dos XIL SS Korps (7.bzw 15.Armee, HeeresgrupPe B) westlich und an der Roer VOM 20.X.r944 31. 1.1945* (General der Infanterie Guenther Blumentritt): MS # P-065b (Reinhardt); and MS # A 994 (Koechling).

[8] Strength Rpts, 1 Nov 44, *XLVII Pz Corps 0. Qu., KTB Anlagen, Einzelbefehle, 17.X. z8. XI 44.*

[9] Lieutenant Colonel C. G. Patterson, GSC. AAA IN Air-Ground Teamwork, p. 19. "Air Force Combat Units of World War II," Office of Air Force History, HQ USAF, 1961; Roger A. Freeman. *The Mighty Eighth War Diary.*

[10] Houston, *Hell on Wheels*, pp. 28–38.

[11] BA-MA RH 24-81/114, 121, and 123, KTB LXXXI Corps, 16 Nov 1944.

[12] 1st Div FO 53, 6 Nov, 1st Div G-3 Opns Rpt, Nov 44.

[13] "Ninth United States Army, 1–30 November 1944." General Corlett Foundation. Ibid.

Chapter 9

Operation Clipper
(November 18–23)

As the Allies' November offensive north of Aachen advanced east and north from their Wurm River positions, the town of Geilenkirchen remained a fortified, unwavering German position. Deep in Ninth Army's left flank, its existence as an enemy stronghold threatened American rear echelon forces and constricted the frontage for follow-on formations as they entered the combat zone. With the salient conforming generally to the Wurm and Maas Rivers southwest of Roermond, and strengthened by the numerous pillboxes and fortifications of the *Westwall*, it physically separated the British XXX and US XIX Corps as they respectively focused on taking Geilenkirchen and crossing the Roer. Simpson, as Ninth Army commander, had favored an encirclement of the town. As this would have meant a coordinated operation between different nations, a compromise was reached in which XIII Corps' 84th Infantry Division was temporary attached to XXX Corps.

Originally slated for the day after the main offensive to the south, the attack was postponed until November 18 to allow German units in its sector more time to be moved to seemingly more threatened sectors. This expected shift did not occur, and in fact German forces around Geilenkirchen increased their strength as *Army Group B's* reserve, *15th Panzergrenadier Division,* was repositioned to confront XIX Corps.[1]

Allied Planning
Since the launching of the two-pronged British Operation Nutcracker/Mallard on November 14, German forces had been drawn from the area where Operation Clipper, as the assault on Geilenkirchen was codenamed, would soon commence. Foreseen as an alternate thrust of converging attacks, it was intended to force the numerically weaker Germans to move to meet new threats and so weaken their ability to effectively resist.

155

THE ROER RIVER BATTLES

Having assumed control of the 27km stretch from the Maas River to Geilenkirchen, Horrocks' XXX Corps had positioned 43rd (Wessex) Infantry Division northwest of Geilenkirchen. During a meeting on November 12, Major General Sir Ivor G. Thomas, the division's commander, had conducted an "O" Group (Orders Group) meeting to discuss the four phases of the upcoming operation. The US 84th Infantry Division, with tank support from the Sherwood Rangers Yeomanry, was to initiate the attack by passing through the narrow, temporary frontage held by 405th Infantry Regiment (on loan from 102nd Infantry Division). With 335th Infantry Regiment having been sent to the Würselen sector, 333rd Infantry Regiment would advance along Geilenkirchen's eastern edge, through the *Westwall* defenses, to the north of Prummern.

Following 204th Field Company's removal of some 1,400 mines that 84th Infantry Regiment had recently laid, 334th Infantry Regiment (Colonel John S. Roosma) was to make straight for Prummern and the surrounding high ground.[2] The British 43rd (Wessex) Infantry Division would follow-up with a strike to the high ground northwest of Geilenkirchen, and once it was encircled 84th Infantry Division would move into the town itself. Finally, the 43rd (Wessex) would clear the Wurm's west bank to the *Westwall* as far north as Hoven.

Thomas planned to use the entire 214th Brigade from near Nijmegen plus one battalion from 130th Brigade, namely the 5th Battalion Dorset Regiment, under command of 214th Infantry Brigade. Meanwhile, 129th Brigade was given the job of holding the start-line, which included the village of Gillrath, and the remaining two battalions of 130th Brigade were held in reserve. 214th Infantry Brigade was given the job of cutting off all exits from Geilenkirchen.

Because of its delayed start, XXX Corps could not be allocated the same level of aerial support as was available two days before. For 10 days prior to the start of its offensive napalm had been dropped around Geilenkirchen. On the 18th, the Second British Tactical Air Force and two groups from Ninth Army's XXIX TAC were to hit Linnich and Heinsberg. XXX Corps' artillery, as well as that of two battalions from XIII Corps, would also support the 84th Infantry Division.

In conjunction with the attack on Geilenkirchen, 2nd Armored Division would attempt to capture Gereonsweiler to broaden the Ninth Army's frontage up to 10km. The division's early success had been tempered by arrival of the *9th Panzer Division*, but if the "Hell on

156

Wheels" could make further headway, 102nd Infantry Division would then follow up by closing the last four kilometers to force a crossing of the Roer River at Linnich. The 113th Cavalry Group, with additional tanks and artillery, was to cover the corps' north flank, while 84th Infantry Division and the refurbished 7th Armored Division were to join the 102nd Division in the Roer bridgehead at Linnich.

German Planning

With so many of the German reserves in the West unavailable due to future commitment in the Ardennes, *OB West* continued to have difficulty plugging the seemingly unending Allied penetrations along the line. Having to reposition formations already at the front to reinforce threatened sectors was an unsustainable solution, but until mid-December little else could be done. Since the British effort in Market Garden had ceased, von Rundstedt moved *10th SS Panzer Division* from the Arnhem sector to *Army Group H's* far left where it would be better able to contest future Allied offensives north of Aachen. Additional formations followed, including a Volksgrenadier and two infantry divisions.

XII SS Corps commander, *General der Infanterie* Günther Blumentritt (sitting in for the sick *SS-Obergruppenführer* Curt von Gottberg), believed an Allied offensive targeting Jülich and Düren would begin in early November. With each day this did not occur, *XII SS Corps* worked hard to establish defensive positions, but only completed a single line in the time allotted before Operation Queen commenced. Without a defense-in-depth, mobile reserves, or protective minefields, these positions were unlikely to offer much of a deterrent.

176th Grenadier Division (essentially a replacement and training division) was positioned north of the town under its popular commander, *Generalmajor* Christian-Johannes Landau. *183rd Volksgrenadier Division* was placed to the southeast, where it was hoped its lack of adequate training and morale could be overcome by the skilled organizer and motivator, *Generalmajor* Wolfgang Lange. In support, Blumentritt placed most of *XII SS Corps'* artillery nearby. Along with its interim commander, two-thirds of the staff and its subordinate *176th Grenadier* and *183rd Volksgrenadier Divisions* were affiliated with the *Waffen-SS*.[3]

With very few terrain features in the Geilenkirchen sector, the Germans made prodigious efforts to control any high ground, bridge, or road hub, and the low-lying area between Rurich and Wassenberg was often flooded to create an effective tank obstacle. The Wurm Bach Creek, flowing north from Geilenkirchen, physically bisected *XII SS Corps*, although several small bridges allowed for lateral movement when they were not destroyed by Allied air attacks. Although it was not wide, the creek's marshy banks and plentiful trees made observation difficult. Blumentritt considered Landau's western position, with its extended frontage, in danger of being cut off should the British break through Heinsberg. The strongest German positions were on either side of Geilenkirchen, where a small mobile reserve was retained for emergencies.

November 18

British

214th Infantry Brigade (43rd (Wessex) Infantry Division)
Commander: Brigadier General Hubert Essame
Brigade HQ
B Squadron 4/7 Royal Dragoon Guards, 1st Worcestershire Battalion
C Squadron 4/7 Royal Dragoon Guards, 5th Duke of Cornwall Light Infantry Battalion
A Squadron 4/7 Royal Dragoon Guards, 7th Somerset Light Infantry Battalion
4th/7th Royal Dragoon Guards HQ

Support
Squadron 13th/18th Hussars, 5th Dorset Battalion (detached from 130 Brigade)
2 Royal Artillery 25pdr Batteries

129th Infantry Brigade

US

84th Infantry Division
Commander: Major General Alexander R. Bolling
Div HQ & HQ Company

Infantry: 333rd (with Sherwood Rangers (British)); 334th (with Drew-force, two troops of M4A4 Sherman Crabs (flail) and Churchill VII Crocodiles (flamethrower) (British) and one troop of 357th Searchlight Battery, Royal Artillery (British)); 405th Infantry Regiment (from 102nd Infantry Division)
Field Artillery: HQ & HQ Battery, 325th, 326th, 909th FA Battalions (105mm Howitzer), 327th FA Battalion (155mm Howitzer)
Special: HQ Special Troops, 84th Reconnaissance Troop (Mechanized), 84th Quartermaster Company, 84th Signal Company, 784th Ordnance Light Maintenance Company, Military Police Platoon
Other: 309th Engineer Combat Battalion, 309th Medical Battalion, 84th Counter Intelligence Corps Detachment

Elements of 79th Armored Division

German

176th Grenadier Division
Commander: Generalmajor Christian-Johannes Landau
Div HQ
Infantry: 1218th, 1219th, 1220th Grenadier Regiments
Field Artillery: HQ, 1176th Artillery Regiment (105mm, 155mm Howitzers)
HHC, 1176th Antitank Battalion, 176th Füsilier Battalion, 1176th Engineer Battalion, 1176th Signal Battalion, 1176th Feldersatz (Replacement Training) Battalion, 1176th Services

104th Panzergrenadier Regiment, 15th Panzergrenadier Division)
10th Panzergrenadier Regiment, 9th Panzer Division)

388th, 407th Volks Artillery Corps

Phase I: Prummern
At 0445 on November 18, British artillery initiated their fire plans in coordination with the forthcoming participation of ground forces. Still clear and frosty at 0600, 357th Searchlight Battery's four searchlights provided hazy "artificial moonlight" as the beams were directed skyward to reflect

off the heavy cloud cover between Geilenkirchen and Immendorf. Two troops of Drewforce's flail tanks (Sherman Crabs possessing rotating chains and wire cutters to clear paths through minefields and wire entanglements, respectively) lumbered into "no-man's land" to clear paths using their heavy, rotating chains. As the muddy terrain might impede the vehicles' effectiveness, engineers remained close behind with metal detectors should any undetonated explosives remain.

Having arrived at Omaha Beach (Normandy) on November 1, 84th Infantry Division was rushed to the front. Although lacking combat experience, its men were eager to prove themselves. An hour later, after a sharp, five-minute artillery preparation, two battalions of 334th Infantry Regiment began moving through the two gaps in their sector's minefield near Breil. Because of the limited number of Sherman Crabs, 84th Infantry Division's commander, Brigadier General Alexander R. Bolling, was forced to initiate a column advance to retain a small frontage. Traditional British armor could not readily follow due to the muddy terrain. 2nd Battalion continued its linear march behind 79th Armored Division's "funnies" and broke into groups to present small targets and improve movement.

German resistance was minimal owing to the limited daylight visibility, and by mid-morning 2nd Battalion had gained the high ground east of Geilenkirchen and cut the road to Immendorf. On the right, ten pillboxes along the railroad temporarily halted 1st Battalion, but its commander, Lieutenant Colonel Lloyd H. Gomes, moved among his platoon leaders and motivated them to not seek shelter along the embankment but to advance. The 1st Battalion men soon renewed their attack, firing as they went, and soon overran the German trenches, followed by the fortifications.

Still concerned about *9th Panzer Division* making a counterattack from Geilenkirchen, Roosma delayed 334th Infantry Regiment's final push to Prummern until he could send his reserve battalion to hold the high ground along the right. Though this did not develop, he remained concerned as XXX Corps artillery observers had seen a 4,500-man column from *15th Panzergrenadier Division* apparently making for Geilenkirchen.[4] The XIII Corps commander, Gillem, alerted two regiments from 102nd Infantry Division that they might be needed to resist a German counterattack.

334th Infantry Regiment resumed its attack through the *Westwall* fortifications and open terrain toward Prummern with its 1st and 2nd

German box mines in the 7th Armored Division's sector near Schmidt on Feb. 11, 1945. (US Signal Corps)

Battalions moving against Hill 101 and the village, respectively. *183rd Volksgrenadier Division* and *10th Panzergrenadier Regiment* stood in the way, but with help from what Sherwood Rangers Yeomanry Fireflies (M-4 Shermans up-gunned to 17pdr main armaments) could be brought forward, the regiment took both objectives and a considerable number of prisoners by the end of the day. Disorganized, cold, and hungry, they were ordered to continue their momentum.

1st Battalion pushed a company northwest of Hill 101 to gain high ground overlooking Süggerath, while 2nd Battalion moved northeast of Prummern toward "Mahogany Hill" (Hill 92.5) near Beeck. 334th Infantry Regiment managed to push just north of their possessions, which was now nearly on line with Task Force X, 2nd Armored Division following their recent capture of Apweiler. With these successes, Horrocks ordered 84th Infantry Division to combine the third and fourth phases of the operation.

Blumentritt instituted a quick reorganization of his command to reflect the changing battle situation. *9th Panzer Division* was sent east of the Wurm Bach, and *15th Panzergrenadier Division* would take its place in the west, where it brought the remaining combat elements from *183rd Volksgrenadier Division* under its control. When the area around Heinsberg was threatened, every effort was made to contain the situation. Unbeknownst to Blumentritt, Maastricht was to be a secondary thrust, as part of the upcoming Ardennes Offensive, and the salient west of the Wurm Bach needed to be retained.

Table of Organization & Equipment for late 1944[5]

British Rifle Brigade (2,632)—3 battalions, HQ
Infantry Battalion (845)—HQ, 4 rifle companies (A-D), 1 support company + possible divisional assets (25pdr battery (8 25pdrs), ATG troop (4 17pdrs), AA troop (8 40mm), MG platoon (4 Vickers MGs), engineer platoon, scout troop)
Rifle company (127)—HQ, 3 rifle platoons
Support company (192)—HQ, mortar platoon, carrier platoon, AT platoon, pioneer platoon
Rifle Platoon (37)—HQ, 3 rifle sections
Rifle Section (10)—(6 .303 Lee Enfields (rifle group), 1 Bren (LMG Group))

Phase II: Bauchem, Süggerath, and Tripsrath

After deploying at their forming-up point for a hot meal, B and D Companies of the 7th Somerset Light Infantry moved out at 1230 on the 18th to cross the open terrain before Niederheide. A half hour later the Worcestershires, also from 214th Infantry Brigade, formed up to advance on Tripsrath and Rischden.

At 1400 the 1st Battalion commander, Lieutenant Colonel Robert E. Osborne-Smith, ordered B and C Companies to lead the formation toward the woods near Rischden. With only sporadic resistance from *183rd Volksgrenadier Division*, and due to the fact that many of the enemy's teller mines had been uncovered by the rainy weather and thus were easily avoided, progress was quick. Some casualties resulted from *Schuh* mines, but the engineers attached to C Company were able to mark paths for the follow-up tanks of 4/7 Royal Dragoon Guards. These were to support A and D Companies as they provided support.

With all going well, two *Sturmgeschütze* suddenly appeared in the distance to obliterate the brigade's carrier platoon. A follow-up German infantry/armor/artillery counterattack spread confusion among 214th Infantry Brigade, especially the 5th Duke of Cornwall Light Infantry Battalion under Lieutenant Colonel George Taylor, as they tried to get out of the nearby woods and its treetop explosions. After being absent during the initial fighting, 4/7 Royal Dragoon Guards' tanks arrived late in the afternoon to disperse the attacking enemy.

After weathering German artillery (including the corps-allocated *388th* and *407th Volks Artillery Corps*, each of five to six battalions of three batteries of mixed calibers) for much of the afternoon, A and D Companies were called forward for an infantry attack on Tripsrath, which was some 1,000m distant.[6] Many of the German infantry groups were appearing to rely increasingly on artillery to subdue the enemy. Although there was a plentiful (by contemporary standards) two-day supply of ammunition for the guns, the infantry would soon have to pull its own weight lest these stocks be unduly depleted.[7]

At 1715, British 5.5-inch guns bombarded German positions at Bauchem. Although some erroneously fell on D Company and caused casualties, what fell on the town was heavy, amounting to some 1.8 tons per 100m square.[8] By day's end the British controlled Bauchem, and waited for the familiar counterattack. Now that the town was nearly surrounded, the German defense of Geilenkirchen was essentially compromised.

While the previous day had been miserable and wet, November 19 saw a continual downpour that severely impaired movement, especially that of armor. All British reinforcements and supplies had to be moved to the front using M-3/M-5 Honeys or Weasels. Only Shermans with extended track connectors could operate, and five of these managed to move up to Tripsrath. Three were destroyed by *Sturmgeschütze*, and a fourth succumbed to a *Panzerfaust*, as the *104th Panzergrenadier Regiment* contested the British advance.

At 1100 a second German counterattack was launched from the woods 5th Dorset Battalion had been trying to secure just west of Tripsrath. A company of infantry was supported by two Tiger IIs (*506 Heavy Panzer Battalion*) and two *Sturmgeschütze*, against which the nearby C Company had not been able to move up antitank guns because of the extremely muddy terrain.[9] As the Germans found movement equally difficult, the British were able to use antitank guns and some Shermans from the rear to counter this new threat.

Phase III: Geilenkirchen Virtually Encircled

84th Infantry Division's objective for November 19 was to capture Geilenkirchen and Süggerath, as well as Müllendorf, Würm, and Beeck. With possession of Hill 101, 334th Infantry Regiment had an excellent observation point from which to observe the area over which it would be attacking. As the 2nd Armored Division remained largely inactive, in anticipation of a counterattack from *9th Panzer Division*, and because a MSR through Setterich had not been opened, Bolling provided the 405th Infantry Regiment, even though it was to be used "only in case of emergency."[10] When the expected counterattack never materialized, because *15th Panzergrenadier Division* had been delegated to just support *9th Panzer Division*, the offensive continued to its inevitable conclusion.

With 334th Infantry Regiment having achieved such success the day before, the 333rd attacked at Geilenkirchen at 0700 with high hopes. As it advanced up the valley, B Company rushed the defenders and took the town within a few hours. The 333rd continued toward Süggerath, Müllendorf, and Würm, all within the *Westwall*. For all its success, 84th Infantry Division's offensive suffered from a lack of artillery support. According to Woodyard, "After the artillery preparation for the jump off we received no artillery support because it was considered that our own troops, on the flanks, were too close..."[11] Though two attached troops of tanks from the British Sherwood Rangers Yeomanry provided close support, they could not make up entirely for lack of artillery. 84th Infantry Division's actions had nevertheless resulted in a "perfect operation."[12]

While the 2nd Battalion mopped up in Geilenkirchen, Woodyard's battalion continued northeast on either bank of the Würm toward Süggerath. Crocodiles (A22 Mark VII Churchills that had been modified to shoot flame, in addition to their 75mm main guns) utilized their flamethrower capability to secure two pillboxes guarding the road into Süggerath. The tanks could shoot 80 one-second bursts between 80 and 120 meters, and although these were very helpful in convincing some enemy soldiers to surrender, German resistance in the area was stiffening.[13] It was nearly noon before Roosma's reserve battalion could be sent against "Mahogany Hill" and its three pillboxes. Combined with two more pillboxes northeast of Prummern, field fortifications to the east of the village halted the assault. The hill was generally ignored as combat focused on Prummern, but two days later it fell to a surprise assault.

Within Süggerath, German strongholds held out against Woodyard's

A crew from B Battery, 135th AAA Battalion is tracking a friendly aircraft using an M7 director (auxiliary predictor) near Geilenkirchen on Feb 16, 1944. During combat this electromechanical analog computer determined firing solutions that were passed to the battery's four 90mm guns. (US Signal Corps)

assault, which was becoming disorganized by the heavy fighting. He continued to push for the high ground northeast of the town. Regimental commander Colonel Timothy A. Pedley, Jr. managed to get a second battalion into the fight, and the pair was able to secure Süggerath during the night. The 333rd Infantry Regiment's final goal of Würm was captured the next day with help from the flame-throwing Crocodiles.

On November 20, with the Geilenkirchen salient nearly eliminated, the 333rd Infantry could better coordinate with the British to the northwest. Once the 334th Infantry Regiment cleared the last enemy strongholds at Prummern, both regiments would be free to renew the attack against Müllendorf, Würm, and Beeck.

With the American offensive fading, the Germans were able to regroup as well. *10th SS Panzer Division* arrived in individual battalions, and Blumentritt organized it and the other two armor-heavy divisions under the control of the adjacent *XLVII Corps* commander,

General der Panzertruppe Heinrich Freiherr von Luttwitz, so that the trio could be used as a unified force.

Phase IV: Hoven, Müllendorf, Würm and Beeck

On the fourth day of the offensive around Geilenkirchen, heavy rains and wind remained the norm. Mines along the road from Süggerath to Müllendorf and Würm added to British troubles as the tanks supporting 333rd Infantry Regiment attempted to use an alternate road along the rail line, but debris at a demolished underpass in Süggerath blocked movement in that direction. Pedley's regiment also ran into a cluster of pillboxes that issued devastating grazing fire.

After working through the night, engineers finally cleared the underpass with explosives and bulldozers around mid-afternoon on the 22nd. The tanks that had been held up from supporting 84th Infantry Division's continuing attack were finally able to get into the fight. A rolling artillery barrage from the 84th Infantry Division and XXX Corps was also added to help protect the infantry and armor that was forced to cross open, water-soaked terrain. With so many vehicles embedded in the mud, Shermans were often called in to pull them out, while trying not to get stuck themselves in the process.

As the attacking units approached to within 500m of Müllendorf, the regular and flame- throwing tanks soon convinced the defenders of three pillboxes that blocked their way to surrender. However, the heavy fuel wagons that the Crocodiles towed were likewise getting stuck, and their commander refused to continue. When the unsupported infantry tried to go it alone they ran into heavy machine-gun fire that hampered movement once again.

This increased German resistance continued beyond the Müllendorf sector, and the 43rd (Wessex) Infantry Division was halted short of gaining its final objectives beyond the Wurm River. Intelligence seemed to be correct in its belief that the *15th Panzergrenadier Division* was increasing its presence in the area, in particular with its *104th Panzergrenadier Regiment.* Having first employed the *panzergrenadiers* in counterattacks against XIX Corps, the Germans had then committed most of the division to fixed defenses in front of the 84th.

Concern about the 84th Infantry Division's southeastern flank was not alleviated by this identification, so Bolling got permission to reinforce his attack with the 405th Infantry Regiment. On November 22, he sent two battalions to flank Beeck by seizing high ground on the east and north of the town, while the remaining battalion struck frontally. Two battalions of 84th Infantry Division provided fire support, but exposed ground and mud continued to confound their efforts, especially among the hills between Prummern and Beeck.

As of November 23, 84th Infantry Division and its attachments reverted to XIII Corps' control, but it was still unable to take Müllendorf and Beeck. Gillem directed the division to assume a defensive stance, and for the next five days it remained fixed as the 113th Cavalry Group gradually took over the duty of staying in contact with the British. With 84th Infantry Division worn down from recent combat, and 102nd Infantry Division's regiments temporarily dispersed, XIII Corps' final push to the river would have to wait a bit longer.

Against tactical common sense, the Germans in the shrinking battle zone west of the Roer River were forced to continue fighting as per Hitler's "hold all ground" orders. With much of the ground to his immediate rear soft and partially flooded, Blumentritt worried that if his forces were not crossed to the east bank they would soon be trapped and destroyed.

Footnotes

[1.] OB WEST KTB, 18 Nov 44.

[2.] Louis M. Scully. *The Battle for Tripsrath: 1st Battalion Worcestershire Regiment.* 2009, p.8

[3.] MS# B-290. "The XII SS Corps West of, and on the Roer" (20 October 44–31 Jan 45). 1947.

[4.] CG XIII Corps, 1030, 18 Nov, XIII Corps G-3 Jnl file, 17–20 Nov 44.

[5.] "War Establishment for an Infantry Battalion," ref II/233/3, notified in Army Council Instructions 29th November 1944, effective date 12th November 1944.

[6.] MS# B-290. "The XII SS Corps West of, and on the Roer" (20 October 44–31 Jan 45). 1947.

[7.] Ibid.

[8.] Major General Jonathan B.A. Bailey. *Field Artillery and Firepower.* Naval Institute Press. Annapolis Maryland. 2004, p. 320.

[9.] Louis M. Scully. *The Battle for Tripsrath: 1st Battalion Worcestershire Regiment.* 2009.

[10.] Msg, 84th Div to XIII Corps, 0850, 19 Nov, XIII Corps G-3 file, 17–20 Nov 44. NUSA Opns, IV, 106.

[11.] Wes Gallagher. Associated Press.

[12.] Peter Chamberlain and Chris Ellis. *British and American Tanks of World War Two.* Cassel & Co. London, 1969.

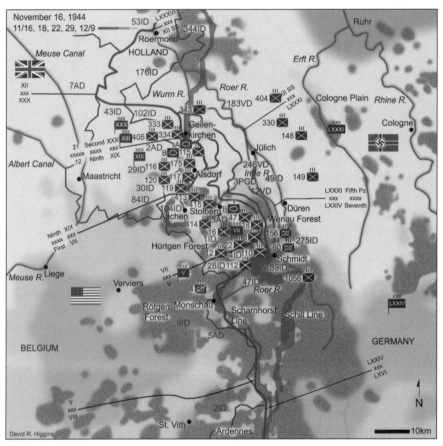

The US First and Ninth Army's push to the Roer River as part of Operation Queen (November 16–December 9, 1944).

Chapter 10

Ninth Army (Queen)
(November 19–26)

With the 2nd Armored Division's front running between Apweiler and Puffendorf, it was slightly ahead of 29th Infantry Division on its right. Until this flank was brought up on par, Harmon sent CCA/2 due east to capture Ederen and Freialdenhoven as a precursor to the main drive on Gereonsweiler. Task Force A from Puffendorf was to negotiate a gap in an extensive tank ditch between Gereonsweiler and Freialdenhoven. At three meters in width, and almost as deep, the obstacle was incorporated into the defenses of the surrounding entrenchment that included deep minefields and dense concertina wire. A second task force would push through Setterich in an effort to bypass a second tank trench. Even after avoiding or penetrating these obstacles, over 200 antitank fortresses had been established to the west of the Roer, many with cupolas and concrete-protected 88mm guns.[1]

As CCA/2 prepared to advance on November 19, Task Force X, CCB/2 was hit by a battalion-sized armor/infantry *Kampfgruppe* from the *15th Panzergrenadier Division* near Apweiler. I Company, 67th Armored Regiment, rose to the occasion and helped blunt the German force. A second German counterattack against CCA/2's Task Force A that advanced during the afternoon was similarly stopped. Task Force A, CCB/2 moved up from Puffendorf, apparently undetected, and struck the enemy in the flank. With German efforts against 2nd Armored Division yielding negligible results, their limited numbers would likely have been put to better use remaining on the defensive. CCA/2's Task Force A, however, only achieved limited gains during the day as German observers at Ederen were able to call in accurate artillery fire. That night American engineers and bulldozers were brought up to create new paths over the ditch.

To the south, CCA/2's Task Force B (mostly a battalion of the 66th Armored Regiment and another from 119th Infantry Regiment) attacked at 1245 from the bridgehead across the antitank ditch northeast of Setterich. Against sporadic resistance the task force quickly secured the Geilenkirchen-Aldenhoven road just shy of Freialdenhoven. An extensive enemy minefield blocked further progress, and that night engineers were brought up to clear paths.

Gereonsweiler Falls

On November 20, the 2nd Armored Division's CCB/2 set off for Harmon's primary objective of Gereonsweiler. Persistent, heavy rain brought into question whether to postpone the drive, but Harmon would not relent, believing that it would justify the heavy fighting of the last few days. With the town in American hands, 2nd Armored would likely forfeit its gains to XIII Corps, and be repositioned behind 29th Infantry Division to exploit any bridgehead over the Roer.

Task Force B, CC/2 brought up four Crocodiles to lead the infantry through the minefield, and even though the vehicles were eventually disabled, the Americans managed to take Freialdenhoven by late afternoon. At 1100, three task forces from CCB/2 advanced toward Gereonsweiler. TF 1 advanced from Puffendorf to take the high ground along the road to the town before turning due east. TF 2 moved up the center, and Task Force X attacked from Apweiler to capture the northern half of Gereonsweiler.

Ten minutes before the jump-off, six artillery battalions fired five rounds per gun into the western fringe of the village, followed by a 15-minute bombardment from corps-controlled guns around the target. Finally, the six divisional pieces began a rolling barrage over the village.

With the village isolated, TF 1 took the high ground along the Puffendorf-Gereonsweiler road. When TF 2 encountered machine gun and long-range tank fire, Brigadier General Isaac D. White directed Task Force 1 to deviate from its objective and move on Gereonsweiler. Having relieved the pressure on Task Force 2, both groups penetrated the village within the hour. British Crocodiles used their flamethrowers to pave the way for TF X's assault into Gereonsweiler.

To the southeast, CCA/2's pair of task forces managed to reach Ederen just after sunset on the 21st. With the Roer now just 2km distant, 2nd Armored Division would remain in place for several days until XIII Corps arrived. The next day, the 771st Tank Battalion (minus A Company) was placed under 2nd Armored Division, where it was to support 406th Infantry Regiment in the coming assault on Gereonsweiler.

A pair of US M-4 medium tanks from 2nd Armored Div firing at German positions in Biekesdorf on Feb 19, 1945. Given their inaccuracy, the T-34 (Calliope) 60x107mm (4.5-inch) rockets were used against area targets. (note the soldiers taking cover at the front of each vehicle) (US Signal Corps)

On to Aldenhoven

With the 29th Infantry Division having taken Siersdorf and Battendorf the day before, both it and the 2nd Armored continued eastward against the *246th Volksgrenadier Division*. As the US 415th Infantry Regiment approached Dürboslar the Germans launched a counterattack with twelve assault guns.[2] Like the others, it failed to effectively halt the enemy's advance, this time due to a combination of US bazooka teams and aerial support from XXIX TAC.

At Schleiden, the 3rd Battalion (Lieutenant Colonel William O. Blanford), of the 175th Infantry Regiment (Colonel William C. Purnell) advanced under the covering fire of every regimental machine gun and 81mm mortar. A forward observer with the initial infantry companies coordinated artillery fire on the target until they got to within 300m of the village. In support, a platoon of M-4 Shermans from 747th Tank Battalion remained on a parallel course 350m to the north, where they suppressed the German defensive positions with a steady rate of fire.

Early on November 20 a battalion of 175th Infantry Regiment took Niedermerz, and followed it up with a two-pronged attack against Aldenhoven. Another German counterattack comprising some hundred infantrymen and up to nine tanks was also stopped. When Purnell took this major road hub the next night, the second (intermediate) defensive arc protecting Jülich was breached, and the fall of the city seemed imminent. 29th Infantry Division was now less than four kilometers from the Roer River.

Though von Zangen, the *Fifteenth Army* commander, frequently exhorted the *LXXXI Corps* to eliminate 29th Infantry Division's penetrations, Köchling had only inadequate resources with which to work. He attempted to reinforce the *246th Volksgrenadier Division* by committing a battalion from *3rd Panzergrenadier* and another from the *12th Volksgrenadier Division*. At Niedermerz, US intelligence confirmed that elements of the *116th Panzer Reconnaissance Battalion* were arriving, and that the remainder of the division could be expected to follow. In reality, this was part of *Panzer Group Bayer,* which Köchling took from the *47th Volksgrenadier Division*.

The 30th Infantry Division had made considerable progress over the last few days, and it was not until November 19 that the divisions on its flanks were able to come abreast. Impressed by its achievements, the XIX Corps commander gave the division a new assignment. Redrawing his division boundaries, McLain directed Hobbs to renew his attack on the Roer two days later, now along a front narrowing to 2km. As Gerhardt continued his advance on the 21st, intelligence was beginning to believe that the Germans were preparing to pull behind the Roer, now a mere 2km to the east. Gerhardt responded by ordering his regiments to throw out patrols to the river.

Linnich to Jülich

With the Roer River in sight, XIII Corps took up a position between the British XXX and US XIX Corps on November 24. The 84th Infantry Division remained around Geilenkirchen and Prummern, while the 102nd moved up along its right. 7th Armored Division was still recuperating in corps reserve from its earlier fight in the Peel Marshes. Prior to the commitment of his corps to 12th Army Group, Gillem had planned

Aerial view near Linnich on Feb 13, 1945 showing the flooded Roer River Valley.
(US Signal Corps)

on using the 113th Cavalry Group as part of a task force under Colonel William S. Biddle, which would precede the 2nd Armored Division into Gereonsweiler, and later serve as its primary reconnaissance element. Thereupon, 102nd Infantry Division was to have captured Linnich on the Roer and to have prepared to cross the river. The 7th Armored and 84th Infantry Divisions were to have been available to exploit a bridgehead.

By nightfall, Gillem had assumed responsibility for about 10km of front, from the Wurm River at Müllendorf to the new boundary with the XIX Corps below Ederen. Nevertheless, the hard fighting experienced by the 84th Infantry Division in Operation Clipper and the disorganized state of the 102nd Infantry Division made it impossible for the XIII Corps to be ready to attack until November 29. Major General Frank A. Keating, commander of the 102nd thought more time was needed as two of his infantry regiments had just completed heavy combat.

Once the degree of German resistance was found to be weak,

Gillem dissolved TF Biddle on the 21st, and attached the 113th Cavalry Group to 84th Infantry Division, which was to become XIII Corps' main effort. 102nd Infantry Division was to simply push to the northeast to secure Linnich, and occupy the high ground overlooking German supply routes around Brachelen astride the Teich Creek. US intelligence believed that following the Allied failure to take Arnhem in September, additional formations might be arriving in the area, especially the remnants of the *9th Panzer, 15th Panzer Grenadier,* and *183rd Volksgrenadier Divisions.*

After the recent unsuccessful counterattacks from the *9th Panzer* and *15th Panzergrenadier Divisions,* both were transferred from *XLVII Panzer Corps* to *XII SS Corps.* Blumentritt once again assumed control from the Maas to the Roer Rivers near Flossdorf. The front was strengthened by the *407th Volks Artillery Corps* near Linnich, and a *Volksgrenadier* division, enroute to the Ardennes, was diverted to the Roer's east bank from which it could reinforce *XII SS Corps.*

Abandoning the hope of enemy withdrawal, the XIX Corps on November 23 adopted a cautious, almost leisurely pattern of operations. Despite close support from a company of tanks, a battalion of the 41st Armored Infantry Regiment was only able to take half of Merzenhausen along the Merz Creek. With that, Harmon decided that a consolidation was needed, and 2nd Armored Division spent the next few days reorganizing for the coming push over the Roer River.

German

340th Volksgrenadier Division
Commander: Generalleutnant Theodor Tolsdorff
Div HQ
Infantry: 694th, 695th, 696th Volksgrenadier Regiments
Field Artillery: HQ, 340th Artillery Regiment (75mm, 105mm, 155mm Howitzers)
Antitank Battalion (75mm AA and AT), Engineer Battalion, Signals Battalion, Feldersatz (Replacement Training) Battalion, Füsilier Company, Support Regiment

Securing the Inde River
Unlike the 2nd Armored and 30th Infantry Divisions, the 29th Infantry

Medics of the 102nd Infantry Division cross the Roer at Linnich on Feb 23, 1945. Members of 279th Eng Combat Btn, 407th Infantry Regiment are in the center. (US Signal Corps)

would continue to push ahead. Against *340th Volksgrenadier Division* it fought a slogging battle across the cold, muddy ground near Bourheim. One of two attacking battalions of 175th Infantry Regiment finally entered the village late on November 23. Just after midnight, the Germans initiated a heavy, 15-minute artillery barrage, supplemented by mortars. This was soon followed by a counterattack that, although failing to dislodge the Americans, formed a pattern that was to continue for three more days. 29th Infantry Division replied in kind. Even with the general shortage of ammunition, especially for larger guns, US artillery disrupted German concentrations along the Roer's west bank. These artillery battles had been common over the last week, with German estimates for *LXXXI Corps'* sector amounting to an average daily ammunition expenditure of 27,500 rounds for the American artillery and 13,410 rounds from the German guns.[3]

To the north, the 115th and 116th Infantry Regiments fought

around Koslar on November 25, with the latter attacking with a bayonet charge that scattered the defenders. The most intense fighting for these two villages would come at dawn on the following day. Köchling ordered counterattacks against the pair in an effort to reestablish the inner defensive ring protecting Jülich. Both regiments of *340th Volksgrenadier Division* attacked with support from 14 artillery battalions and 28 armored vehicles from *301st Heavy Panzer Battalion*, *341st Assault Gun Brigade*, and *3rd Panzergrenadier Division*. Its commander, *Generalleutnant* Theodor Tolsdorff, was a holder of the Knight's Cross with Oak Leaves, Swords and Diamonds, one of only 27 men to receive the high honor.

The Germans burst into the American artillery concentration, and soon spread into the villages. At 1030, with the weather finally clear, US fighter-bombers stopped the German advance, but two companies from 116th Infantry Regiment were nearly surrounded in Koslar. Until 116th Infantry Regiment sent a battalion to break through to the beleaguered companies on the 27th, they had to be supplied from the air. When the rest of 116th Infantry Regiment entered the village the next morning, the Germans had left.

At the same time, Gerhardt had the 115th Infantry Regiment move on Kirchberg. While a battalion in Bourheim made a feint by fire, another moved from Pattern during the morning of 27 November without artillery preparation but behind a smoke screen. By this stratagem the 115th Infantry achieved almost complete surprise. By late afternoon, Kirchberg was secure, and a three-village defensive arc before Jülich was established. *340th Volksgrenadier Division* withdrew its two regiments to the east bank, leaving only a rearguard in the two strongpoints east of Jülich.

30th Infantry Division adopted a similar pattern: one day of attack followed by consolidation. A battalion of 120th Infantry Regiment had taken Lohn, which it held against two counterattacks. While a battalion of the 119th Infantry Regiment moved into 29th Infantry Division's zone to strike southeast against Pattern, a battalion of 120th Infantry in Erberich opened fire, catching the German defenders off guard. Preceded by a barrage from 11 artillery battalions, 119th Infantry Regiment took the village without a casualty.[4] With only Altdorf remaining under German control, McLain got approval to have the 30th Infantry Division stand down until the flanking villages of Inden and Kirchberg could be secured.

Footnotes

[1] MS# A-997 "Combat Operations in the Aachen Sector" (September to December 1944).

[2] Joseph H. Ewing. *29th Infantry Division: A Short History of a Fighting Division.* 1992.

[3] LXXXI Corps KTB, Arty.-Lage u. Art.Gliederungen.

[4] "Ninth United States Army, 1–30 November 1944." General Corlett Foundation.

A sergeant with the radar unit of 135th AAA Gun Battalion checks the collimation of scope on a friendly aircraft near Geilenkirchen on Feb 16, 1944. The SCR (Signal Corps Radio)-584 was by now the Army's primary antiaircraft gun laying system. (US Signal Corps)

Chapter 11

First Army (Queen)
(November 19–26)

Having been tasked with clearing the Eschweiler-Weisweiler industrial triangle, the 104th Infantry Division had pushed across open terrain for the last three days, and was now just west of Röhe and Eschweiler. On the 18th the division overran Hill 287 near Donnerberg, pleasing its commander, Terry Allen, a man who Bradley described as "someone who was stubborn, independent, skillful, adept, aggressive, and who frequently ignored orders and fought in his own way."[1] The 104th Infantry Division could now work directly with Hobbs' 30th Infantry Division. At dawn on November 19, the 413th Infantry Regiment (Colonel Welcome P. Waltz) squared off against the *12th Volksgrenadier Division* with the goal of taking Eschweiler. To its right the 415th Infantry Regiment (Colonel John H. Cochran), was to clear the northern half of Stolberg and wooded high ground beyond, while the 414th Infantry Regiment moved up against elements of the *3rd Panzergrenadier Division*. As the Germans in the sector had previously pulled back, resistance was not consistent, but rubble and mines delayed the fall of Stolberg until the end of the day.

With the German defense of Eschweiler expected to melt away once its flanks were compromised, Collins felt that the 104th Infantry Division should let the town fall on its own. Having learned not to wait until his flanks were secured and that everything was in order before advancing, the VII Corps commander hoped to maintain a good rate of advance. Allen, however, saw no reason to skip this objective since 415th Infantry Regiment was available to take it. Although the Germans initially held the position, when 413th Infantry Regiment moved north of the city on the 21st, *OB WEST* ordered a withdrawal to a new line east of the town. Although in contradiction of Hitler's "no withdrawal" policy, small retirements were occasionally permitted if it meant conserving forces that could be committed to the Ardennes.

Dürwiss to Laufenberg

Toward the end of November 22, 104th Infantry Division had mostly cleared the industrial region between its sector and 30th Infantry Division. Only Putzlohn, Hill 154, and some towns along the Inde River remained to be taken. Allen had made considerable progress with minimal casualties. The 104th had moved up on par with the 1st Infantry Division, and Collins, saw an opportunity and changed his original plan. Instead of having 1st Infantry Division secure the corps' left as it moved to the Inde, 104th Infantry Division would now continue beyond the river near Hücheln, with help from CCA/3, and make for the Roer. 1st Infantry Division (now with the 47th Infantry Regiment) would seize the Langerwehe-Merode road.

To Allen's right, CCB/3 continued to defend its objectives at Werth, Scherpenseel, and Köttenich. As Hastenrath was mopped up, heavy German artillery and small arms fire continued to offer harassment. CCA/3 moved from defensive positions at Stolberg to assembly positions at Mausbach. The 83rd Reconnaissance Battalion assumed responsibility for the defense of Stolberg.

1st Infantry Division's progress achieved similar results, and was indicative of the fighting in that it was slow and casualty heavy. The German defenders were given time to organize counterattacks, which further eroded American gains. Huebner, the strict disciplinarian with a dry sense of humor, was pressured to use his reserve 18th Infantry Regiment. While 3rd Battalion, 47th Infantry Regiment (Colonel Donald C. Claymen) advanced between Hill 232 and Nothberg, its effort to assist 1st Battalion's struggling attempt to take Hills 187 and 167 amounted to little. 16th Infantry Regiment, 1st Infantry Division continued to make progress. While its 1st Battalion was ordered to stand down, the 3rd and 2nd were sent ahead toward Hamich and Hill 232, respectively.

16th Infantry's commander, Colonel Frederick W. Gibb, reacted by sending his remaining battalion to strike immediately for Hill 232. Preceding the assault, several field artillery battalions laid an impressive time on target barrage on the height, in which numerous rounds struck individual targets at virtually the same time. The men of the stunned *12th Fusilier Battalion*, having been brought up to support the wavering *48th Grenadier Regiment*, would need time to regain their wits.

At 1000 Claymen advanced into the woods after capturing Hill 232. German artillery and mortar fire stalled US progress, especially

A PFC from F Coy, 413rd Inf Regt, 104th Infantry Division inspects a pillbox near Düren on Feb. 25, 1945. (US Signal Corps)

around Bovenberg and the surrounding woods. Poor coordination between 16th Infantry Regiment and the division created some of the problems. The use of US 8-inch guns from corps artillery finally settled the matter.

47th Volksgrenadier Division's commander planned to retake Hamich and Hill 232. Forces were still being organized for a two-pronged counterattack, which was to hold First Army's advance along the Simmerath-Düren road. At 0530 part of *104th Grenadier Regiment* pushed onto the Hamich Ridge, but after several hours of close combat the attack was forced back. The second prong became disorganized prior to combat. It ended up at Hamich where it was hammered by US artillery.

At 1945 on November 19, Köchling was told by *Fifteenth Army* that he would receive a tank destroyer company, and that it was only to be used with infantry. The following day 12 vehicles were moved to Langerwehe-Luchem as a corps reserve.[2] By the afternoon, these were thrown against 1st Infantry Division as they were pinching off the Bovenberger Forest, where they held up the American attack in that sector for the next three days.

On November 21, Köchling had been receiving reports of attacks all along his front. *Fifteenth Army* had little choice save to pull back to a line along Bourheim-Pattern-Dürwiss, and to evacuate the Eschweiler salient. The following day *340th Volksgrenadier Division* relieved the battered *246th*. The *12th* and *47th Volksgrenadier Divisions* were to remain in place. In the six days since Operation Queen began, German intelligence estimated that they had suffered some 12,000 casualties, and that the enemy had lost 20,000 and 320 armored vehicles.[3]

The Push to the Inde (11/22–26)

As the 104th Infantry Division renewed the attack before daylight on November 23, German defenses consistently hampered rapid movement across the Roer Plain. Many of the towns and villages were mutually supporting. Conquest of Putzlohn was influenced by the progress of the adjacent 30th Infantry Division against Lohn; the capture of Weisweiler by the degree of success in 1st Infantry Division's sector against Hücheln and Wilhelmshoehe.

At Weisweiler, the 414th Infantry Regiment encountered less, but equally stubborn resistance. As it moved on Weisweiler, the capture of Putzlohn and Hill 154 on the 23rd provided observation of the town. 2nd Battalion, 47th Infantry Regiment entered Nothberg, but as it continued the ground was open, with little protection beyond the castle at Frenzerburg. The Germans shifted their defenses south of Langerwehe to a line between Hill 203 and Schönthal, and the US 18th Infantry Regiment was thrust into a fight for the elevation. Morale remained a problem on both sides as the fight seemed to have no end, and self-inflicted wounds correspondingly rose.

After dawn on November 25, 1st Infantry Division's Task Force Richardson took Hücheln and Wilhelmshöhe. By the afternoon, the Germans were seen withdrawing from Weisweiler. IX TAC fighter-bombers exploited a rare break in the weather to interdict this movement. With *12th Volksgrenadier Division* reduced to some 800 combat effectives, it was soon integrated into the *47th Volksgrenadier Division*, with the resulting formation being called *Gruppe Engel*.

On the 26th, 414th Infantry Regiment, 104th Infantry Division captured Frenz with minimal effort. At Lamersdorf and Inden, however,

Covered by a smokescreen the "Pursuader," a 155mm M-12 GMC (Gun Motor Carriage), crosses an M2 treadway bridge over the Roer River at Linnich on Feb. 26, 1945. (US Signal Corps)

the Germans had been able to organize a stronger defense before the Inde River. 413th Infantry Regiment tried to roll up the enemy flank by striking Lamersdorf, but ran into opposition that would last for the next three days. 414th Infantry Regiment around Frenz also suffered setbacks as heavy German artillery east of the river forced the Americans to abandon their position. Separate regimental assaults were ordered against the two objectives, but even with tactical aircraft and divisional and corps artillery, the German batteries could not be silenced.

By nightfall of 28 November, a rifle company had taken a portion of Inden and an intact bridge. *3rd Panzergrenadier Division* moved up, and with help from assorted divisional and *LXXXI Corps* elements, counterattacked the American position. During the night, the grenadiers managed to cut off the rifle company from any reinforcement. Just before dawn the Germans captured additional US forces that had tried to make a stand in a nearby factory. With two companies from 413th Infantry Regiment badly mauled at Inden, a relief force was sent in during the afternoon. A reserve battalion under Colonel William M. Summers, and a company from 750th Tank Battalion advanced against heavy enemy fire that, combined with the muddy terrain, halted the armored effort. The infantry component was able to continue, however, and soon entered the village. Summers subsequently assumed command of the five infantry companies in Inden and coordinated an effort to clear the village.

Summers soon found the task of getting the Germans out of Inden to be a tall order. Rested infantry reinforcements from *246th Volksgrenadier Division* began arriving to take over for *3rd Panzergrenadier Division*, making his job of opening the way to the river for the 104th Infantry Division more difficult. Over the next few days, however, Summers was able to wrest control of the village from enemy hands, and the Germans pulled back to the east of the river.

Smoke, confusion, and a steady stream of casualties would remain constant until November 29. Only then did the Germans finally withdraw to the Inde River's east bank. After leaving a small rearguard in Lamersdorf, they destroyed the bridges in their wake. Near midnight the village was taken over by US forces.

Spearhead

On November 24, CCB/3 continued its assault southeast of Eschweiler, and soon occupied Werth, Hastenrath, Scherpenseel, and Köttenich. At 1445 it continued to the northeast to secure the high ground between Langerwehe and Frenz. CCA/3 achieved similar results, having advanced against strong German resistance to secure Hücheln along 104th Infantry Division's right.

Over the next two days, CCA/3 attacked with the 67th Armored Field Artillery Battalion, moving to secure the high ground between Langerwehe and Frenz. Progress remained slow, again due to mud and enemy artillery, mortar, and small arms fire. Because vehicles were so handicapped by the extremely soft terrain, and German antitank guns were taking an increasing toll, American armor was pulled back. Reused to provide direct fire support for the attacking infantry, the latter finally reached their objective at 1630 on November 26. Only on December 2 were the last Germans finally pushed out of the area west of the Inde River.

German

3rd Fallschirmjäger Division
Commander: Generalmajor Walther Wadehn
Div HQ
Infantry: 5th, 8th, 9th Fallschirmjäger Regiments
Field Artillery: HQ, 3rd Artillery Regiment (105mm, 155mm Howitzers)
HHC, 3rd Antitank Battalion, 3rd Antiaircraft Battalion, 3rd Engineer Battalion, 3rd Signals Battalion, 3rd Feldersatz (Replacement Training) Battalion, 3rd Medical Battalion, Services

Merode

As the 1st Infantry Division prepared to finally exit the Hürtgen Forest, all that stood in its way were the enemy defenses around Merode. The 26th Infantry Regiment eagerly pushed on to the southeast of Merberich to quickly secure the position. With the goal in sight a battalion was sent ahead, but after being brutalized by two weeks of forest fighting, it did not make much of an impact. 26th Infantry's remaining battalions were temporarily out of the immediate picture. One was at Jüngersdorf to the north, and the other needed to secure the regiment's right flank in the woods because the adjacent 4th Infantry Division had not yet reached the eastern edge of the forest.

Behind the support of 1st Infantry Division artillery, the 2nd Battalion's commander, Lieutenant Colonel D.M. Daniel, sent two companies toward Merode before noon on November 29. The German *5th Parachute Regiment* made a tough fight of it, backed up by aggressive artillery fire of their own. Its parent formation, the rehabili-tated, and nearly full-strength *3rd Fallschirmjäger Division* (*Generalmajor* Walther Wadehn) had recently arrived to take over from *Gruppe Engel* to defend the approaches to Düren.[4] The American companies had steadily penetrated the village by the afternoon, but they had yet to subdue Merode's defenders.

That night small groups of US infantrymen tried to help get armor and additional infantry forces forward, but the single road into the village was extremely muddy and would not permit the movement of heavy vehicles. German artillery continued to hamper the effort, and the two companies were eventually cut off. With 26th Infantry Regiment's push to secure Merode tapering, patrols were sent toward the village over the next two days to help the apparently trapped companies, without success. On December 1, Daniel lobbied to use a full-strength battalion to settle the matter, but his regimental commander, Colonel John F.R. Seitz, would not commit additional forces. He believed that only unsupported infantry was available to make the attempt and that "what is in town may be annihilated by now."[5]

With these men abandoned to their fate, the next day Collins ordered that the worn-out 1st Infantry Division was to cease further activity and simply straighten its front lines. The 47th Infantry Regiment was sent back to the 9th Infantry Division, and Merode would not be taken for another week. The Roer was still nearly 5km away.

Footnotes

[1.] Bradley, *A Soldier's Story*, p. 81.

[2.] BA-MA RH 24-81/114 KTB LXXXI Corps, 19 Nov 1944.

[3.] BA-MA RH 19 IV/82, Anl.944, KTB Sup Cmd-west, 22 Nov 1944.

[4.] 26th Inf Unit Jnl, 30 Nov 44.

[5.] Opns Order for 1 Dec 44, *Fifteenth Army (Gruppe von Manteuffel)* to *Corps Group Blumentritt* and *LXXXI Corps*, 0115, 1 Dec 44, *LXXXI Corps KTB, Befehle Heeresgruppe und Armee an Gen. Kdo., 1.-31.XII-44.*

Chapter 12

Escape from the Hürtgen Forest
(November 17–28)

Aas the US XIX and VII Corps slowly but surely made their way across the open, largely urbanized terrain to the north, Major General Raymond O. Barton's 4th Infantry Division looked to finally break free from the constrained environment of the Hurtgen Forest in order to move up to the Roer River, upstream from Düren. In the days leading up to Operation Queen, 4th Infantry Division had been moved from V to VII Corps, where its 12th Infantry Regiment (Colonel James S. Luckett) had hurriedly taken over for the 109th Infantry Regiment, which had recently been battered along with its parent 28th Infantry Division around Schmidt. Unable to properly reconnoiter the new, heavily wooded surroundings, and with the front lines very close to the enemy, Luckett had considerable difficulties organizing, deploying, and preparing his command for combat.

When First Army established a new inter-corps boundary on November 10, 12th Infantry Regiment was returned to 4th Infantry Division. Having consolidated their newly regained positions around Kommerscheidt and Schmidt, the Germans soon launched a counterattack. Luckett was unable to control his regiment as a unified force. With one of his battalions pushing northward, the Germans were able to pinch off two-thirds of the force, and repeat the process on November 12 with a two-company relief force from 12th Infantry Regiment. These four companies would hold on until finally extracted on the 15th, the day before Operation Queen was to commence. In just a few days of fighting, 12th Infantry Regiment had not only lost ground, but also took roughly 1,000 casualties due to battle, disease, or exhaustion. In anticipation of the regiment having its combat capabilities so reduced, Hodges had previously attached CCR/5 to VII Corps.

On November 16, XIX and VII Corps began what they hoped would be their final push to the Roer River. Luckett was ordered to renew his attack to regain the ground he had lost and secure control either of the Weisser Weh or the Germeter-Hürtgen roads to allow armor to move on Hurtgen. In its depleted state, the 12th Infantry Regiment proved able to achieve only the first of its goals, and even this gain was limited. For his inability to complete his mission, Luckett was relieved of his command on the 21st, and transferred to another division.

As the 4th Infantry Division's General Barton prepared to continue with his remaining two regiments, he requested reinforcements to accomplish his mission of advancing 12km to the Roer, half of which was through dense forest. With First Army covering an extended front, it could only allocate CCR/5. Working with what it had, 4th Infantry Division moved off to achieve its objectives, while maintaining contact with the 1st Infantry Division along its left. For this task, Barton allocated the 8th Infantry Regiment (Colonel Richard G. McKee), to buttress the 26th Infantry Regiment. From just south of Schevenhütte, the colonel was to attack northeast 3km through the forest to high ground around Gut Schwarzenbroich.

To fill the gap between his flanking regiments, Barton sent in his remaining regiment, the 22nd (Colonel Charles T. Lanham). To best support 1st Infantry Division, Lanham was to attack towards Kleinhau and Grosshau on a two-battalion front. With his main effort to be on the left, his reserves were weighted to the north as well. 24th Cavalry Reconnaissance Squadron kept the area north to the regimental boundary clear. 12th Infantry Regiment would, hopefully, plug the gap along Lanham's right flank. Once beyond the initial villages, the 22nd and 8th Infantry Regiments would re-connect before moving to the Roer. Each would have to contend with a single road as a MSR, even as there was limited intelligence coming from the German lines due to increased security related to their buildup in the Ardennes.

The *275th Grenadier Division*, once again, prepared to meet the latest threat, having already bested the US 9th and 28th Infantry Divisions. Ordered to control a frontage from Schevenhütte to the Germeter Plateau, Straube's *LXXIV Corps* was virtually without reserves. Except for the *Kampfgruppe* sent north to *LXXXI Corps'* reserve, the depleted *116th Panzer Division* remained available, but higher headquarters was becoming increasingly insistent that this division be released for refitting for use in the Ardennes. Although a mixed bag of various units and types, *275th Grenadier Division* still possessed roughly 6,500 combat effectives. Two of the division's organic regiments were basically intact, and with a smaller one in reserve, the division's heavy weapons amounted to 106 tubes of artillery, 21 assault guns, and 23 antitank guns of 75mm or larger.[1]

Out of the Forest

Even though Barton was reinforced with four artillery battalions, he decided to forego a preliminary bombardment and rely on surprise instead. The only support scheduled in 4th Infantry Division's zone was for fighter-bombers to target Hürtgen, Kleinhau, Grosshau, and Gey.

On 4th Infantry Division's left, the 8th Infantry Regiment tried to pierce the German line along the Weh Creek. The leading battalion (Lieutenant Colonel Langdon A. Jackson, Jr.) was harried by 120mm mortar fire as it moved up a wooded slope east of the creek. When Jackson's command came upon the well-organized German position surrounded by a 3m tall pyramid of concertina wire, further movement was barred. A dense minefield, complete with Schuh mines, and machine gun fire countered every American effort to come to grips with the enemy position.

After a failed attempt at breaching the perimeter using a Bangalore torpedo, the battalion's Ammunition and Pioneer Platoon was finally able to blast a gap through the wire, but little more. On November 17, the battalion assaulted the German position three times, but each was driven back. Having suffered 200 casualties by noon, every effort was made to create another breech and divide the enemy's attention.

To the southwest, the 22nd Infantry Regiment was also advancing under fire, as it moved on Grosshau and Kleinhau. Though the enemy line here was primarily a series of outposts, the going was far from easy. With no axial roads for the first 2km, supply problems quickly became apparent, and by nightfall of D-Day the leading battalion of 22nd Infantry still was some 300m short of the Weisser Weh.

On November 17, Lanham directed another battalion to move ahead to secure a nearby ridge along a firebreak to be used as an additional supply route. On reaching a junction of several of these cleared strips, coined "Five Points," the battalion was able to turn east and cross the Weisser Weh. As the lead battalion continued toward Grosshau, German artillery rained down, causing several casualties and a loss of communications. Lanham sent in a platoon of light tanks as support, but the first two struck mines and blocked the passage of the remaining vehicles.

On November 18, 22nd Infantry Regiment's lead battalion made greater progress, but continued to be dogged by problems. After rebuffing a small counterattack against its exposed southern flank, the battalion discovered an extensive antipersonnel mine field. Trying to find a path around the obstruction, one company got lost and could not be located until late in the day. By then enemy fire had claimed the battalion commander, and eventually much of his staff. Only after the S-2, Maj. Howard C. Blazzard, arrived in late afternoon to assume command, was the battalion at last able to move. With darkness falling, the depleted formation crossed the Weisser Weh and climbed the steep slope beyond. To alleviate the supply issue, 8th Infantry Regiment was to cease offensive operations and help clear a lateral route to the 22nd Infantry Regiment.

With the concertina obstacle and the German position eliminated, McKee's 8th Infantry Regiment continued its advance. To enhance his command's effectiveness, he ordered a fresh infantry battalion forward, with help from a platoon each of light and medium tanks, and three tank destroyers. As the regiment turned south toward Grosshau, another pocket of German resistance appeared. Although it appeared to be another elaborately prepared defensive position, the lack of mines allowed American armor to provide a base of fire, through which the light tanks and an infantry company maneuvered to outflank the enemy, who soon succumbed to the pressure. 8th Infantry Regiment continued on, now little more than a kilometer from its objective of Gut Schwarzenbroich.

By November 19, the more successful gains by the 8th and 22nd Infantry Regiments were indicative of the degree to which the overextended *275th Grenadier Division* was losing its ability to effectively resist. Reinforcements, long denied, were finally becoming available, but by now it was a losing battle. Having to stretch its defensive lines dangerously thin, the adjacent corps to the south was able to allocate *344th Grenadier Division*, and a day later a *Volksgrenadier* division arrived in the *Seventh Army's* southernmost corps to relieve *353rd Grenadier Division*. The Germans rushed first the *344th*, then the *353rd*, to the forest. Over the next two days, *344th Grenadier Division* would replace the exhausted *275th Grenadier Division*.

When both American regiments continued to push to the east and northeast the next day, neither achieved much success in getting through the German defenses before Gut Schwarzenbroich. Enemy resistance, and a tenuous line of supply, hampered Lanham's efforts as well. By assembling a bridge within the nearby woods, and then transporting it to its destination, engineers finally created a stable crossing over the Weisser Weh later on the 20th. 22nd Infantry Regiment, however, still had an inadequate supply route, and would until Lanham's regiment made contact the next day.

Courtney Hodges, having transferred Hürtgen and Kleinhau into V Corps' zone of responsibility, believed the shift would ensure their capture, while decreasing 4th Infantry Division's frontage. Being relatively fresh, he 4th could then be used to expand the offensive, and help enable V Corps in exploiting any breakthrough.

V Corps' Turn

Since November 20, the rested, full-strength 8th Infantry ("Golden Arrow") Division under Major General Donald A. Stroh, and the attached CCR/5 was given the mission of capturing Hürtgen, Kleinhau, and the Brandenberg-Bergstein Ridge before V Corps was to reach the Roer. The rest of the corps (the 9th and 99th Infantry Divisions, and elements of the 5th Armored Division) would remain available to exploit any success. The Roer dams were still not an objective as senior US commanders continued to believe that only one more push would be required to break the German front and their will to continue the fight.

The 21st dawned characteristically wet and gray as V Corps artillery, with support from VII Corps, fired some 4,500 rounds against known and suspected enemy gun positions.[2] All were time on target missions with an average of five battalions of artillery on each target. Reinforced by guns of CCR/5, and by two companies of chemical mortars, 8th Infantry Division's organic artillery fired on the enemy's front lines and the villages beyond. US artillery attempted to pave the way for 8th Infantry Division, but it made little difference. Terrain and enemy defenses hampered American efforts, and by the end of the day only a portion of 3rd Battalion, 121st Infantry Regiment (Colonel John R. Jeter) had reached its objectives after negotiating the formidable "Wild Pig" minefield.

On November 23, Hodges called a meeting with Gerow, Collins, and others to discuss progress. He fumed against the 8th Infantry Division's Stroh, believing that the plan was sound and that lack of progress was due to a failure of leadership. With German reinforcements believed enroute, the 8th Infantry Division, and CCR/5, needed to capture Hurtgen as soon as possible. When the 4th Infantry Division arrived to help cover 121st Infantry Regiment's flank, Hodges approved Collins' and Gerow's plans for a coordinated attack to seize the town. To advance quickly Stroh ruled out the Weisser Weh Valley due to 2nd Battalion's lack of progress, and instead chose the Germeter-Hurtgen road, through the positions of 3rd Battalion, 121st Infantry Regiment. CCR/5's commander, Anderson, didn't believe the advance would keep a good pace as engineers would have to remove hundreds of mines along the route. Nevertheless the attack proceeded.

At first, 121st Infantry Regiment's left wing seemed to make good progress where a battalion was trying to drive up the Weisser Weh Valley so that a follow-up by armor might be made up the adjacent road instead of the exposed Germeter-Hürtgen highway. Soon after, however, the battalion was hit by heavy artillery fire that was magnified by tree bursts, followed by an aggressive German counterattack that drove the weary Americans back.

At 0730 the next day, CCR/5 headed out on the Germeter-Hurtgen road, only to be halted by additional enemy artillery fire from several calibers. Being unable to quickly clear a large crater that blocked vehicular traffic, the armored infantry tried later to advance alone. Unable to make additional headway against mines and enemy artillery, and having lost scores of soldiers over the last few days, CCR/5 withdrew as well.

Taking Hürtgen

The Americans closed in on the town of Hürtgen on November 26, and after receiving reports that the enemy had withdrawn, organized a push to finally take it. Although slow, 121st Infantry Regiment's efforts had brought it into a more defensible position. 4th Infantry Division had also made similar progress as it outflanked Germans units in the woods along 121st Infantry's left flank. By juggling troops on the defensive fronts held by the 8th Infantry Division's other two regiments, Stroh had freed the 1st Battalion (Lieutenant Colonel Morris J. Keesee), 13th Infantry Regiment, to assist in renewing the attack, which he gave to Colonel Cross, the new 121st Infantry Regiment commander. He then ordered Keesee to circle around through the forest into the 4th Infantry Division's zone, and on 27 November to strike for Hürtgen along the left flank of 121st Infantry Regiment from the wood line northwest of the village. As the attack unfolded, it was found that the Germans had evacuated the nearby woods and the Americans were able to move up to Hürtgen virtually unopposed. A rumor that the town had been abandoned as well, however, soon proved to be false.

Finding that resistance remained within Hürtgen, US forces prepared for their final assault. After Keesee's battalion was rebuffed while trying to cut the Germeter-Hurtgen road, 2nd Battalion, 121st Infantry Regiment managed to occupy the western part of the town. US tank destroyers moved into the nearby woods to provide covering fire as a platoon of Shermans moved up with the lead infantry battalion. Artillery took quick advantage of improved observation. By nightfall the Germans still held the bulk of a mostly destroyed Hürtgen, but Keesee had finally cut the Hürtgen-Kleinhau highway and gained a toehold in the northeastern edge of the village. A battalion of 121st Infantry under Lieutenant Colonel B. Kunzig moved into a few buildings in the western edge. German reinforcements from Kleinhau could not be contested due to darkness, and both sides held part of Hürtgen.

In the meantime, Lanham decided to envelope Grosshau, first by having the 1st Battalion support the 3rd to seize the high ground north of the town. 2nd Battalion would remain in place, but at 1100 the regiment jumped off for the high ground. 45 minutes later Barton ordered it to attack Grosshau directly.

Even after Keesee seized Hill 401 at dawn on November 28, the Germans continued to hold out in part of Hürtgen. Only after Kunzig's reserve company, riding M-4 Shermans from the 709th Tank Battalion, arrived on the scene in the afternoon did the last of the Germans withdraw. At 1800 Cross announced that Hürtgen was now under American control. Kleinhau and Grosshau would fall two days later. It would soon be found that the German defenses, although bent and battered, remained intact.

Footnotes

[1] MS # B-810 (Schmidt).

[2] V Corps Operations in the ETO, p. 316; V Corps Arty Per Unit Rpt 164, 21–22 Nov, V Corps G-3 file, 21–23 Nov 44.

Chapter 13

Operations up to the Ardennes Offensive
(December 7–17)

During the first week of December the US Ninth and First Armies had reached the Roer River (XIII and XIX Corps between Linnich and Jülich, and VII and V Corps along a small stretch around Bergstein). On December 7 Eisenhower met in Maastricht with Montgomery and Bradley to plan an all-out offensive for the early weeks of 1945. The Supreme Allied Commander decided that Montgomery would make the main effort, with 21st Army Group staging a secondary offensive in the south. The Field Marshal argued that the past few months had shown that only one attack could be adequately supported. Much as he had coordinated a single thrust at Arnhem, he again called for a concentrated thrust across the Rhine north of the Ruhr.

With the remaining uncleared west bank predominantly in VII Corps' sector, Collins would make every effort to catch up with his peers. Along the flat terrain to the north, 104th Infantry Division was to cover the remaining 5km between the Inde and Roer Rivers. To its right, 9th Infantry Division, and a combat command of 3rd Armored Division, was to operate in a zone less than 6km wide that technically was assigned to just the 9th Infantry Division. This pair was to open a route to Düren, while on VII Corps' southern flank, the 83rd Infantry ("Thunderbolt") Division prepared to sweep the southwestern approaches to the city. After gaining additional roads on the fringe of the Hürtgen Forest, the 83rd was to relinquish the extreme right of the corps zone to 5th Armored Division so that the armor might bridge a gap between the infantry's objectives near Düren and the point on the Brandenberg-Bergstein ridge where V Corps had reached the river.

To supplement the division's guns, Collins added his corps artillery, which although weaker than in the past, was still considerable compared to the Germans. With 14 artillery battalions available, he parceled out one to each of his five divisions, with the remainder remaining under VII

Corps control. An additional separate battery was divided between the 9th and 104th Infantry Divisions.

Whether V Corps could persuade the Germans to withdraw to the east of the Roer remained to be seen. According to VII Corps' G-2, it was more a question of "how long can the enemy continue his defense in the face of his present rate of losses and the new demand for troops in the south [to counter the US Third Army]." He believed that the Germans had considerable artillery that amounted to some 20 light artillery battalions, 5 medium battalions, and 15 to 20 self-propelled guns, plus some 10 tanks and likely assistance from the guns of the reserve SS divisions.[1]

Instead of withdrawing to the relative safety of the Roer's east bank, the Germans continued to resist on the west side with what forces were available to them. A new boundary was established to place the Düren sector entirely under Köchling's *LXXXI Corps,* as well as to accommodate the *3rd Parachute Division,* which arrived in late November to relieve *Gruppe Engel* (remnants of the *12th* and *47th Volksgrenadier Divisions*). Nearly brought up to full strength by replacements, the parachute division was directed to provide two battalions for the specific task of defending Düren. North of the paratroopers, *246th Volksgrenadier Division* had been returned to the line after having been reconstituted with a few reserves and some rest, but little more.

South of Düren, Straube's *LXXIV Corps* consisted of the *353rd Grenadier Division*, with a few remnants of *344th Grenadier*, and the *272nd Volksgrenadier Division*. The *85th Grenadier Division* would soon arrive from Holland to relieve the *89th Grenadier Division,* south of the *272nd,* which in turn was recommitted along *Fifteenth Army*'s left on December 15.

Along the Aachen-Cologne Reichsautobahn

As the Allies advanced ever closer to the Roer River, the terrain became increasingly open, especially the plain from Alsdorf to Jüngersdorf, and the northeastern fringe of the Hürtgen Forest. The 3rd Armored and 9th Infantry Divisions worked in concert as equals to reach the river, as a combat command was to feign an attack along the left half of the infantry division's sector. The armor was to capture Geich, Obergeich, and Echtz. 60th Infantry Regiment, 9th Infantry Division was then to relieve the combat command, presumably as a prelude to taking

Near Germeter members of B Coy, 12th Eng Combat Btn, 8th Infantry Division dig holes for placing mines on Dec 30, 1944. These are filled with logs, which would be replaced with mines should a German attack be forthcoming. (US Signal Corps)

Mariaweiler and Hoven along the river's west bank. To 9th Infantry Division's right, unaccompanied infantry would forge ahead, but to remain aware of an American armor thrust against Obergeich lest the flank be left open.

On December 10, after the armor had run into trouble from a combination of mines and mud, Craig sent a battalion of his 60th Infantry Regiment to assist. Together this battalion and a contingent of the 33rd Armored Infantry Regiment pushed into the first objective of Obergeich. The battalion helped the tanks and armored infantry in securing the next village of Geich, while Craig sent another infantry battalion to assist more armor in securing Echtz. By nightfall, American forces were able to occupy all three objectives.

At 0730 on the 11th, CCR/3 attacked toward Echtz, but the advance was hampered by extremely muddy terrain. At Obergeich a task force under Lieutenant Colonel Samuel M. Hogan ran into a minefield and heavy, anti-tank, and small arms fire that halted their advance. Infantry entered the town ahead of the tanks and mopping-up operations were completed by 1700 hours. The advance on Geich was continued, but at the edge of town heavy fire was encountered so that the forces withdrew for the night to a position between Obergeich and Geich. At 1400 a task force under Lieutenant Colonel Matthew W. Kane was ordered to attack across country to seize Echtz. The advance was successful and Task Force Kane entered the town at 1700 hours. Mopping-up operations were completed by 2100 hours.

Within half an hour, TF Kane, CCR attacked from Echtz with the mission of seizing Hoven. On crossing the line of departure this force was immediately brought under fire from anti-tank guns. At 0800 Task Force Hogan attacked and seized the town of Geich, and within two hours had secured its prize and established roadblocks. Along with TF Kane, the pair continued their thrust, but soon encountered antitank guns and armor. The forces regrouped in Echtz, and on December 12 tried again with help from 1st Battalion, 60th Infantry Regiment attached to the 3rd Armored Division at 1700.

The 1st Battalion stayed north of Hamich to directly support CCR/3 in its attack to seize Hoven. The battalion fired 13 salvoes, with the result that all of the German antitank guns fired upon were reportedly knocked out. Smoke was created to designate targets for loitering fighter-bombers. On December 12, CCR/3 continued its assault on Hoven. TF Kane attacked at 0800 and advanced steadily against heavy tank, antitank, and artillery fire, and lead elements entered the town at 1040. Six hours later it was mopping up and establishing roadblocks.

Collins created a plan for taking the two remaining villages west of the Roer. A battalion of 60th Infantry Regiment was sent to support CCR/3, while the remainder of the regiment was slated for capturing Mariaweiler. Regarding the latter, over the last day two refurbished companies from *47th Volksgrenadier Division* had steadily reinforced their comrades in Hoven and Mariaweiler. German observers occupied the high ground in their shrinking zone, and brought in devastating artillery fire onto American positions around Hoven. On December 12, this fire caused additional losses to 60th Infantry Regiment attacking

A US sergeant fastens primacord to a booby trap release while working with A Coy, 327th Eng Combat Btn, 102nd Infantry Division to relocate a minefield on Jan 4, 1945. (US Signal Corps)

Mariaweiler. To the north, regimental elements laid smoke and were finally able to secure Hoven. By nightfall CCR/3 and the 60th Infantry Regiment would also secure their sector, save for German holdouts at a factory at Mariaweiler that did not fall for another two days.

In the meantime, while armor and infantry had been coordinating in the main push, the 39th Infantry Regiment had been attacking alone to clear Derichsweiler and Merode. Remembering the problems with the previous American attempt to push on Merode, 39th Infantry Regiment (Colonel Van H. Bond), directed his battalions to delay until the capture of Obergeich anchored his northern flank and opened additional roads. Bond also considered initiating a thrust to the south to help trap German forces lingering in the Wenau Forest.

VII Corps to the Roer

On December 10, Joe Collins ended his command's period of inactivity. Early in the day a battalion from the 44th Infantry Regiment attacked out of Inden toward Schophoven and Pier. The *246th Volksgrenadier Division* had incorporated the villages into elaborate entrenchments. Fire from the fortifications at Schophoven pinned down one battalion, but a second advanced behind a rolling artillery barrage and penetrated into Pier, only to be forced out after nightfall by a counterattack supported by three self-propelled guns.

The 104th Infantry Division continued with its nighttime activity, something of a specialty as of late. With help from precise artillery fire designed to box-in a route of advance, a battalion from the 415th Infantry Regiment approached its target several hundred meters northwest of Merken. With white phosphorus rounds landing as markers in the darkness, a platoon dropped off to clear the hamlet while the main body effected an abrupt change of direction in the darkness to move southeast on Pier. Again, white phosphorus guided the American advances, and both locations quickly gave way before surprise assaults. In advancing to Merken, the 415th Infantry had passed southeast of Pier, thereby opening a route for a flanking force to hit that village from the south.

At dawn on the December 12, while the bulk of a battalion continued to strike Pier from the west, a company of infantry supported by tanks approached from the south. The Germans, however, had already begun to withdraw across the Roer, and 104th Infantry Division artillery hastened their progress. German defenses at Schophoven offered greater resistance. A flanking thrust across the newly opened path from the south eventually eliminated the threat. By mid-afternoon the next day 104th Infantry Division had reached the Roer and secured a 6km strip of the west bank.

From the Hürtgen to the Roer

The newly committed 83rd Infantry and 5th Armored Divisions finally emerged from the Hürtgen Forest near Gey and Strass. Schmidt and the surrounding area, however, remained German-controlled, and Hodges was finally understanding just how important it was to secure the Roer dams. Air attacks had proven ineffective in solving the problem, so Hodges decided to try a ground approach using V Corps, prompting Gerow to plan an envelopment of the dams. Major General Edwin P. Parker, Jr.'s 78th Infantry ("Lightning") Division had just arrived on scene and was directed through the Monschau corridor to the eastern edge of the Hürtgen Forest. After securing Schmidt, the 78th was to attack the dams from the north. Further south, Major General Walter M. Robertson's 2nd Infantry ("Indian Head") Division would attack into the Monschau Forest from Krinkelt and Rocherath, and approach the dams from the southeast.

By December 15 the Allies were suffering from a lack of riflemen, which in 12th Army Group amounted to a shortage of some 17,000.[2] As a solution to losing combat forces from disease, exposure, and the like, Eisenhower reclassified many support personnel as infantrymen. This decision meant that the system that supported the front line formations would be reduced. It also meant that the numerous African-American soldiers that had been relegated to rear echelon duties would now be given a chance to prove their worth in combat.

At 0530 on December 16, a massive German bombardment heralded their strategic counterattack in the Ardennes-Eifel. By 0800, three German armies burst into the unsuspecting American lines along a 112km front between Monschau and Trier. Many GIs wondered whether the activity of which they were hearing was the real thing or just some unfounded panic. As a precaution, roadblocks were established against possible German paratrooper activity, and extra guards were put on watch.

Hodges tried to continue with his offensive by reattaching 5th Armored Division (minus CCR) to VII Corps, while V Corps was to quickly capture the Brandenberg-Bergstein Ridge and Hill 400. The situation along Gerow's right, however, necessitated that this endeavor be cancelled. As was the case along the entire Western Front once the Germans had burst into the Ardennes, the Allied effort to establish bridgeheads beyond the Roer River would have to wait.

Footnotes
[1] Annex 2 to VII Corps FO 13.
[2] CMH Pub 72-25. "Rhineland, The US Army Campaigns of World War II," p. 26.

Chapter 14

Operation Blackcock
(January 14–27)

By mid-January 1945, the US First and Third Armies had blunted the German counteroffensive in the Ardennes and had nearly pushed the bulge back to its starting line. With 71 divisions in the field, and 14 more expected by spring (61 US, 16 British, and 8 French), Eisenhower looked to exploit the fact that the enemy had expended his strategic reserve in the West. First the Allies would destroy all German forces lingering west of the Rhine River before seizing crossings between Mainz and Karlsruhe.[1] From there the route to Frankfurt and Kassel would be open, and with their capture a seizure of the Saar Basin would be effected. In the north, Rhine bridgeheads would be established from Emmerich to Wesel as a springboard to finally advance into the plains of northern Germany, and in so doing capture the Ruhr as well.

Before this great drive in the north could commence, crossings over the Roer River remained to be established in the US sector, and a large triangular salient before the British XII Corps needed to be eliminated. This area within Roermond, Maaseik, and Geilenkirchen had been created by the US Ninth and British Second Army's offensive during Operation Queen the previous November. When American formations had to reorient southward to contain the Ardennes sector during the preceding month, the British XII Corps extended southward to compensate.

For the past four months the Germans in the Roermond sector had been largely left alone behind the formidable Maas River. To the south, its tributary, the 6m-wide Saeffeler Creek, presented another hurdle to an attacker where its marshy edges made the barrier an effective tank trap. There were few places for heavy armored vehicles to attempt a crossing, and the main road bridge at Hongen had been blown. The Germans had put their time to good use, and extensive minefields, blown bridges, tank ditches, and various fortifications now covered the region. Numerous streams, especially along XII Corps' left, and cold winter weather added to the potential difficulties the British would have to overcome, and acted as a combat modifier for the outnumbered German defenders. Nevertheless, on December 31, British senior commanders determined that Lieutenant General Sir Neil M. Ritchie's XII Corps needed to clear the salient. This would considerably shorten the corps' frontage, and allow the building of mobile reserves for the expected push beyond the Roer River.

British Planning

Against an estimated 16,500 Germans consisting of two *Volksgrenadier* divisions and assorted formations, the British offensive would amount to some 46,200 soldiers.[2] XII Corps consisted of the 7th Armoured ("Desert Rats") Division west of Sittard, with the 52nd and 43rd Infantry Divisions (supported by a detachment from the US 1141st Combat Engineer Group) on the center and right, respectively. With the latter, it was hoped the Germans would expect the main attack from Geilenkirchen against Dremmen and Heinsberg. To ensure a quick completion of the mission, the Sittard-Heinsberg and Sittard-Roermond roads would need to be secured, as would the wooded region in the salient's center.

The operation was to break through along XII Corps' left, and be followed by a series of turning operations from the north and west. D-Day was to be at 2100 on January 15, and would unfold along three axis comprising 10 objectives, each of several sub-goals: Angel (D+1 (1/15)), Bear (D+1), Crown (D+2-3), Dolphin (D+2-3), Eagle, Fleece, Globe, Hart (on completion of Eagle), Jug, and Kettle.

West of the Maas, the British could count on the assistance of 1st Commando Brigade, comprising three Army and one Royal Marines Commando. Totaling some 1,200 specialists in clandestine and nighttime operations, the force was increasingly used as shock troops.

Three Canadian Typhoon squadrons were available for air support, but as poor weather was expected over the course of the operation, their help was not to be expected. Tactical medium bombing would likely provide intermittent day and night area bombing against enemy communications and reinforcements, as well as isolating the battlefield. Regardless of air support, British ground forces were expected to continue fighting.

In addition to XII Corps artillery, the Commander Corps of Royal

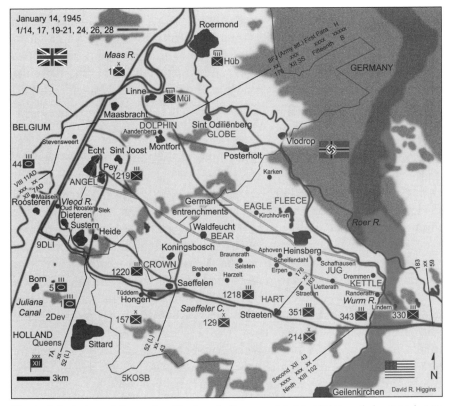

Tactical depiction of Operation Blackcock (January 14–28, 1945) and the British XII and VIII Corps' efforts to clear the Roermond bulge.

Artillery (CCRA) was given executive control over each division's organic complement. During each operational phase, some 250 guns from up to eight field and six medium artillery regiments, a limited-range mattress battery of 3-inch rockets, and various howitzers, heavy, and super heavy guns would be used. The US XIII Corps was to provide artillery on the right, while the British VIII Corps supported 7th Armoured Division near Maaseik. To this were added roughly 560 Cromwells and Fireflies.[3]

Having readjusted their frontline positions prior to the battle, the British hoped to make the Germans believe that the main attack would come from Geilenkirchen toward Dremmen and Heinsberg. The 43rd (Wessex) Infantry Division replaced The 52nd (Lowland) Infantry Division along XII Corps' right, which in turn did the same to the 7th

205

Armoured Division. Two Wessex brigades were subsequently in a conspicuous placement as the apparent strike force. Fighting was to continue during the dark hours of the days and the nights as much as possible. Antiaircraft searchlights were used to indirectly illuminate the battlefield by shining them at a certain angle on the low hanging clouds, otherwise known as "Monty's Moonlight."

German Planning

Under the command of *General der Infanterie* Günther Blumentritt, *XII SS Corps* prepared to defend the triangular salient that remained after the US Ninth Army's offensive the previous November. Three lines of defenses had been constructed. The most southern ran from Lindern and along the Saeffeler Creek and consisted of a line of trenches, weapon pits, and mines. Behind that, a second line of fighting and communication trenches snaked its way from the *Westwall* at Uetterath to Echt. The final line of trenches ran from Dremmen to Haaren. Numerous pillboxes and other trenches connected the three defensive lines into a formidable obstacle between Linnich and Heinsberg. Roermond was also prepared with an all-around defense, with two tank ditches with wire entanglements to the south of the town. Echt, Schilberg, and Montfort were similarly prepared for an all-around defense, and were strengthened by mines and booby traps in the intervening terrain.

Along Blumentritt's right, *8th Fallschirmjäger Division* positioned two regiments, each under Huebner and Mueller, totaling some 1,500 paratroopers. The *176th Grenadier Division* occupied the center with its three regiments, each with two grenadier battalions. Reduction from the original nine infantry battalions per division was partly alleviated by substituting a füsilier battalion for the old reconnaissance unit. This new fusilier battalion was organized like a rifle battalion except for one company, which was equipped with bicycles, but in practice the fusiliers were often regarded as the seventh grenadier battalion. The *183rd Volksgrenadier Division* was similarly composed on the left/rear, with both formations at around seventy percent of full strength. By mid-1944 the ratio of combat versus service troops in German infantry divisions had been raised to seventy-five or eighty percent, and was thus much higher than for US and British infantry divisions. On the eve of battle, artillery along the front consisted of roughly 90 field guns, 36 mediums, and 18 7.5mm guns, while armor support amounted to some 28 Hetzers, 30 StuG IIIs, and 27 Tiger IIs.[4]

On Jan 8, 1945 soldiers of K Coy, 406th Inf Rgt, 102nd Infantry Division pound barbed wire posts south of Geilenkirchen. (US Signal Corps)

January 14

British

43rd (Wessex) Infantry Division
Commander: Major General Ivor Thomas

Attached
6th Guards Tank Brigade
C Squadron, 141st RAC
B Squadron, Dgns
16th Assault Squadron RE (less one troop)
344th SL Battery
C Flt, 653rd Air OP Squadron
100th Radar Unit Detachment

52nd (Lowland) Infantry Division
Commander: Major General E. Hakewill-Smith
HQ
52nd Reconnaissance Regiment
Infantry: 155th, 156th, 157th Rifle Brigades
Field Artillery: HQ, 79th, 80th, 186th FA Regiments (25pdrs)
Other: 54th Antitank Regiment (17pdrs, 6pdrs), 108th Light
Antiaircraft Regiment (40mm), 52nd Reconnaissance Regiment, 7th
(MG) Battalion (MMGs, 4.2-inch mortars), Manchester Regiment,
Royal Engineers (241st, 554th, 202nd Field Companies; 243rd Field
Park Company; 17th Bridging Platoon), 52nd Signals

7th Armored Division
Commander: Major General L.O. Lyne
HQ
Armor: 22nd Armored Brigade (340 mostly Cromwells), 8th King's
Royal Irish Hussars
Infantry: 131st (Queens) Infantry Brigade, 3rd Independent MG
Company, Northumberland Fusiliers)
Field Artillery: HQ, 3rd, 5th Royal Horse Artillery
Other: 7th Armored Signals, 4th, 621st, 143rd Field Squadron Royal
Engineers, 7th Bridging Troop, 65th Antitank Regiment, 15th Light
Antiaircraft Regiment, 7th Armored Signals

1st Commando Brigade
8th Armored Brigade (Brig Gen Prior-Palmer) 220 tanks (Shermans and Fireflies)
6th Guards Tank Brigade (Brig Gen Greenacre) (Churchills)
155th Brigade
31st Armored Brigade- elements of 79th Armored Division (Crocodiles and Flails)

German

341st Sturmgeschütz Brigade
301st Heavy Panzer Battalion
407th Volks Artillery
59th Grenadier Division (Generalleutnant Walter Poppe)

8th Fallschirmjäger Division
Fallschirmjäger Regiment Hübner

Angel

What had been a seemingly unending string of cold, rainy days during November was now replaced by bitter cold, snow, and fog. On January 15, Phase Angel, an attempt by the 7th Armoured Division to seize the area from Echt to Schilberg and establish a "Class 40" (able to support armor) route from Sittard, was to have commenced at 2100, so as to allow enough time for a bridge to be constructed over the Vloed River during the hours of darkness. Poor weather and thaw soon forced a postponement to 0730 the following morning.

On the morning of the 16th, the assaulting British battlegroup built around the 9th Durham Light Infantry made good progress against minimal resistance. By 1045 it had crossed an intact bridge over the Roode Creek, captured Dieteren, and provided security for the engineers constructing a new bridge over the Vloed River. The bridge was built in about 12 hours, but German mortar and artillery fire soon destroyed it. Another counterattack was beaten off, and a second "Class 40" bridge was not finished until dawn the next day.

Preceding the second phase because of the delay imposed by constructing a primary crossing over the Vloed River, Angel III got underway at 0600 on January 17. A battlegroup built around 1/5 Queens attacked Susteren and within a half hour had penetrated its northern outskirts. A pair of enemy assault guns or tanks was quickly supported by an infantry counterattack of battalion strength. The British position was hit hard, but within the hour two troops from 1st Royal Tank Regiment arrived to blunt the German force. Although seven tanks succumbed to *panzerfaust* teams, the Germans were forced to retire. By 1500 Susteren was nearly completely occupied by 1/5 Queens, which nearly six hours later linked up with 1st Rifle Brigade. During the afternoon the 5th King's Own Scottish Borders (5KOSB) was placed under the 131st Infantry Brigade to clear Oud Roosteren, and to take over Dieteren from 9th Durham Light Infantry, as it was to go into Brigade reserve. By 1800, 5 KOSB had taken the town, and thereby secured the division's left flank along the Juliana Canal.

Earlier that morning, Angel II began when armor was thrown across the Vloed River atop bulldozed crossings. With a reserve to their rear, 2nd Devonshire Regiment's battlegroup advanced in two columns. The left advanced along the Dieteren-Echt road, and it captured Echt around midnight. The right moved from Susteren to Schilberg, where it ran into greater resistance.

By 0300 on the 18th, the last bridge south of Susteren was complete. At 0630 2nd Devonshire Regiment attacked Schilberg with help from the 1st Royal Tank Regiment and flame-throwing Crocodiles. Enemy resistance held on and heavy fighting took place at the Schilberg-Pey crossroad. Only in the afternoon did the defenders withdraw, but fighting continued over the crossroad until darkness.

Bear

With the goal of capturing Koningsbosch from the west, Bear Phase was comprised of four columns from 7th Armoured Division, each with a mix of armor, infantry, and support units. At 1400 Group "Black" moved up. Germans running between British column vehicles to distribute mines hampered progress, and it was not until dawn on January 19 that "Black" reached the town. "Brown" and "Red" advanced at 0930, but not along their intended route. Mines and roadblocks necessitated that the group follow "Black's" path north. "Red" encountered German assault gunfire at 1140 from a swampy area known as "Bloven," but got going again after a four-hour attack. The 9th Durham Light Infantry had now cleared Schilberg and Pey, while to

Reinforcements from 121st Inf Rgt move up to join the 8th Infantry Division deployed between Germeter and Hürtgen. (Note the camouflaged 75mm Pak 40 antitank gun to the left.) (US Signal Corps)

the west, 3rd Commando crossed the Meuse River to raid Stevensweert.

For the rest of the day British forces contended with confused, often heavy fighting as they pushed north. Their armor, forced to remain in existing tank lanes, if possible, to avoid the ubiquitous landmines, was often without adequate infantry support and vulnerable. By evening "Black" and "Red" had made it to the wooded area north and east of Koningsbosch near Waldfeucht, and linked up with part of the 52nd Infantry Division. By nightfall, 8th Armored Brigade was pulled back from its sector after further progress was considered limited given its present direction.

Dolphin

At 0630, elements of the 156th Rifle Brigade moved from Tüddern toward the small hamlets of Lind and Stein. Here the Saeffeler Creek was crossed under heavy German mortar and machine gun fire. At midday Dolphin Phase was to commence with the 9th Durham Light Infantry (under 22nd Armored Brigade), which was moved up to Schilberg for an attack slated for 1430.

In the afternoon one troop of 3rd Commando Brigade crossed the Maas River and captured the village of Stevensweert, situated in the no-man's land between the Maas and the Juliana Canal. During the night, 1/5 Queens moved from Susteren to take over right flank protection around Slek-Heide from 5KOSB, which took 155th Infantry Brigade and went back under the 52nd Infantry Division. The 5th Dragoon Guards were placed under the 131st Infantry Brigade to hold Susteren in replacement of 1/5 Queens. At this point Hitler ordered that all division-sized and larger attacks—or retreats—must have his approval.

On January 20, in cold and misty weather, 22nd Armored Brigade launched what it thought would be a comparatively easy assault against two rather young companies of the *2nd Battalion, Fallschirmjäger Regiment Hübner*. Operating in the town, 200 German infantry and a number of assault guns provided a stout defense, in part as they received regular reinforcement from *Regiment Hübner* in Roermond.[5] Sint Joost was along 7th Armoured Division's path as it advanced on Montfort. On January 21 and 22 Royal Canadian Air Force (RCAF) Hawker Typhoon 1B fighter-bombers hit the town, and lost two planes for the effort. The British did not receive such replacements and it would ultimately require four attack waves to clear the village; the final attack would commence at 1930 on January 21. The 9th Durham Light Infantry and 1st Rifle Brigade suffered heavy casualties around Sint Joost. On the other side, Hübner had an entire company erased from his rolls, and a second nearly so. Such fierce combat led many who participated to consider it the hardest battle of the Blackcock operation.

British patrols were soon sent from Sint Joost northeast through Slek. Two destroyed bridges over the Vloot Creek that skirted Montfort were repaired later in the afternoon, and 22nd Armored Brigade was able to continue into Aandenburg, but no further. Heavy fighting continued throughout the night and into the next day. 1st Commando Brigade, and a squadron from 8th Hussars, had left Echt that morning, and by 1330 had captured Maasbracht and Brachterbeek. When a German attempt to cut 22nd Infantry Brigade's MSR back to Sint Joost, 2nd Devonshire Regiment was ordered up to contest it, with the commandos taking the vacated position at the town. Only when 1/5 Queens arrived to link up with 2nd Devonshire Regiment on the 24th

British tankers from 8th Armored Battalion assist the US 406th Infantry Regiment at Brachelen on January 26, 1945. (US Signal Corps)

was Aandenburg finally cleared. Montfort fell soon after. On the following day 1st Commando Brigade would take Linne as well. The British had by now erased roughly half of the German salient.

Crown

The thaw that had begun on January 17 continued as 156th Rifle Brigade, with a battalion from the 157th, set off at 0630 to clear a path through the minefield near Stein, and erect two assault bridges across the Saeffeler Creek. By 0843 one bridge was in place and British infantry assaulted Line and Stein. On crossing, the first few Crocodiles and Flails immediately bogged down, a scenario repeated when the second bridge went up at 1030.

Line and Stein proved a difficult undertaking for the British, whose infantry had to attack without adequate armor support. Trenches that allowed the German defenders to move about with relative ease connected buildings. Slowly, however, 156th Infantry Brigade was able to move into the expanding bridgehead. Hongen was captured that night.

Eagle

Phase Eagle I was the movement of the 52nd (Lowland) Infantry Division's artillery north of the Breberen-Saeffeln road to support Phase Eagle II. Here, a battlegroup built around the 8th Armored Brigade would capture Braunsrath and Haaren, and clear the woods to the north. 156th or 157th Rifle Brigades, with supporting Flails and Crocodiles, would take Selsten and Aphoven if ordered.

The 5th King's Own Scottish Borderers of the 52nd Division occupied Waldfeucht early on January 21 without meeting serious resistance. At 0630 the Germans launched a counterattack of battalion strength on the village, supported by about 15 self-propelled guns and six Tiger tanks. German artillery began to shell the village heavily. The battle for Waldfeucht was a bitter affair, but 5KOSB stoutly defended the village for 18 hours.

Eventually the Germans gained a lodgement in the east of Waldfeucht and B Company of 5KOSB was cut off. The Germans, however, withdrew in evening, and the British secured the village again on January 22. The defense of Waldfeucht was considered by many to be the most aggressive and largest counterattack the 52nd Division experienced during the operation.

The division made good progress during January 22 and got to within 5km of Heinsberg. Braunsrath was soon occupied, with Haaren soon to follow. Just before dark, the 5th Highland Light Infantry, supported by tanks of the Sherwood Rangers Yeomanry, one troop of Churchill VII Crocodiles, and some M4A4 Sherman Crabs, captured Laffeld.

Fleece

On completion of Phase Eagle, the 8th Armored Brigade and 52nd Reconnaissance Regiment, and corps artillery would provide armor support for 156th or 157th Rifle Brigades. 8th Armored Brigade would seize Karken, Kempen, Heinsberg, and Kirchhoven, while 52nd Reconnaissance Regiment would cover the left flank, and make contact with the 7th Armoured Division, which was completing Phase Globe by capturing Posterholt to Sint Odilienberg

Hart

With the elimination of the salient winding down, 43rd (Wessex) Infantry Division continued with its Phase Hart objective of clearing German resistance south of the Roer, and taking the area from Harzelt to Straeten. The 129th Rifle Brigade was used to secure a route south of Breberen through which 130th Rifle Brigade would pass.

Jug

As per Jug I's objectives, the 43rd (Wessex) Infantry Division was to take the region between Schafhausen and Erpen. 129th Rifle Brigade battlegroup would then capture Scheifendahl, Straeten, and Uetterath, while maintaining contact with the 52nd (Lowland) Infantry Division. The second phase, Jug II, consisted of 130th Rifle Brigade extending its gains from Phase Hart to capture the villages around Schafhausen, establish a front line between Lindern and Heinsberg, and relieve 129th Rifle Brigade near Schleiden. Phase Kettle completed operations in the salient as the 43rd Infantry Division and XIII Corps captured the Randerath spur.

By January 25, British engineers had opened a "Class 40" route from Sittard to Heinsberg. All bridges across the Roer, save a trestle bridge near Roermond, were now British-controlled. The only area still possessed by the Germans was a small bridgehead at Vlodrop, and another at Herten. Both were protected by German positions north of the Roer. With all the Allied objectives completed successfully, they possessed the entire length of the Roer River's west bank. Their plans for the capture of the Rhineland could now be put into effect.

Footnotes

[1] CMH Pub 72-75. "Rhineland: The US Army Campaigns of World War II."

[2] Har Gootzen / Kevin Connor, "Battle for the Roer Triangle." 2008.

[3] Ibid.

[4] Report on "Operation "Blackcock" 12 Corps. 15–26 Jan 45.

[5] Ibid.

Chapter 15

Capturing the Dams and Crossing the Roer
(February 1–27)

With the German salient in the Ardennes eliminated, the Allies prepared a strategic counterattack to achieve their long-standing goals of reaching the Rhine River, penetrating Germany in depth, and concluding the war. February was to be a month of considerable activity along the Western Front from Nijmegen in the north to the Saar area in the south. Initially, the primary offensive would be undertaken by the Canadian First Army, with attached British forces, in Operation Veritable. In concert, the US Ninth Army's Operation Grenade would push northeast to act as the southern pincer designed to encircle, or drive out, German resistance between the Roer and Rhine Rivers. Once First Army secured the Roer dams it was to go largely over to the defensive, while elements of VII Corps advanced as protection for Ninth Army's right flank.

With the inability of the Americans to capture the dams in a coup de main, they would have to come up with an alternative plan. One solution was to simply bomb the dam at Urft to create a rise in the water behind the Schwammenauel Dam, and rely on erosion to drain the reservoir enough to greatly reduce the danger. Hodges favored this approach, but after the idea made its way to Eisenhower, and then to the RAF, it was deemed impractical. Eisenhower persisted, and the RAF reconsidered, but a string of days with poor weather made aerial targeting impossible. When the dam was actually hit, only superficial damage was done, and further efforts seemed unnecessary. The dams would have to be captured by ground forces.

On February 2, SHAEF's plan for Veritable and Grenade was accepted, after Eisenhower assured Montgomery that the principal effort would remain in the north, and that crossing the Rhine was not contingent on clearing the entire area west of the river. This eased Montgomery's concern that the dual effort would dissipate his assault. Major General

Clarence R. Huebner (now in command of V Corps after Gerow left for the newly created Fifteenth Army) ordered Major General Edwin P. Parker to have his rather inexperienced 78th Infantry Division capture Schmidt in the Hürtgen Forest as well as the Schwammenauel Dam.

At 0300 on February 5, the 78th Infantry Division started out for Schmidt, while elements of the 82nd Airborne and US 7th Armored Divisions provided support. The next day, the 9th Infantry Division captured the Urft Dam intact, and it looked as if the one at Schwammenauel would follow suit. Parker's efforts were hampered by the close combat environment that minimized artillery and armor support. In an effort to punch through German resistance, and appease the exhortations from his superiors, all three of 78th Infantry Division's regiments were put on the front line.

Parker had the 310th Infantry Regiment go all out for Schmidt, and it pushed through the 309th after the latter's effort had stalled against determined resistance. Subsequently, all three regiments overwhelmed the *272nd Volksgrenadier Division*, as Schmidt was attacked from three sides.

February 8

US

78th Infantry Division
Commander: Major General Edwin P. Parker
Div HHC
Infantry: 309th, 310th, 311th Infantry Regiments
Field Artillery: HHB, 307th, 308th, 903rd FA Battalions (105mm Howitzer), 309th FA Battalion (155mm Howitzer)
Other: HQ Special Troops, 78th Reconnaissance Troop (Mechanized), 78th Signal Company, 303rd Engineer Combat Battalion, 78th Counter Intelligence Corps Detachment
Trains: 778th Ordnance Light Maintenance Company, 78th Quartermaster Company, Military Police Platoon, 303rd Medical Battalion

Attached
552nd Antiaircraft Artillery Battalion AW
774th Tank Battalion
893rd TD Battalion

German

272nd Volksgrenadier Division
Commander: Generalleutnant Eugen Konig
Div HQ
Infantry: 980th, 981st, 982nd Grenadier Regiments
Field Artillery: HQ, 272nd Artillery Regiment (75mm, 105mm, 155mm Howitzers)
Other: 272nd Antitank Battalion (75mm AA and AT), 272nd Engineer Battalion, 272nd Signal Battalion, 272nd Feldersatz (Replacement Training) Battalion, 272nd Füsilier Battalion, 272nd Support Regiment, Services

85th Grenadier Division
Commander: Generalmajor Helmut Bechler
Div HQ
Infantry: 1053rd, 1054th Grenadier Regiments
Field Artillery: HQ, 185th (105mm, 155mm Howitzers)
Other: 185th Antitank Battalion, 185th Engineer Battalion, 185th Signal Battalion

Fourth Schmidt

Although the 309th Infantry Regiment had reached Kommerscheidt the day before, Parker was still not achieving results to the degree required by Eisenhower and other senior Allied commanders. With Operation Veritable set to commence on February 8, the dams needed to be secured as soon as possible. Parker responded by sending an RCT from Louis Craig's 9th Infantry Division to Schmidt to take over the 78th Infantry Division for another push for the Schwammenauel Dam. The 310th and 311th Infantry Regiments moved to clear the approaches, while the 309th teamed up with the US 82nd Airborne Division, rebuffed elements of *272nd Volksgrenadier Division* around Schmidt, and finally took the town.

Even with the new commander, 9th Infantry Division's progress fared little better. Only during the night of February 9 was 1st Battalion, 309th Infantry Regiment able to approach the target. Two groups from the 1st Battalion were sent ahead, with one moving across the top of the

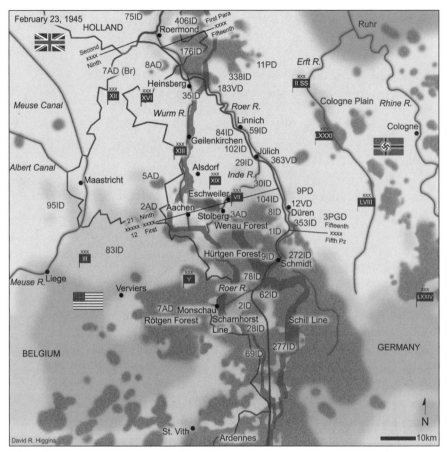

The February 23, 1945 position along the Roer River prior to its crossing by the US First and Ninth Armies.

dam and the other along the bottom. Under German small arms fire a quick check was made for demolitions, but none were found. Instead of blowing the dam up, the machinery that controlled the structure's water flow had been destroyed. The Roer River Valley steadily flooded and effectively blocked the Allied advance to the Rhine. Hodges' recent cancellation of the slated 0530 jump-off had proven wise.

With the Americans temporarily fixed, German commanders were able to send additional forces north to contest the Veritable offensive. *General der Fallschirmtruppe* Alfred Schlemm, commanding *First Fallschirm* (Parachute) *Army*, was free to use his reserve, *XLVII Corps*, to counterattack the Anglo-Canadian forces. With Operation Veritable

Ninth Army medics crossing the Roer in an assault boat after the bridge was destroyed by an M-4 Alligator that had rammed it in the strong current on Feb 23, 1945. (US Signal Corps)

having been under way for the last day, the anticipated quick break-through by the Canadians had not happened, and the operation quickly bogged down against a stubborn German defense. Montgomery was faced with a crisis.

If he renewed the attack, infantry casualties were bound to increase, possibly threatening the future viability of Second British Army. If he waited for the Americans the enemy would have time to create new defenses and bring up more reinforcements. In any case, until the water receded, Montgomery was similarly halted. Once the Allied path was reopened US forces would probably encounter a reduced number of defenders, and the farther east they moved the less resistance the British would encounter as well.

Although the Germans had not destroyed the dams to release a massive, yet shorter flood, the result was instead a steady flow of water that gradually inundated the Roer River Valley. What was normally between

30m and 300m width soon broadened threefold, with a swift 3m per second current.[1] At least First Army had finally extricated itself from the Hell that was the Hürtgen Forest. To the north, Simpson's Ninth Army, under the operational control of the British 21st Army Group, made final preparations for Operation Grenade. When news of the damaged dams became apparent, however, the jump-off scheduled for 0530 on February 10 was understandably postponed until the water receded.

Crossing the Roer (February 21–28)

During the nearly two-week wait for the inundated Roer River to recede, Ninth Army trained its soldiers for scenarios such as crossing rivers and destroying fortifications, and accumulated large amounts of supplies, including 46,000 tons of ammunition and 3,000,000 gallons of fuel.[2] Unit commanders were also flying in light observation planes to observe and study the areas over which they were soon to attack.

On February 21, Simpson's engineers notified him that the Roer's water level would be back to normal in three to four days. Figuring that the Germans were also aware of this, Simpson planned to put Ninth Army on the offensive two days earlier to achieve surprise. Stretched along nearly 50km of the Roer's west bank, the most northern XVI Corps was to take Roermond from the southeast, and butt up against Crerar's First Army before heading east. XIII and XIX Corps would thrust to the northeast to clear the Rhineland, and make for the Rhine River south of Wesel. Collins' VII Corps (First Army) would make for Cologne, while also providing support along Simpson's right.

In another projected river assault along the Roer, just south of Linnich the 102nd Infantry Division readied to lead XIII Corps across the river and into the open Cologne Plain beyond. The 407th Infantry Regiment was to lead Gillem's XIII Corps, where civilian casualties were not expected near the river as the numerous villages had been evacuated. Further east, only some fifty percent of the civilians had been evacuated.[3] Keating went on to outline how the division, after seizing its initial bridgehead, would then swing north and later be passed through by the 5th Armored Division, which would attempt to break through to the Rhine.

In the lead-up to 102nd Infantry Division crossing the Roer, the 237th Engineer Combat Battalion cleared mines and pillboxes, improved roads, and coordinated with the 84th Engineer Camouflage Battalion to better conceal the division's preparations.

First Army medics take shelter on the Roer's east bank as shells fly overhead on Feb. 23, 1945. (US Signal Corps)

Assault Crossing

The objectives required of a river assault crossing often blend into each other. Each phase was designed and planned to ensure the establishment of a secure bridgehead across the river. The first phase consisted of keeping the Germans from employing direct fire against the crossing, followed by preventing observed, indirect artillery fire. The third phase focused on stopping the sustained fire from enemy ground weapons, and on gaining sufficient space on the far bank to secure a bridgehead.

Several steps were then required to affect an assault crossing. Once the far bank was secured, footbridges, raft approaches, and light and heavy vehicular bridges would be constructed. Since armor and self-propelled guns were usually needed in a crossing's initial stage, heavy "Class 40" bridges were often given priority status. Most rivers in this part of Europe were manageable, and only required an M2 floating treadway bridge that could be constructed in about five hours.

The Roer and Beyond

On February 23 (D-Day), the 237th Engineer Combat Battalion, with help from the 1141st Engineer Combat Group, made its final preparations to support the crossing. At Linnich the 297th Engineer Combat Battalion was to provide assault boat crews. Two companies were to advance abreast, and once across the river the engineers were to construct narrow bridges for follow-on infantry, with the 989th Treadway Bridge Company providing the equipment.[4]

At 0245, Ninth Army began its offensive to finally cross the Roer River with a 2,000-gun bombardment, the largest such artillery grouping by the US to date.[5] In front of 102nd Infantry Division's projected path, its organic artillery regiments, and some from XIII Corps, totaled some four battalions of 105mm howitzers; four battalions of armored field artillery howitzers; four battalions of 155mm howitzers; one battalion of 4.5-inch guns; two battalions of 155mm towed guns; one battalion of 155mm self-propelled guns; one battery of 240mm howitzers; one battalion of 76mm tank guns; three companies of 90mm tank-destroyer guns, and one company of 3-inch towed guns.[6]

For the next 45 minutes the barrage steadily crept westward to a pre-designated line to subdue enemy defenses along the east bank. Many of the Allied guns fired time on target bombardments to have their shells land on a given area at essentially the same time. This made it virtually impossible for those on the receiving end to seek shelter.

Fifteen minutes after the US bombardment began, the Germans regained enough of their senses to hit back with counter-battery and mortar fire. As they had pre-registered their artillery to cover the anticipated bridgeheads, much of it fell in these areas. The leading battalions were the 1st of the 405th Infantry Regiment at Rurdorf, and the 1st and 2nd of the 407th at Linnich. The first wave crossed entirely in assault boats manned by the 327th and 279th Engineer Combat Battalions.

The 1st Battalion, 407th Infantry Regiment was to capture Gevenich, and at 0330 they sent in two waves of two companies abreast. 1st Squad, 2nd Platoon, K Company, 407th Infantry Regiment led, with two more squads right behind. Ten infantrymen and two combat engineers were crowded into each boat, which after it disgorged its passengers, would be returned by the engineers for subsequent trips.

The Germans responded with small arms fire, as well as rockets and mortars, to contest the crossing. Some boats were hit, and others drifted downstream in the heavy current. After a 16-minute trip, the lead squad

Ninth Army engineers prepare a pontoon bridge crossing over the Roer River on Feb 26, 1945. (US Signal Corps)

from 407th ("Aux Arcs") Infantry Regiment scrambled up the muddy embankment to silence a harassing German machine gun team on the east bank. After more than five months of mistakes, improvisations, and determination, the Allies had finally crossed the Roer River and reached the open Cologne Plain beyond.

Footnotes

[1] Major Norman C. Carey. *The European Theater, Part V. The Campaign for Central Europe.*

[2] Ibid.

[3] "Report After Action Against Enemy—February 1945." Headquarters 5th Armored Division APO No 255 7 March 1945.

[4] "HQ 327th Engineer Combat Battalion After Action Report." APO 102 US Army 3 March 1945. p. 12.

[5] John B. Wong. *Battle Bridges*, p. 233.

[6] Major Norman C. Carey. *The European Theater, Part V. The Campaign for Central Europe.*

Afterword

Having outrun their logistics following the Normandy breakout, Allied forces had few options to prevent a lull in the fighting that might give the *Westheer* an opportunity to reorganize an effective strategic defense. Had US commanders made a concerted effort to weaken some mechanized units to provide sufficient ammunition and fuel for a select few, operational momentum could have been maintained along selected sectors. Such narrow penetrations would have kept the Germans off balance, and likely made it all but impossible for them to maintain positions west of the Roer River, and probably along the Cologne Plain as well. With no choice but to cancel their build-up for an offensive through the Ardennes (December 16–January 28, 1945), the Germans could have used these strategic reserves to significantly bolster existing defenses, especially in Poland where the Soviet Vistula-Oder offensive (January 12–February 2, 1945) brought the Red Army to within 40km of Berlin.

Maintaining Eisenhower's, "broad front" strategy, seemingly restrictive in such a situation as it promoted maintaining a steady, unified advance, actually helped the Allied cause in an unanticipated way. By not bypassing battlefield quagmires such as the Hürtgen Forest, the Germans were denied areas from which to influence the fighting during the "Battle of the Bulge." Hitler, uncompromising in his desire to effect a decisive blow against the Western Allies and force a favorable armistice, squandered vital men and material that would have been better used in defense of the homeland. Offensive operations, although possessing a temporary element of surprise, were not in line with German late-war capabilities. Even more modest operations, such as von Rundstedt's proposed counterattack to retake Aachen, would not have had the necessary resources to exploit success beyond the short term. A strategic defensive stance in late 1944 would have better preserved and prolonged Germany's combat effectiveness (and correspondingly its destruction via aerial bombing), but General Staff decisions had long since been subordinated to the Supreme Commander's will and logic was not always a factor.

By February 1945, German forces, much as during the previous September, were worn out, in disarray, and looking to withdraw behind the seemingly formidable barrier of the Rhine River. This time, however, they would not be given an opportunity to recover. Within two weeks of crossing the Roer River, the US First and Ninth Armies pushed past the Cologne Plain to finally reach the Rhine along a broad front. With the Reich's eastern and western borders having been penetrated by enemy forces posturing for their final push to win the war, the Allied capture of the only intact Rhine crossing at Remagen, and subsequent bridgehead, sealed Germany's fate in the west. Although many German units continued to offer fierce opposition across all fronts, the increasing lack of support and command and control resulting from the Reich being overrun meant that it was of limited duration. It was only a matter of time before the loss of resources, manufacturing capability, and the will to continue a hopeless fight would force Germany's capitulation.

Appendix

The *Westwall*

As early as the Franco-Prussian War (1870–71), Germany had emphasized the need for a physically secure border with France. What started out as a series of fortifications around key urban centers such as Metz and Strasbourg gradually expanded to other areas of the German border, including that running along Belgium and the Netherlands.

Following Hitler's 1935 reoccupation of the Rhineland, which had been taken by France as part of its reparations for the First World War, Germany set about modernizing and expanding its old border fortifications. Initially, the fortified region at the Ober-Warthe Bend became a place for fortress engineers to actualize their new but untested designs. Showing promise, additional defenses were created over the next year. Additional manpower and technicians were increasingly required, and the Fortress Engineer School was hard-pressed to meet the need.

While the Siegfried Line (so called by the Allies in reference to the First World War Hindenburg Line) presented a strategic obstacle to an Allied offensive, the viability of such static field fortifications remained in doubt. However, unlike the equally outdated solution of France's Maginot Line, with its linear, curtain wall approach, the *Westwall's* defenses were distributed into zones up to a depth of 32km and integrated into the surrounding terrain, especially along an enemy's most likely avenues of attack. Numerous small and large bunkers were backed by a host of additional defenses. Interlocking fields of machine guns, minefields, wire entanglements, and antitank ditches not only helped funnel enemy armor into killing zones, but separated them from any accompanying infantry.

When the Second World War erupted in September 1939 the Siegfried Line (*Westwall* to the Germans), served its purpose by dissuading France or Britain from interfering with Hitler's ambitions in

Czechoslovakia and Poland. Over the course of its usefulness, the *Westwall* consisted of the following construction phases:[1]

Fortress Engineer (1936): Consisting of light constructions with B1, C, and D strength until the beginning of the "Limes" Phase.

Border Watch: A progression of initially light D-Class bunkers at important roads or rivers crossing the border. C-Class fortifications were next installed. They were to protect against sustained machine gun fire, and had roofs that were double the thickness of "D" versions. These *Ausbaustärken* were soon outdated, and the installation of "D" and "C" bunkers ceased after June and August 1938, respectively.

Pioneering Program (1938): Constructed along Germany's 1936 western border, the program was under the control of army engineers, with an end-date progressively estimated to be 1952! Bunkers were predominantly C and B1 varieties, but these were already considered obsolete, being only effective against small arms and shrapnel. The program was carried out by the *Grenzwacht* (Border Watch), a small military troop activated in the Rhineland immediately after it was remilitarized.

Limesprogramm (1938): Added 3,471 1,500mm-thick Type 10 concrete bunkers, which had a separate entrance and allowed up to 12 soldiers to fight atop stepped embrasures with carbines and machine guns. A new generation B1-Neu design was implemented. Between 1939 and 1940 four standard bunker types were under construction along the *Westwall*: machine-gun, antitank, personnel or ammunition, and headquarters bunkers. The bunkers varied in size and accommodated from six to forty men. The smallest weapons used in these fortifications were machine guns, although some apertures were large enough to permit the use of the hand-held *panzerschrecke*.

Aachen-Saar Program (1939): In late 1938 Saarbrücken and Aachen were selected for receiving additional protection, as neither was east of the existing fortifications. This program established more bunkers, some with double machine gun casemates, side embrasures, heavy metal doors, and concrete walls up to 3,500mm thick, as part of a second defensive belt.

Geldernstellung (1939/40): The Geldern Emplacement extended the *Westwall* as far north as Kleve on the Rhine. Most construction consisted of concrete dugouts, with many local farms and urban areas being incorporated as camouflage.

Kriegsregelbauten (1939): A new construction concept aimed at standardization, and making use of limited building materials once the war started. It enabled Organization Todt to best adapt fortifications to local conditions and requirements.

44/45 Program: In 1944, as Allied armies were closing in on the German homeland, a largely ineffectual effort was made to get the *Westwall* up to fighting condition.

Western Air Defense Zone (Luftverteidigungszone (Air Defense Zone) West) (1938): The establishment of an air defense zone of anti-aircraft guns, barrage balloons, and early warning systems extended from 15 to 50km behind the *Westwall* proper. These were integrated into the "ring of steel" that protected Germany proper from air attack. Backed by 4–5 *gruppen* of fighter aircraft, the German command placed primary reliance on light and heavy anti-aircraft guns, sound detectors, and searchlights, together billed as a "gapless barrier." The incorporation of flak turrets forced Allied planes to operate at higher altitudes. The commander reported directly to Goering as a way to organize the efforts of *Luftflotten* 2 and 3, whose commands included parts of the *Westwall*.

Entmilitarisierte Zone

The extensive length of the *Westwall* meant that an exact configuration was not attained throughout, but did consist of degrees of the following:

Advance Position (Field Fortifications) consisted of trenches, barbed-wire entanglements, machine-gun and artillery emplacements, and observation posts of between 2,000 and 4,000m in depth.
Fortified Belt between 5,000m and 10,000m behind the Advance Position, and consisted of concrete and steel works, and mutually supporting artillery emplacements.

Second Fortified Belt was roughly similar, but less heavily defended than the forward belt roughly 10,000m to 15,000m ahead, while the intervening ground contained fortified works located at critical points on natural avenues of advance.

The *Westwall's* individual defenses consisted of two basic varieties. A decentralized type was characterized by firepower, with concrete bunkers or steel turrets united into a center of resistance that was capable of continuous machine gun and antitank fire, and interconnected tunnel networks that facilitated movement of personnel, ammunition, and wounded. The second, "closed type" applied to large underground concrete shelters, which possessed no gun emplacements, and were largely used for ammunition storage and personnel protection in preparation for action.

Structures
Type A: Concrete (3,500mm); Steel (600mm)
Type A1: Concrete (2,500mm); Steel (350mm)
Type B: Concrete (1,500mm–2,000mm); Steel (250mm)
Type B1: Concrete (1,000mm); Steel (120mm)
Type B1: Neu: Concrete (500mm); roof (150mm)
Type C: Concrete (600mm); Steel (60mm)
Type D: Concrete (300mm); Steel (20mm)

Supplemental defenses included reinforced concrete "dragon's teeth" or "pimples" (in German *Höcker*, or "humps") stretched along the Siegfried Line in several rows on a single foundation. These were Type 1938 (four teeth) and Type 1939 (five teeth), with each row getting higher toward the back. Welded steel bars were worked into tank obstacles that could penetrate the vehicle's thinner bottom armor. Terrain permitting, water-filled ditches were dug instead of tank traps, especially along the Wurm River between Aachen and Geilenkirchen.

In anticipation of the need to present an adequate border defense against Eisenhower's broad front, Hitler issued a levy on August 22 for "people's" labor for the *Westwall*. Two days later he ordered the renewed construction of the Siegfried Line. 20,000 forced laborers and teenagers from the *Reichsarbeitsdienst* (Reich Labor Service) joined with locals to reequip the line for defensive purposes. Several single-man, concrete "Tobruk" dugouts were built along the western edge of the

Westwall. Allied air superiority, however, largely negated these efforts.

Streams and ravines were turned into antitank obstacles by deepening and widening them to an average depth of three and a half yards and an average width of six to eight yards.

In its final incarnation the *Westwall* stretched more than 630km between Kleve on the Netherlands border to Weil am Rhine before Switzerland. It was between 13km and 32km in depth and consisted of some 18,000 bunkers, tunnels, and tank traps. More with propaganda in mind than for any strategic reason, construction involved five developmental stages, all of which were pushed forward with the highest priority, using every resource available.

Footnotes

[1.] Dieter Bettinger and Martin Büren, 1990. *Handbook on German Military Forces, US War Department 1945.*

Bibliography

Books

Ambrose, Stephen E. *Citizen Soldiers: The U.S. Army from the Normandy Beaches to the Bulge to the Surrender of Germany*. New York: Simon & Schuster, 1997.

Baumann, Guido, Bönnemann, Otto, and Meven, Walter. *Die Tragödie von Aachen*. Verlag D+C, 2003.

Bergstrom, Christer. *Bagration to Berlin: The Final Air Battles in the East: 1944–1945*. Surrey: Ian Allen, 2007.

Bettinger, Dieter R. and Büren, Martin. *Der Westwall*. Verlag, 1990.

Blumenson, Martin. *World War II: Liberation*. Alexandria, VA: Time Life, 1978.

Boog, Horst, Krebs, Gerhard, and Vogel, Detlef. *Germany and the Second World War: Vol. VII: The Strategic Air War in Europe in the West and East Asia, 1943–1945*. Militargeschichtliches Forschungsamt. Oxford University Press, 2006.

Chaitt, Art. *View From the Other Side*. Bridgehead Sentinel. Summer 1965.

Collins, J. Lawton, General, U.S. Army. *Lightning Joe: an Autobiography*. Baton Rouge and London: Louisiana State University Press, 1979.

Connor, Kevin and Gootzen, Har. *Battle for the Roer Triangle*.

Cooper, Matthew. *The German Army 1933–1945*. Lanham, Maryland: Scarborough House, 1978.

Creveld, Martin L. Van. *Fighting Power: German and US Army Performance, 1939–1945*.

Delaforce, Patrick. *Churchill's Desert Rats: from Normandy to Berlin with the 7th Armoured Division*. Stroud, UK: Alan Sutton, 1994.

D'Este, Carlo. *Decision in Normandy: The Real Story of Montgomery and the Allied Campaign*. London: Penguin Books Ltd, 2004.

Doubler, Michael D. *Closing with the Enemy: How GIs Fought the War in Europe, 1944–1945*. University Press of Kansas, 1995.

Dunn, Walter S. *Heroes or Traitors: The German Replacement Army, The July Plot, and Adolf Hitler*. Praeger Publishers, 2003.

Eisenhower, John S.D. *The Bitter Woods: The Battle of the Bulge*. De Capo Press, 1995.

Gabel, Christopher R. *Knock 'em All Down: The Reduction of Aachen, October 1944.*

Military Operations on Urbanized Terrain: The 2d Battalion, 26th Infantry at Aachen, October 1944.

Haalser, Timm. *Hold the Westwall or Perish With It . . . The History of Panzer-Brigade 105, September 1944*. JJ Fedorowicz, 2007.

Hoffmann, Peter. *History of the German Resistance, 1933–1945*. McGill-Queen's University Press, 1996.

Karmp, Hans. "Operation Blackcock—Clearing the Area Between the R. Maas and the R. Roer, 15th–26th January 1945" by 21st Army Group. *Rurfront 1944/45.*

Kaufmann, J.E., Jurga, Robert M. *Fortress Europe: European Fortifications of World War II*. Cambridge, MA: De Capo Press, 1999.

Kroener, Bernhard R. Generaloberst Friedrich Fromm. *der starke Mann im Heimatkriegsgebiet*. Schöningh, 2005.

MacDonald, Charles B. *Breaching the Siegfried Line*. Washington, DC: Office of the Chief of Military History Dept. of the Army, 1963.

Martin Lindsay & M.E. Johnston. *History of 7th Armoured Division, June 1943–July 1945.*

Mansoor, Peter R. (1999). *The GI Offensive in Europe: The Triumph of American Infantry Divisions, 1941–1945*. Lawrence, Kansas: Kansas University Press.

Neillands, Robin. *The Battle for the Rhine 1945*. London: Orion Publishing Group, 2005.

Scheuer, Helmut. *Wie war das damals? Jülich 1944-1948*. Verlag des Jülicher Geschichtsvereins, 1985.

Schirmer, Horst, & Boesch, Paul. *Hurtgen: A Look at World War II's Cauldron of Death From the Other Side: A Joint Effort*. Houston, Texas: n.p., 1949.

Smith, Steven. *2nd Armored Division: "Hell on Wheels."* Hersham, UK: Ian Allan Publishing, 2003.

Spiller, Roger J., ed. *Combined Arms in Battle Since 1939*. U.S. Army

Command and General Staff College Press. 1991

Wilt, Alan F. *War From the Top: German and British Military Decision Making During World War II.* 1990.

Wood, James A. *Army of the West: The Weekly Reports of German Army Group B From Normandy to the West Wall.* Harrisburg, PA: Stackpole Books, 2007.

The Editors of *Command* Magazine. *Hitler's Army: The Evolution and Structure of German Forces, 1933–1945.* Conshohocken, PA: Combined Books, 1995.

Booklets

VII Corps, US Army Staff. *Mission Accomplished: The Story of the Campaigns of the VII Corps, US Army, in the War Against Germany, 1944–1945.* Merriam Press: Bennington, VT, 2008.

Ordnance Department. *Flaming Bomb: The Story of Ordnance in the ETO.* Paris: Desfosses-Neogravure, 1945.

The First! The Story of the 1st Infantry Division. GI Stories series. ETOUSA. Desfosses-Neogravure, 1944.

29 Let's Go! The Story of the 29th Infantry Division. GI Stories series. ETOUSA. Desfosses-Neogravure, 1944.

IX Tactical Air Command Achtung, Jabos!: The Story of the IX Tactical Air Command Paris: printed by Curial-Archereau, 1945.

Manuscripts

Bieroth, Ella. "The Battle of the Hurtgen Forest." English trans of German writer's account 1944.

Coakley, Robert W. "The Administrative and Logistical History of the European Theater of Operations. Part II, Organization and Command in the European Theater of Operations." Historical Division, U.S. Army Forces, European Theater, 1945–1946.

Daniel, Derrill M. "The Capture of Aachen," CARL manuscript collection.

Denkert, Walter. "The 3 Panzer Grenadier Division in the Battle of Aachen (October 1944)." Heidelberg: Historical Division, United States Army, Europe.

Knickerbocker, H.R, et al. "Danger Forward: The Story of the First Division in World War II" (Washington, DC: Society of the First Division, 1947).

Köchling, Friedrich. "The Battle of the Aachen Sector (September–

November 1944)." Heidelberg: Historical Division, United States Army, Europe, 1945.

Wendt, Col. William R., and others. "Organization and Command Relationships During World War II." A committee study done at the U.S. Armed Forces Staff College, 17 December 1951.

1st Infantry Division, "G-3 Report, 114, 118–119." Report of Breaching the Siegfried Line, 11.

1st CIC Detachment, "CIC Operations in Aachen and Vicinity September, October, and November," 1.

"The War Against Germany: Europe and Adjacent Areas (United States Army in World War II)," by Center of Military History, United States Army, 1994, Brasseys, Inc.

CIC "Operations in Aachen and Vicinity: Sep, Oct, Nov 1944."

European Theater Historical Interrogations (ETHINT)-1 "From Invasion to the Siegfried Line." By General der Artillerie Walter Warlimont; 48 pp; 19 20 July 1945. The Allied landing; Cherbourg; replacement of von Rundstedt; breakthrough and Mortain; fall of Paris and retreat.

ETHINT-18 "116th Panzer Division from the Seine to Aachen." By Generalleutnant Gerh. Graf von Schwerin; 59 pp; Oct Nov 1945.

ETHINT-53 "Seventh Army; Siegfried Line Defense of the Siegfried Line." By Generalmajor Rudolf Frhr. von Gersdorff; 8 pp; 24 Nov 1945.

Report of the General Board, United States Forces European Theater. "Study of the Organization of the European Theater of Operations." Study No. 2. 1945.

"Organization and Functions of the Communications Zone." Study No. 127, Bad Nauheim, Ger, 1945–1946.

US War Department. "A Manual for Commanders of Large Units, (Provisional)." Vol. 1. Operations. Washington, DC Government Printing Office, 1930.

CMH-140 Center of Military History, U.S. Army. "Army Command and Control, 1940–1975."

"Bomb Effectiveness Analysis, Phase 1, Final Report." 3 Vols. Statistical Lab of Purdue Univ, 1 Apr 1952.

"Fighter Bomber Control," a compilation of procedures used by the Ninth Air Force during Opns on the European Continent. 1945.

"River Crossings 1939–45: An Historical Study and Analysis of British and American River Crossing in the Second World War." British

War Office, Aug 1950.

"Combat Operations Data, First Army, 1944–1945."

"Operations IV Offensive in November 1944." Pt 2. HQ Ninth U.S. Army, Feb 1945.

"G-4 data, First U.S. Army (SOP's, etc), 1944." Personal ref book, COL R.W. Wilson, G-4, First Army.

"Roer River Crossing Conducted by the Ninth U.S. Army, XIII U.S. Corps, and the 84th Infantry Division, 23 February 1945." Offensive, Deliberate Assault, River Crossing.

Ninth Air Force, "Summary of Air Plan," 7 Nov 44, NUSA G-3 Jnl file, 1-11 Nov 44; FUSA, Air Support, Annex 4 to FO 12, 8 Nov, VII Corps Admin and FO file, Nov 44; FUSA Rpt, Vol. 1, pp. 73-74; *Conquer The Story of Ninth Army*, pp. 80-81; NUSA Opns, IV, 34.

A-872 "Strength, Organization, Armament, and Equipment of Troops in Battle." By General der Panzertruppen Hasso von Manteuffel; 51 pp; OCMH multilith; 1946.

A-981 Gersdorff, R.V. "The Battle of the Hurtgen Forest." USAREUR Foreign Mil Study. FgnMSColl.

A-982 "Questions for Consideration and Reply." FgnMS. FMSColl.

A-988 "LXXXI Corps" (Sep 1944 Apr 1945). By General der Infanterie Friedrich Koechling; 5 pp; 1945. Order of battle.

A-989 to A-993 "The Battle of the Aachen Sector (Sep–Nov 1944)." By General der Infanterie Friedrich Koechling; 7 vols, 38 pp; 1945. Questionnaires on the action of LXXXI Corps in the Aachen area answered by the corps commander.

A-994 "Counterpreparation to Meet American Attack on the Roer," 16 Nov 1944."

A-995 "Germany, flooding of the Roer, Nov 1944."

B-034 4 Nov, "OKWIWFSt, KTB Ausarbeitung, der Westen i.IV. 16.XII.44."

B-053 "Germany, Roer River."

B-058 "116th Panzer Division (21 Aug–19 Sep 1944)." By Generalmajor H. Voigtsbergel 17 pp; 1946. From the Falaise pocket to the West Wall. An account of rearguard action by an armored mobile unit against enveloping pursuit.

B-730 "Northern France—Vol X; Seventh Army (1–20 Sep 1944)." By General der Panzertruppen Erich Brandenberger; 111 pp, 7 illus; 1947. Seventh Army in Belgium and retreat to the West Wall.

B-792 "49th Infantry Division (2 Sep–10 Oct 1944)." By

Generalleutnant Siegfr. Macholz; 46 pp; 1948. From the Meuse to the West Wall (north of Aachen).

B-793 "89th Infantry Division (13 Sep–1 Oct 1944)." By Oberst Hasso Neitzel; 23 pp; 1948. In the West Wall near Monschau; a picture of general conditions.

B-811, B-812 "Roer and Rhine, Fifteenth Army defensive battles, 22 Nov 1944-9 Mar 1945."

D-069 "Ten Points to be Remembered by the Leader of a Reconnaissance or Combat Patrol in Difficult Wooded Terrain." By Oberstleutnant i. G. Hans Roschmann; 6 pp; 1947. Based on field experience in Russia.

P-065a "The Volksgrenadier Division and Volkssturm." By Generalmajor Reinhardt; 22 p; 1950. A concise study on the organization of these two types of German units.

P-065b "The Volksgrenadier Division and the Volkssturm." By Generalmajor Hellmuth Reinhardt; 16 pp, 1 illus; 1950. Additional information on the infantry and artillery of the Volksgrenadier division.

Manuals

"FM 7-5, Infantry Field Manual: Organization and Tactics of Infantry, The Rifle Battalion" (Washington, DC: Government Printing Office, 1940), 99.

"FM 100-5, Field Service Regulations, Operations" (Washington, DC: Government Printing Office, 1944).

"FM 100-20 and Employment of Air Power" (US Army, 1944)

U.S. Army. Field Artillery School. S-2 Section. "Siegfried Line: A Compilation of Information from Various Sources." 1944.

VII Corps. "Engineer Operations by the VII Corps in the European Theater. Vol IV: Pursuit Into Germany." n.p., 1949.

XIX Corps. "Breaching the Siegfried Line." n.p., 2 Oct 1944.

U.S. War Dept. Military Intelligence Division. "German Doctrine of the Stabilized Front: Special Series No. 17." Washington, DC: GPO, 1943.

Eckstein, Walter. "Fortifications of the Lower Rhine (15 September 1943 to 17 October 1944)."

Kraemer, Fritz. "I SS Pz Corps in the West in 1944."

Zimmerman, Bodo. "OB West, Atlantic Wall to Siegfried Line: A Study in Command." Special ed. Vol I.

TM 30-306, German Language Guide. "Cracking the Siegfried Line," 13–19 September, based on interview with Col. Leander Doan and Lt. Col. William Orr., Intelligence summary, 9 November, Koln campaign plans, Messages from Gen. Maurice Rose, 13 December.

Papers

Fix, Major Robert G. "Reconnaissance in Force: A Key Contributor to Tempo." School of Advanced Military Studies. Fort Leavenworth, Kansas. 1993.

Forrest C. Pogue, "The Supreme Command, United States Army in World War II" (Washington, 1954).

Heichler, Lucian, "Germans Opposite VII Corps in September 1944," Research Section, Office of the Chief of Military History, Washington, D.C. December 1952.

McGregor, Edward W. "Operations of the 1-18th Infantry in Vicinity of Crucifix Hill, Northeast of Aachen, Germany 8–10 October 1944." 1950.

Parrish, Maj. Monte M. "City Fighting Tactics: The Battle of Aachen." Field Artillery Journal 44 (September–October 3.976).

"Report of Breaching the Siegfried Line and the Capture of Aachen." Headquarters, 1st U.S. Infantry Division, APO# 1, U.S. Army, 1944.

"Selected Intelligence Reports, Vol I, June–November 1944." By Assistant Chief of Staff, G-2, lst Infantry Division. 1944.

"Unit Report of Action 1–31 Oct 1944." 1st Infantry Division. 4–5 November 1944.

"Intelligence Activities—1 October 1944 to 31 October 1944," 1 November 1944.

Fort Leavenworth, Kansas Command and General Staff College Library Archives Section. Document No. R-11235. "Headquarters 1st U.S. Infantry Division APO 1 U.S. Army."

Fort Leavenworth, Kansas Command and General Staff College Library Archives Section. Document No. N-16631-D. Headquarters VII Corps, Office of the Engineer APO 307 U.S. Army. "Engineer Operations by the VII Corps in the European Theatre, Vol IV, Pursuit into Germany," 18 October 1944.

Unpublished Government Document, "The Operations of VII Corps in September 1944." Office of the Chief of Military History. Department of the Army, 1953.

Periodicals

Blumenson, Martin. "Coordination and Muscular Movement in the Hedgerows." *Army* 7 (May 1957).

Ferrell, Bruce K. (1 November 2000). "The Battle of Aachen." *ARMOR Magazine* (Fort Knox, Kentucky: US Army Armor Center).

Hobbs, L.S. "Breaching the Siegfried Line." *Military Review* XXVI (Jun 1946): Action of 30th Inf and 20th Arm Divs.

Parrish, Monte M. "The Battle of Aachen." *Field Artillery Journal* 44 (Sep–Oct 1976).

Ramsey, Winston G. "The Battle for Aachen," *After the Battle,* No. 42, 1983.

Sterba, Antonin M. "Breaching the Siegfried Line." *Military Engineer* XXXVII (May 45).

Trees, Wolfgang. "Schlactfeld Zwischen Maas und Rhein." *Triangel Verlag,* Aachen. 1995.

Whitlock, Flint (December 2008). "Breaking Down the Door." *WWII History* (Herndon, Virginia: Sovereign Media) 7 (7).

26th Infantry Regiment Association. *Aachen: Military Operations in Urban Terrain.* 4th Edition. Lititz, PA, 1999.

Stolberg: Penetrating the Westwall. 3d Edition. Lititz, PA, 1999.

Cantigny Military History Series. *Blue Spaders: the 26th Infantry Regiment, 1917–1967.* Votaw, J.F., ed. Cantigny First Division Foundation, Wheaton, IL. 1996.

Rheinisches Amt für Bodendenkmalpflege. *Der Westwall — Vom Denkmalwert des Unerfreulichen.* Landwirtshaftsverband Rheinland, Rheinland-Verlag GmbH, Köln. 1997.

Reports

Bykofsky, Joseph and Larson, Harold. "The Transportation Corps: Operations Overseas," US Army in WWII Series. Washington, DC: US Government Printing Office, 1957.

Gross, Manfred. "Der Westwall zwischen Niederrhein und Schnee eifel."

Luttichau, Charles V. P. von. "The Ardennes Offensive, Germany's Situation in the Fall of 1944, Part II, The Economic Situation," MS in OCMH.

Ross, William F. and Romanus, Charles F. "The Quartermaster Corps: Operations in the War Against Germany," US Army in WWII Series. Washington, DC: US Government Printing Office, 1965.

Ruppenthal, Dr. Roland G. "Logistical Support of the Armies, May 1941–September 1944, United States Army in World War II, Vol. 1." Washington, DC: OCMH, 1953.

"The Tyranny of Logistics, September 1944–February 1945," Vol. 2. Washington, DC: OCMH, 1959.

General Marshall's report: "The Winning of the War in Europe and the Pacific, Vol. 3." United States. War Dept. General Staff, George Catlett Marshall. 1945.

No. 2 ORS Report No. 22, "The Effect of Artillery Fire on Enemy Forward Defensive Positions in the Attack on Geilenkirchen, in Operational Research in North-West Europe."

"War Diary, 5th Dorsetshire Regiment," Nov 1944, PRO WO 171/1287.

Omar N. Bradley and the US 12th Army Group Air Effects Committee, "Effect of Air Power on Military Operations, Western Europe" (15 July 1945) p. 42, PRO AIR 40/1131.

US XIX Corps, quoted in "The AF Evaluation Board in the ETO, The Effectiveness of Third Phase Tactical Air Operations."

Folders 2–7: "After Action Reports—33rd Armored Regiment, September 1944–February 1945."

Folder 10: "Log Book—2nd Battalion, 33rd Armored Regiment, 1944–45."

Folder 12: "Evidence in Camera," Aerial photograph reports, British Air Ministry, 1944–45.

Folder 13: "Copies of Radio Messages from Manuel Baker, 1944–45" 54 AFA September 17, 1944–March 27, 1945.

Folders 14–19: "After Action Reports—486th AAA Battalion, September 1944–February 1945."

Folders 19–24: "Journal and Log—32nd Armored Regiment, 1944 September 1944–February 1945."

Folder 23: "A History of the 143rd Armored Signal Company, 1941–45 Written by Francis B. Grow and Alfred Summers, Summer 1945."

Folder 25: "Journal and Log—32nd Armored Regiment, 1945."

Folder 27: "War Diary—Company "D" 32nd Armored Division, 1944–45" Abstracts by Stuart Thayer.

Folder 27: Letters and Publications—"Combat Intelligence Report," 1945 Combat Intelligence Report by Col. Washington Platt, XIX corps, 19 July.

Folder 28: Letters and Publications—"Organization, Equipment and

Tactical Employment of the Armored Division," 1945.

Folder 30: "36th Armored Infantry Regiment History, 1941–45."

Folder 31: "36th Armored Infantry—After Action Reports, September 1944."

Folders 32–37: "G-2 Periodic Reports September 1944–February 1945."

"Organization, Equipment and Tactical Employment of the Armored Division," study #48, ca. December 1945.

September 1944 issue of *Intelligence Bulletin*. "The German Replacement Army (*Ersatzheer*), April 1944," a publication of the Military Intelligence Division, War Department.

Intelligence Bulletin. "Pillbox Warfare in the Siegfried Line." Vol. III, No. 5: January 1945.

"Weekly Reports by COSSAC to the Chiefs of Staff Committee of the War Cabinet" (File COSSAC/3243/Sec).

"Minutes of COSSAC Weekly Meetings" (File COSSAC/3131/1/Sec).

G-2 (Intelligence) Div. A useful record, consisting of brief notes of important developments on British Army Form C.2118, supported by copies of important documents as appendices, covering the period from 26 July 1943.

G-3 (Operations) Div. Brief notes of important developments on British Army Form C.2118.

G-4 (Administrative) Div. "Movement & Transportation Branch." Weekly Progress Reports.

G-5 (Civil Affairs) Div. A chronological list of chief developments from 5 September 1943.

G-6 (Publicity & Psychological Warfare) Div. A chronological list of chief developments from 29 April 1943.Aachen, 16, 19, 22-24, 27-30, 31-32, 35-36, 38-43, 46-50, 52, 54, 57-61, 64, 67-61, 73-76, 78-79, 83, 87, 94, 97-103, 105-108, 110, 112-113, 115, 117-118, 139-141, 144-46, 148, 151-155, 157, 177, 196, 227, 230, 232

Index

40-43, 48-49, 52, 141, 146,
153, 157, 159, 160, 162, 164,
174
10th *Panzergrenadier* Regiment,
35, 48, 159, 161
10th *SS Panzer* Division, 142,
157, 165
11th *Panzergrenadier* Regiment,
35
12th *SS-Panzer* Division, 31
12th *Volksgrenadier* Division, 48-
49, 51-52, 54, 58, 62, 68,
107, 121, 145, 151-153, 172,
179, 182
15th *Panzergrenadier* Division,
141, 146, 155, 160, 162, 164,
166, 169, 174
16th *Panzer Regiment*, 34, 129,
131-132
29th *Panzergrenadier* Regiment,
107
47th *Volksgrenadier* Division,
152-153, 172, 181-182, 198
48th *Grenadier* Regiment, 50, 180
49th *Grenadier* Division, 32, 35,
40-41, 58, 67, 98, 151
60th *Panzergreadier* Regiment, 38-
39, 43, 127, 133-134
85th *Grenadier* Division, 196
89th *Grenadier* Division, 47, 80,
86, 121, 127, 196
104th *Grenadier* Regiment, 181
104th *Panzergrenadier* Regiment,
163, 166
105th *Panzer* Brigade, 31, 40
116th *Panzer* Division, 31-32, 38,
40, 42-43, 48, 51, 58, 70, 97,
100-101, 106, 121, 127, 135,
138, 152, 188
116th *Panzer* Regiment, 133
130th *Panzer (Lehr)* Division, 142
146th *Panzer* Artillery Regiment,
34, 40

156th *Panzergrenadier* Regiment,
38-39, 43, 133-135
176th Replacement Training
Division, 42
176th *Grenadier* Division, 78,
157, 159, 206
183rd *Grenadier* Division, 58
183rd *Volksgrenadier* Division,
31, 52, 63, 65-68, 157, 161-
162, 174, 206
246th *Volksgrenadier Division*,
51-52, 54, 58, 63, 67-68, 97,
101, 106-107, 110, 115, 151,
153, 171-172, 182, 184, 196,
200
253rd *Grenadier* Regiment, 77
272nd *Volksgrenadier* Division,
121, 196, 218-219
275th *Grenadier* Division, 32, 35,
41, 52, 68, 76, 78, 84, 86, 94,
118, 121, 129, 147, 151, 188,
190
340th *Volksgrenadier* Division,
175-176, 182
343rd *Grenadier* Regiment, 68
344th *Grenadier* Division, 190,
196
347th *Grenadier* Division, 78
352nd *Grenadier* Regiment, 91
353rd *Grenadier* Division, 23, 32,
35-36, 39-41, 43, 49-52, 76-
77, 85, 95, 190, 196
388th *Volks* Artillery Corps, 163
404th *Grenadier* Regiment, 68,
152
407th *Volks* Artillery Corps, 159,
163, 174
416th *Grenadier* Training
Regiment, 47
526th *Grenadier* Division, 32
536th Replacement Training
Division, 41
861st *Grenadier* Regiment, 78